Closing the Gap in Education?

Improving Outcomes in Southern World Societies

Closing the Gap in Education?

Improving Outcomes in Southern World Societies

Edited by Ilana Snyder and John Nieuwenhuysen

© Copyright 2010.

All rights reserved. Apart from any uses permitted by Australia's Copyright Act 1968, no part of this book may be reproduced by any process without prior written permission from the copyright owners. Inquiries should be directed to the publisher.

Monash University Publishing
Building 4, Monash University
Clayton, Victoria 3800, Australia
www.publishing.monash.edu

This book is available online at www.publishing.monash.edu/cge

ISBN: 978-0-9806512-2-5 (pb)
ISBN: 978-0-9806512-3-2 (online)

DESIGN
Les Thomas

COVER IMAGE
© 2010 Gary Moore/realworldimage.com
A young boy peers through the shutters of a school in Palo Amarillo, Cabarete, Dominican Republic (February 2010)
realworldimage.com image number 15270
Used with permission.

PRINTER
Griffin Press

Contents

Foreword	vii
Notes on Contributors	ix
Closing the Gap in Education? *Ilana Snyder & John Nieuwenhuysen*	xv

Section 1:
The scope and substance of marginalisation in education

Challenges and Opportunities in Australian Indigenous Education *Mick Dodson*	1
My Story Should Not Be Unusual The Education of an Australian Aboriginal Girl *Inala Cooper*	12
Bridging the Gap in South African Education *Graeme Bloch*	17
Scholastic Heritage and Success in School Mathematics Implications for Remote Aboriginal Learners *Robyn Jorgensen & Peter Sullivan*	23

Section 2:
The structure and entrenchment of disadvantage

Old Gaps are Closing, New Gaps are Opening Education, Ethnicity and Gender in New Zealand, 1986–2006 *Richard Bedford, Paul Callister & James Newell*	39
The Structure and Entrenchment of Disadvantage in South Africa *Thobeka Mda*	56
Gendered Violence and Pedagogical 'Resources for Hope' Mothers' and Daughters' Stories From the Fringe of an Australian City *Jane Kenway, Lindsay Fitzclarence & Johannah Fahey*	68
Two Orientations to Education System Reform Australian and South African Politics of Remaking 'the Social' *Terri Seddon*	85

Section 3:
The challenges facing Indigenous education

Indigenous Australians as 'No Gaps' Subjects   109
Education and Development in Remote Australia
   Jon Altman & Bill Fogarty

Closing the Gap in Education by Addressing the Education   129
Debt in New Zealand
   Russell Bishop

If This Is Your Land, How Do You Teach Your Stories?   149
The Politics of 'Anthologising' Indigenous Writing in Australia
   Adam Shoemaker

Beyond the 'Digital Divide'   158
Engaging with New Technologies in Marginalised Educational Settings in Australia
   Ilana Snyder

Closing the Quality Gap in South African Education   174
An Analysis and Critique of the Education Roadmap
   Leon Tikly

Section 4:
Enhancing social justice and equity

Stronger Smarter Approaches to Indigenous Leadership in
Australia   195
   Chris Sarra

Redressing Marginalisation   204
A Study of Pedagogies for Teaching Mathematics in a Remote Australian Indigenous Community
   Peter Sullivan, Robyn Jorgensen & Rebecca Youdale

Marginalisation of Education Through Performativity in South Africa   217
Towards a Radicalisation of Education
   Yusef Waghid

Index   229

Foreword

In November 2009 a notable conference was held at the campus of Monash South Africa, near Johannesburg. It was the third international conference in a highly successful series of partnerships between the Monash Institute for the Study of Global Movements (MISGM) and Monash South Africa.

Entitled *Closing the Gap in Education?*, the conference attracted distinguished international speakers, including the 2009 Australian of the Year, Professor Mick Dodson AM, who is among the most eminent of Monash University's graduates. In addition, leading scholars, officials and educationalists from South Africa, New Zealand, Australia and Britain participated, and this volume of refereed papers, published by Monash University Publishing, is the outcome of their presentations.

The themes of the conference were the pressing challenges facing education systems in three southern world societies – Australia, South Africa and New Zealand. Of special concern was the way in which the needs of marginalised students in both urban fringe and remote regional areas are being met.

The comparisons between these three different countries are set against the background of their considerable underlying similarities, including colonial settlement histories, multicultural societies, and separate dualistic pockets of poverty and affluence.

On behalf of Monash University, I would like to thank all the contributors who participated in the conference and subsequently produced papers for refereeing and publication. The university owes them a particular debt of gratitude.

A special feature of the conference, as of others mounted by MISGM at Monash South Africa in 2008 and 2006, was the attendance of local students, who added immeasurably, I understand, to the quality and interest of questions and debate. I wish to express my special pleasure in their welcome participation.

I would also like to acknowledge the vocal group Sweet Oasis, composed entirely of Monash South Africa students, who entertained the conference delegates with their fine performance; and all those at Monash South Africa, under the leadership of Professor Tyrone Pretorius, as well as the Monash Melbourne organisers, Irene Thavarajah and Sahar Sana, for their efforts in ensuring the conference's success.

Finally, I thank the conceivers of the conference, and editors of this volume, Professors Ilana Snyder and John Nieuwenhuysen, for this initiative, which once more shows the value of Monash's international spread in enabling scholarly networking and comparative publications of great importance for economic development and social justice.

Professor Ed Byrne AO
Vice-Chancellor and President
Monash University

Notes on Contributors

Jon Altman has a background in economics and anthropology. He has been involved in research relating to Indigenous Australians since the late 1970s. In 1990 he was appointed Foundation Director of the Centre for Aboriginal Economic Policy Research at the Australian National University, a position he held for 20 years; he is now located at the centre as an ARC Australian Professorial Fellow. Professor Altman, who is a Fellow of the Australian Academy of Social Science, divides his research efforts between national Indigenous economic development issues and those specific to remote Australia, where he has worked for over 30 years.

Richard Bedford is Pro Vice-Chancellor Research at AUT University, Auckland, and Professor of Population Geography in the Population Studies Centre at the University of Waikato in Hamilton. He is a specialist in migration research and, since the mid-1960s, has been researching processes of population movement in the Asia-Pacific region. He is a Companion of the Queen's Service Order, a Fellow of the Royal Society of New Zealand and a member of several research and policy advisory groups.

Russell Bishop is Foundation Professor for Maori Education in the School of Education at the University of Waikato in Hamilton. His research experience is in the area of collaborative storying as a Kaupapa Maori researcher. His book, *Collaborative Research Stories: Whakawhanaungatanga*, reflects this approach. Other research interests include collaborative storying as pedagogy and culturally responsive pedagogies. He has also authored numerous journal articles and research reports on the topic of improving the educational achievement of minorities and Indigenous students. His most recent book is *Scaling Up: Addressing Disparities in Education*.

Graeme Bloch is an education policy analyst at the Development Bank of Southern Africa. Before 1994 he was an executive member of the National Education Crisis Committee as well as the United Democratic Front: for his involvement in the democratic movement he was detained and arrested numerous times. He was banned from 1976 to 1981. He has written and published widely, in particular on education, in both academic and more popular publications. *The Toxic Mix: What is Wrong with South Africa's Schools and How to Fix It* (Tafelberg 2009) is his most recent book.

Paul Callister is Deputy Director of the Institute for Policy Studies at Victoria University in Wellington. He is an economist who has a longstanding research interest in the ethnic and gender dimensions of labour-market and education outcomes in New Zealand.

Inala Cooper is a member of the Yawuru peoples, the traditional Aboriginal owners of land and waters in the Broome area of the southern Kimberley region of Western Australia. She works in the Department of Planning and Community Development Victoria in the Ministerial Taskforce on Aboriginal Affairs. She is also the Executive Officer, Indigenous Advisory Council, Monash University. She was a finalist for the Institute of Public Administration Australia Young Indigenous Leader Award 2009.

Mick Dodson AM is a member of the Yawuru peoples, the traditional Aboriginal owners of land and waters in the Broome area of the southern Kimberley region of Western Australia. He is currently the Director of the National Centre for Indigenous Studies at the Australian National University and a Professor of Law at the ANU College of Law. He is also the Chairman of the Australian Institute of Aboriginal and Torres Strait Islander Studies and Co-Chair of Reconciliation Australia. Professor Dodson was Australia's first Aboriginal and Torres Strait Islander Social Justice Commissioner. He has been a member of the United Nations Permanent Forum on Indigenous Issues for the last six years and is a fellow of the Academy of Social Sciences in Australia. In 2009 he was named Australian of the Year.

Johannah Fahey is a Research Fellow at Monash University. She has a PhD in cultural studies from Macquarie University, Australia. Her latest co-edited book is *Globalizing the Research Imagination*. Her latest co-authored book is *Haunting the Knowledge Economy*. An earlier book is *David Noonan: Before and Now* and she is currently co-authoring 'Moving ideas and travelling intellectuals'.

Lindsay Fitzclarence is an independent researcher, at present undertaking a major writing project that involves re-theorising curriculum theory. Prior to this he worked in teacher education programs in the faculties of education at Monash and Deakin universities and at the University of South Australia, where he was also a lead writer for the *South Australian Curriculum Standards and Accountability Framework*. His research has long focused on the development of alternative approaches to curriculum and pedagogy.

Bill Fogarty is a graduate student at the Centre for Aboriginal Economic Policy Research at the Australian National University. He has extensive experience teaching Indigenous students in urban and very remote settings, in Indigenous education policy and in Indigenous education research in the Northern Territory. He is currently writing up his thesis – 'From pedagogy to production: Indigenous land, youth and education' – as part of an Australian Research Council Linkage project with the Bawinanga Aboriginal Corporation, the Northern Land Council and the Northern Territory Department of Education and Training as Industry Partners.

Robyn Jorgensen is a Professor of Education at Griffith University in Queensland. She has worked in the area of equity and mathematics education for two decades, concentrating on issues of practice and how it is implicated in the exclusion of working-class, remote or rural and/or Indigenous students. Drawing predominantly on the theories of Bourdieu, she seeks to develop new forms of practice to enable greater access for traditionally disadvantaged learners to engage with mathematics and schooling. She is currently on leave from the university and is working as the CEO/Principal of Nyangatjatjra Aboriginal Corporation. The corporation is the only provider of secondary education for Aboriginal students in Central Desert lands of the Northern Territory.

Jane Kenway is a Professorial Fellow of the Australian Research Council and in this capacity is leading an international team to conduct a study called 'Elite independent schools in globalising circumstances: A multi sited global ethnography'. She is also a Professor of Education at Monash University. She is recognised internationally for her research expertise on the politics of educational change in the context of wider social, cultural and political change. Her more recent jointly written books are *Haunting the Knowledge Economy* (Routledge 2006), *Masculinity Beyond the Metropolis* (Palgrave 2006), and *Consuming Children: Education–Advertising–Entertainment* (Open University Press 2001). Her most recent jointly edited book is *Globalizing the Research Imagination* (Routledge 2009).

Thobeka Mda is Deputy Executive Director of the Policy Analysis and Capacity Enhancement (PACE) research program at the Human Sciences Research Council, South Africa. She holds a PhD in Educational Policy and Leadership from the Ohio State University, United States. Her experience includes teaching at high schools in former Transkei, Soweto and East Rand, lecturing at a teachers college in the East Rand and a professorship at the University of South Africa (UNISA). She is a former Dean of the Faculty of Education at UNISA. Professor Mda is a member of various professional committees and is currently the president of the Southern African Comparative and History of Education Society. Her areas of research include language in education, diversity in schooling and teacher development.

James Newell is the Director of Monitoring and Evaluation Research Associates, a Wellington-based statistics and social policy consultancy in New Zealand. He has specialised in studies of the interaction between population, labour market, migration and national, regional and community population dynamics since the 1980s. He has carried out extensive analysis of trends in participation in early childhood, school and tertiary education.

John Nieuwenhuysen is Foundation Director of the Monash Institute for the Study of Global Movements, Visiting Professor, King's College, University of London, and a member of Council, RMIT University in Melbourne. He was previously Foundation Director of the Bureau of Immigration, Multicultural and Population Research, and Chief Executive of CEDA, the Committee for Economic Development of Australia. A graduate of the London School of Economics and a Fellow of the Academy of Social Sciences of Australia, he received an award (AM) in the Order of Australia in 2003 for services to independent public and private research, and the reform of the liquor laws of Victoria.

Chris Sarra has completed a Diploma of Teaching, a Bachelor of Education, a Master of Education and a PhD in Psychology at Murdoch University in Western Australia. In the late 1990s Dr Sarra took on the challenges of Indigenous education as the principal of Cherbourg State School in south-east Queensland. Under his leadership the school became nationally acclaimed for its pursuit of the strong and smart philosophy. He is now the Executive Director of the Stronger Smarter Institute, which is pursuing improved educational outcomes for Indigenous children through engagement with principals, teachers, community leaders and government.

Terri Seddon is a Professor in the Faculty of Education at Monash University. She has built a research program in the field of education (lifelong learning) and work, with a special focus on policies and politics of educational work. Her research is cross-sectoral in orientation, looking at schools, vocational and higher education, and workplace and community learning spaces. She has strong links with European research and is actively engaged in local and transnational partnership work. Her most recent book is *Learning and Work and the Politics of Working Life: Global Transformations and Collective Identities in Teaching, Nursing and Social Work* (co-edited) and she co-edits the *Routledge World Yearbook of Education*.

Adam Shoemaker is Deputy Vice-Chancellor (Education) Monash University and is responsible for the quality, range and impact of the university's academic programs. He was Dean of the College of Arts and Social Sciences at the Australian National University (ANU) and Foundation Director of the ANU Research School of Humanities. He has also been a Visiting Professor at the University of Toulouse-le-Mirail and the University of Antwerp. His sustained research interest is in Indigenous Australian history, literature, culture and politics, and he has published eight books in these areas, including *Black Words White Page* (1992, 2004), *Mudrooroo: A Critical Study* (1993), *A Sea Change: Australian Writing and Photography* (1998), and *Aboriginal Australians: First Nations of an Ancient Continent* (2004, with Stephen Muecke). He is currently writing a study of international Indigenous cultural flows called 'Authenticity? Indigenous culture and globalisation'.

Ilana Snyder is a Professor in the Faculty of Education, Monash University. Her research has investigated the changes to literacy practices associated with the use of digital technologies. Books that explore these changes include: *Hypertext* (1996), *Page to Screen* (1997), *Teachers and Technoliteracy* (2000, with Colin Lankshear and Bill Green), *Silicon Literacies* (2002) and *Doing Literacy Online* (2004, with Catherine Beavis). Her research has also examined the connections between literacy, learning, technology and disadvantage. *The Literacy Wars* (2008), her most recent book, discusses the politics of the volatile media debates around literacy education in Australia and beyond.

Peter Sullivan is Professor of Science, Mathematics and Technology Education at Monash University. He is the author of the shape paper for the new Australian mathematics curriculum, editor of the prestigious

Journal of Mathematics Teacher Education, and between 2005 and 2009 was a member of the Australian Research Council College of Experts for Social, Behavioural and Economic Sciences, including judging the Discovery Indigenous Research Grant program. He was a member of the selection advisory committee for the Future Fellowships program, and is the president of the Australian Association of Mathematics Teachers. His current research interests include the Maths in the Kimberley research project.

Leon Tikly is a Professor of Education and Director of Research at the University of Bristol, England. He also directs a large research program consortium on 'Implementing education quality in low income countries' (EdQual), which has partners in the UK, South Africa, Ghana, Tanzania, Rwanda, Pakistan and Chile. Professor Tikly started his career as a science teacher in London and then at a school for South African refugees in Morogoro, Tanzania. He worked as a policy researcher at the Wits Education Policy Unit during the transition from apartheid to democracy. On returning to the UK, he taught international and comparative education at the University of Birmingham before taking up a post in education management and policy at Bristol. Professor Tikly's research interests include the impact of globalisation on education policy in Africa and on the achievement of black and minority ethnic learners in the UK.

Yusef Waghid is Professor of Philosophy of Education and Dean of the Faculty of Education at Stellenbosch University, South Africa. He holds doctorates from the universities of the Western Cape and Stellenbosch in philosophy, policy and education. His current research focuses on philosophy of education, democratic citizenship, cosmopolitanism, higher education transformations and universal justice in relation to education. He is an elected member (fellow) of the Academy of Science of South Africa, executive member of the International Network of Philosophers of Education, and editor-in-chief of the *South African Journal of Higher Education*. His forthcoming book is entitled 'Education, democracy and citizenship reconsidered: Pedagogical encounters'.

Rebecca Youdale is a teacher in a remote community school in the Kimberley region of Western Australia. She has an honours degree in linguistics and has taught in various countries before coming to this school. She commenced a role as a teacher adviser in 2010.

Closing the Gap in Education?

Ilana Snyder & John Nieuwenhuysen
Monash University

The impetus for this collection was a conference held at the Monash South Africa campus, near Johannesburg, in November 2009. As the title for the conference, 'Closing the Gap?' did the trick. It attracted the participation of international leaders in education and related fields interested in exploring a range of interconnected questions on marginalisation, and highlighted the pressing issues of inequality that urgently require solutions. It was the catalyst for important conversations across national borders and suggestions for moving forward. But the metaphor was criticised by many of the participants, who saw it as unsatisfactory and polarising. They made this point in one way or another and provided compelling elaborations of its limitations.

The two-day conference focused on the numerous challenges facing educational systems in three southern world countries – Australia, New Zealand and South Africa. The central concern was the identification of ways in which educational systems meet the needs of marginalised students. Two main categories of marginalised students were considered: children and young people who live in remote Indigenous communities; and deeply disadvantaged students in low socioeconomic circumstances on the fringes of urban areas. Relevant issues were identified, research findings shared and recommendations made for policy renewal and reform.

Although there are significant differences in educational provision and outcomes between Australia, New Zealand and South Africa, it was evident that there are some remarkable parallels. All three countries were colonised – with the remnants of that experience still evident – and are multicultural. All have marginalised communities that are not benefiting equally from the wealth enjoyed by parts of the population, and all have some examples of success in enhancing educational opportunities and futures for disadvantaged young people. And in each country there is the will to improve education for marginalised students, yet achieving that goal has often been elusive.

Integral to the conference papers and the chapters that developed from them is the belief that education systems have a moral responsibility to take seriously the plight of those who are economically and socially disadvantaged. Communities historically experience marginalisation through colonisation, systemic racism and other forms of structural oppression. Their marginalisation is inherited from past policies: in South Africa, for example, colonisation was succeeded by the long-entrenched oppression of apartheid, while in Australia and New Zealand the invasion of the white settlers carried often terrible consequences for Indigenous peoples.

The chapters in this collection show how marginalisation is experienced and interpreted in schools and how its origins are found in unequal degrees of power established by those whose interest it is to maintain or even extend inequality. Above all, the chapters highlight how complex and various power relationships underlie marginalised education.

Among the indicators of disadvantage in a society, such as poverty, unemployment and poor health, low educational outcomes are among the most important. In the three southern world societies covered by this book, the relative proportions of each total population falling into the disadvantaged category vary, with South Africa displaying the greatest comparative inequality in income, employment, living conditions and educational standards. However, despite these differences in degree, a common question remains: How can the wealth and taxation resources of the affluent, more privileged segments of each economy be employed to help close the gap in education standards between the rich and poor schools, training institutions and universities?

The foundation for the major themes of the conference and the book was provided by two keynote contributions. The first was delivered by Professor Mick Dodson AM, Australian of the Year 2009, from the Australian National University, and the second by Professor Leon Tikly, from the University of Bristol. They spoke about the challenges and opportunities in Australian and South African education respectively. Dodson highlighted the very marked disparities between the educational attainment of Indigenous and other Australian children. He suggested that, while performative measures of competency in literacy and numeracy are an essential part of improving the education of Indigenous students, there is a danger that this approach will become a form of management and regulation that destroys Indigenous culture, failing to confront the deeper social factors affecting Indigenous education. With an eye to the future, Tikly argued that the quality of education is fundamentally a political issue and that its definitions and frameworks need to be informed by vigorous public debate and advocacy. He outlined a social justice framework for analysing the challenges and opportunities facing South African education in the global era, with a special focus on the quality of basic education experienced by disadvantaged learners.

Difficulties associated with closing the gap in education policies are examined in many of the chapters. Jon Altman and Bill Fogarty, from the Australian National University, focus on those adopted in Australia. They identify three main difficulties: the lack of consultation with the people who are to be the subject of the proposed improvement; the statistical goals of closing the educational gap, which have effectively become abstractions quite separate from the daily reality of life for the people concerned, and which have been converted into quests for 'technical, managerialist' solutions; and the principles designed to achieve the closing the gap outcomes, which do not take into account the diversity of circumstances of the disadvantaged, their beliefs and the practices that separate them from 'mainstream norms'. These difficulties illustrate the complexity of closing the educational gap policies in countries that share the experience of colonial settlement and conquest of existing occupants of the land.

Ensuing themes that were explored at the conference and in the book include: the scope and substance of marginalisation in education in Australia, New Zealand and South Africa; the structure and entrenchment of disadvantage; Indigenous educational challenges in Australia and New Zealand; educational disadvantage and gender; education, social justice and equity.

In this collection a number of key questions about marginalisation in education are examined by the contributors:

- What does marginalised education mean? What is its extent? Are there indices to measure it?
- What form does educational disadvantage take? What is the relationship between ethnicity and educational opportunity, relative outcomes and employment income after completion of study?
- Can the substantial financial and other resources of the well-endowed segment of the economy and society bring better standards and opportunities to those in poorer segments?

- Are there gender inequalities in educational opportunities in diverse societies and do these vary according to ethnicity?
- How can social justice and equity be enhanced by altering educational policies?

Many insights emerge from the chapters included in this collection. Chief among them is the need to recognise the complexity of education policy in diverse societies. It is hard to see how one universal approach can succeed or satisfy all. However, there is a common theme integral to all the chapters. All acknowledge the inequalities in education in past years and ask the pressing question: To what extent are these inequalities entrenched today despite the best efforts of governments in Australia, New Zealand and South Africa to close or at least narrow the educational gap?

In her chapter Thobeka Mda, from the Human Sciences Research Council South Africa, vividly highlights the idea of long-term entrenchment by focusing on the structure and persistence of disadvantage in South Africa. In the apartheid era of the past, there was a deliberate, designed educational policy aimed at ensuring that black people would occupy only menial and unskilled positions in the labour market. However, Mda contends that today the unified national South African Education Department does not adequately tackle inequality in the education system:

> Just as South Africa has two nations (haves and have-nots/rich and poor), so is the education system divided into two. Inequality remains between provinces: Gauteng and the Western Cape are the privileged and rich provinces, with better schools, more resources, and better school results. Moreover, the gap between the rural areas and the urban areas is growing wider.

In Australia, this is also evident, as noted by Mick Dodson in his chapter:

> Quite simply, the experience of school for many Indigenous children in Australia is negative. It remains a place for the formal assessment of how far you fall short. The measureable gap in educational outcomes is preceded and produced by subtle, subjective factors – attitudes and beliefs and expectations feeding off and reinforcing low levels of self-esteem. Schools are not frequently seen as integral to Indigenous communities. Our children do not see them as an extension of their home life, but rather as entry into an alien environment that is, at best, indifferent to their culture and identity. At worst, it is antagonistic.

By contrast, Richard Bedford, from the University of Waikato; Paul Callister, Victoria University of Wellington; and James Newell, Monitoring and Evaluation Research Associates NZ, who write about the New Zealand context, conclude:

> Gaps in education attainment in New Zealand between major ethnic groups persist, especially when the standards for attainment used are those for the majority European population. However, there is evidence in the aggregate statistics… that these gaps are narrowing.

They note that rather than an emphasis on gaps to be bridged, the preferred approach in New Zealand is 'strengths based, one that emphasises the potentials of people rather than persistent deficits or gaps… between measures of performance'.

The causes of differing educational outcomes for various groups in comparative countries are, of course, the product of each nation's history, composition, policy and other circumstances. Lessons of achievement in one country in improving educational standards and reducing equality cannot readily be transported as a policy base to another national setting. But the analysis in this book does cast light on different possible avenues of improving educational outcomes in each of the three diverse countries examined.

In addition to the over-riding need to recognise the complexity of education policy in diverse societies, a number of other important insights about marginalisation are developed in this book. First, there are dangers in a diverse society in trying to apply an educational policy that adheres too tightly to national mainstream benchmarks and does not encompass local needs and aspirations.

Second, the ways in which students are empowered to learn in the mainstream classroom setting is sometimes a more critical issue than the idea of 'closing the gap'.

Third, in an unequal society, a sense of national ownership of the difficulties of becoming a 'knowledge' society is necessary and policies regarding funding need to be specific. Effective educational reforms require adequate, continuing, long-term funding.

Fourth, in societies with a 'toxic mix' (see Bloch this volume) of crime and violence in schools, disruptive and ill-disciplined behaviour undermines the scope for learning and creates wider adverse consequences in the general community. An agreed vision and clear plan, with priorities and targets, and national mobilisation to make education a first priority, is one part of the effort required to counter the toxic mix.

Fifth, a variety of background initiatives can help to bolster the quality of educational services in poor, remote societies. These include, for example, better access to material child and health care services, kindergarten facilities, and culturally inclusive learning environments.

Sixth, in disadvantaged communities a broad range of activities needs to be linked to the school experience of children – for example, the school house should be in a central position, encouraging parental participation.

Seventh, there is added scope in dualistic societies to broaden the contribution that schooling can make to social and intercultural as well as economic benefits.

Eighth, social participation depends critically on access to new technologies and their integration into society and its institutions, enabling children and young people to use these technologies in the cultural and economic life of those on the periphery.

In his chapter Yusef Waghid of Stellenbosch University explores the notion of a 'discourse of ethics'. He argues that education has abdicated from its task of engaging in ethical deliberation and imagining the good life. Increasingly, it has become an instrument of performativity within the global economy, concerned solely with transmitting the knowledge and skills needed to prepare for economic productivity. By so doing, Waghid argues that education has relinquished its primary mission of cultivating goodness in people and suggests that the way forward is to undertake 'the monumental task of reclaiming goodness by connecting education to critique'.

He explains what a discourse ethics to guide education might look like. It is not just about imposing views on others, but entails actually engaging students and colleagues by offering some justification for the reasons. A discourse-oriented education is one underpinned by norms of justification through making the point clearer to others, who in turn offer an account of their reasons for agreeing or disagreeing with the arguments.

The educational practice advocated by Waghid captures the mood and spirit of the conference and this subsequent volume. At the conference there was open trans-cultural discussion. It epitomised what Waghid rues the academy is losing in the culture of performativity that prevails. All the contributors recognise that although education often marginalises various groups, it can also be the means for improvement. Even when it disappoints, education has the potential to promote social justice for both individuals and groups.

Section 1:
The scope and substance of marginalisation in education

Challenges and Opportunities in Australian Indigenous Education

Mick Dodson
Australian National University

When I became Australian of the Year in January 2009 I said I wanted to talk about the protection of the rights and human dignity of all Australians. I said that sometimes we don't speak up or act because we think a problem is too hard or that it will somehow go away. I said I believe that we're better than that.

What I said was that I would like to see every Australian child next Australia Day geared up for the start of the 2010 school year. And I said I wanted to be confident that those children were going to get the best education this country can give them. I want it for Aboriginal and Torres Strait Islander children and I want it for other children who are not getting it now because of where they live, because of poverty and because we've failed them. The fact that many of our children are not getting the best education is something none of us should tolerate – or dismiss as inevitable or too hard to fix.

Every child deserves a good education and a country as prosperous as Australia should be able to provide it – and yet we still don't do it. Education is something we've let slide miserably in recent decades. We've failed a lot of children in that time. And many of those children – a disproportionate number – are Indigenous children. We've been failing them for a lot longer.

What I'm saying is that we need to invest in the children and their teachers – the human capital, as people like to say these days – as well as the physical infrastructure. Buildings and roads and computer technology and gymnasiums and science labs are essential to any kind of education revolution. But they're worth nothing without people to occupy them, operate them, teach and learn in them. The education revolution begins and ends with people: teaching them, giving them skills; and, with those skills, the confidence and wherewithal to do their very best for themselves and their communities.

We need more investment in teachers and in their professional development so that we can reasonably expect them to be good teachers; so more good students will grow up wanting to be teachers; and more teachers will believe in the worth of their vocation and in the potential of every child they teach. We need investment in curriculum development. For a start we need curricula that teachers, students and parents can understand, school reports they can understand. That's surely a bare minimum. We need good minds and common sense brought to bear on it – not education theory or bureaucratic fashion. We need curricula that will fit students for fulfilling, useful lives and give them all at least a roughly equal chance at happiness.

It never was an easy task – but the shame is not in failing, it's in not trying as hard or as intelligently as we can. May I also say we should be giving every Australian child a chance to learn about this country's Indigenous history and culture – it is the oldest surviving culture in the world and, as the Prime Minister says, it's a culture all Australians can take great pride in.

I say, let's begin with education: I think we can all agree that a good education is a right and that all Australian children have that right. I think we can all agree that in bestowing knowledge, skills, opportunity and a chance at happiness and self-sufficiency, education also bestows dignity. And all agree, I think, that this right and this dignity are a good deal more than symbolic – they have profound practical effects.

I would like to tell you about a history lesson at Majura Primary School in Canberra. While Canberra is the capital city of Australia, it is a very modest city. Or, at least – it is very modest in size. It has a population of just over 340,000 people. Its surrounds are largely rural, with a number of national parks and a fair bit of bush land.

One day earlier this year, the children of Grade 5 at Majura Primary School went for a bush walk. When they returned to school they discovered that Grade 4 had taken over their classroom. They were told that the desks, the blackboard, their bags and books no longer belonged to them.

The Grade 5 students, confident of what was theirs, asked for it back. The Grade 4 students refused: it all belonged to them now. Not only did they refuse to give the classroom back and the other stuff, but the Grade 5 children were told to stand aside – to stand on the fringes of the classroom – as they now had no right to stand anywhere else. And the teachers supported this.

The Grade 5 students became upset, then angry. They insisted: 'Give us our classroom back'. The other students didn't budge. The anger of the Grade 5s turned to bewilderment and a sense of helplessness. Everything had been turned upside down. Grade 4 seemed to be settling in to stay.

Sound familiar? Like the famous 'blue eyes' experiment that taught students in the US how rapid and devastating institutionalised racial prejudice can be, the colonisation of the Grade 5 classroom at Majura Primary School produced an almost immediate and sharply felt response of injustice and marginalisation in the dispossessed students. The classroom colonisation lesson has the critical experiential dimension of learning that we so often fail to include when teaching our children. It is not just a matter of sparking the imagination and breathing life into the dull facts of text books. It is about an educational experience that reaches and realigns the perspectives and preconceptions that surround and influence our understanding and our ability to learn.

At a deeper level, it is an approach to education that recognises that our perspectives, our attitudes, our understanding, our ability and desire to learn, are all shaped, not only by our access to information and instruction: they are profoundly shaped by our personal experience, our social context and that of our family and community. Just as non-Indigenous children at Majura bring to school background ideas and feelings about the history of Australia and its settlement, so, at a broader level, Indigenous children bring with them certain ideas, feelings and expectations about the formal education system. Within Indigenous families there is a living memory of education as an instrument of disempowerment: dismantling languages, cultures and traditions.

We all come to school from somewhere. Where we come from, what we believe, what we believe about ourselves, significantly – predictably – affects our performance at school. Effective education must have meaning in terms of children's background. It must connect with their real-life experience, the social context and cultural values of their family and community. This critical dimension is often absent in the schooling of Indigenous children in Australia. The central challenge, in my view, is to create an education system and school environment that genuinely connects with the lives of Indigenous peoples.

In Australia the marked difference between the lives of Indigenous and non-Indigenous Australians is known as 'the gap', and it exists in virtually every aspect of existence. Indigenous infant and young-child mortality is two to three times higher than for all Australian infants and children. Our life expectancy is from 17 to 11 years less than other Australians. Our rate of imprisonment is 37 per cent higher. Our rate of employment is 24 per cent lower. In relation to education, 38 per cent fewer Indigenous students complete secondary schooling. Performance in reading, writing and numeracy is substantially lower, and the differential in this performance has remained unchanged for over a decade.

Closing the Gap on Indigenous Disadvantage is a central commitment of the Council of Australian Governments (COAG). Under a national reform agreement, the federal, state and territory governments have identified six objectives:

- closing the life expectancy gap within a generation
- halving the gap in mortality rates for Indigenous children under five within a decade
- ensuring all Indigenous four-years-olds in remote communities have access to early childhood education within five years
- halving the gap for Indigenous students in reading, writing and numeracy within a decade
- halving the gap for Indigenous students in Year 12 attainment or equivalent attainment rates by 2020
- halving the gap in employment outcomes between Indigenous and non-Indigenous Australians within a decade.

To achieve these objectives, seven building blocks have been identified:
- early childhood
- schooling
- health
- economic participation
- healthy homes
- safe communities
- governance and leadership.

Under the COAG agreement we have: objectives, targets, strategic platforms, building blocks, headline indicators and strategic areas; multifaceted inputs, outcomes and outputs; identified roles and responsibilities.

No doubt such things are necessary for the macromanagement of public policy. And the terminology comes with the territory – but it is language very distant from the reality of the lives of Indigenous Australians. It speaks of another kind of gap. I am not simply carping about words. It goes deeper. In my view, this language expresses both a perspective and an approach, where the human dynamics and substance of the issues to be tackled become subordinate to their external description and measurement. The education of our children is predominantly described and assessed in functional, managerial terms: strategic targets, performance indicators, core competencies and levels of attainment.

Take the example of school attendance rates. Measureable improvements in rates of school attendance seem to absorb greater energy than examining Indigenous expectations and experiences when actually attending school. Put bluntly, the issue sometimes seems to be converted from increasing genuine participation to simply getting more bums on seats.

In Australia stringent means have recently been employed to increase school attendance. The idea of making welfare payments to Indigenous people conditional on their children's attendance at school was first introduced under the previous Australian Government's intervention in the Northern Territory in 2007. The intervention was designed to reduce child abuse and encourage 'responsible behaviour and better parenting'. All welfare recipients living in 'prescribed areas' on Aboriginal land – roughly 650,000 hectares, with a population of some 45,000 Aboriginal men, women and children – were subject to income management. A presumption of inadequacy and delinquency was applied geographically, in a form of indirect racial discrimination.

While described by the government as a 'special measure', the operation of the Racial Discrimination Act (RDA) was suspended to ensure that this, and other pre-emptive government measures, could take effect. The government was expected to introduce a Bill into the parliament during the November 2009 sittings, but debate on the Bill will not occur until Parliament resumes in 2010. With the need to go through committee processes, we are likely not to see a change in the law and a reinstatement of the RDA until some time in March [This was the state of play when this speech was given in November 2009]. And there is no guarantee of that, as the government does not control the Senate, which has proven to be generally hostile towards at least some of the government's legislative initiatives.

The current government (for now) has maintained the central imperatives of the intervention and, at the beginning of the 2009 school year, started further trials linking school attendance with welfare payments for Aboriginal parents in six Northern Territory communities. While this management system may produce a reduction in the gap between Indigenous and non-Indigenous attendance rates, it opens a more significant gap. A coercive approach to increasing school attendance rates confuses physical attendance with genuine participation. It reinforces the perception of Indigenous parents and their children that the education system is part and parcel of a wider system of government control over their lives. It plays into and widens the existing social and cultural divide between Indigenous families and their local schools. It drives children into school rather than drawing them in. Most critically, it confirms the negative stereotypes held about – and held by – Indigenous people that are, in my view, one of the most significant and intimate challenges to improving the education of our children. As Charles Davidson, President of the New South Wales Aboriginal Educational Consultative Group, put it:

> [We] cannot think of a single problem plaguing Aboriginal children – from alienation from school, high rates of absenteeism, enjoyment of school, significant underachievement, reduced educational and career aspirations, youth depression and suicide, conceptions about employment prospects and ability to secure rewarding productive careers – that is not traceable, at least in part – to the failure of education systems to maximise our children's identity and self-concept as Aboriginal people. (Craven and Parente 2003)

There is a dynamic interaction between perception and performance. The way we are seen by others and the way we internalise that view has the ability to affect material outcomes. The negative effects of this vicious cycle are most clearly observed in the field of education.

The phenomenon of 'stereotype threat' has been demonstrated in research in the US (Singham 1998, 12). It describes the predictably lower performance of black students when taking tests where they were told the purpose of the tests was to compare their results with those of white students. When the same tests were given without the students being told that the results were for racial comparison, the performance of black students was consistently higher. The same effect was observed where women were told that the purpose of testing was to compare their results in mathematics with those of male students. It was concluded that 'the fear that a poor performance on a test will confirm a stereotype in the mind of an examiner imposes an anxiety on the test-taker that is difficult to overcome' (Singham 1998, 12). The anticipated expectation of lower-level performance is confirmed in practice.

Other research suggests that the perceived link between effort and the benefit in return has a direct effect on education outcomes. There is a correlation between educational effort and the strength of 'the belief that educational effort leads to academic credentials, which in turn lead to gainful employment' (Singham 1998, 12). Where this chain of connection is perceived to be weak, there is a lower commitment to academic effort.

In plain terms, unless you see that there is a realistic prospect of achievement leading to real employment, why bother? Significantly, this perception of a weak belief in the connection between effort in the schoolroom and employment transcends socioeconomic background. Poor educational outcomes were seen to have less to do with poverty than with the strength of racial stereotypes and expectations of success.

Quite simply, the experience of school for many Indigenous children in Australia is negative. It remains a place for the formal assessment of how far you fall short. The measureable gap in educational outcomes is preceded and produced by subtle, subjective factors – attitudes and beliefs and expectations feeding off and reinforcing low levels of self-esteem. Schools are not frequently seen as integral to Indigenous communities. Our children do not see them as an extension of their home life, but rather as entry into an alien environment that is, at best, indifferent to their culture and identity. At worst, it is antagonistic. I can think of no more powerful way to lay a strong pathway between students' homes and their school than for them to start their learning in the language they speak in their family and community.

In the Northern Territory 40 per cent of Aboriginal students speak a language other than English at home. Bilingual teaching programs have been run in the Territory since 1973. In 1999 the government announced the closure of the Bilingual Language Program. Due to the strong opposition of Aboriginal communities, they were maintained in some places, rebadged as the Two-Way Program; but their numbers actually declined substantially.

In 2005 the Minister for Education put bilingual education back on the agenda, recognising it as 'an important teaching methodology'. Then, late in 2009, she announced that all teaching in all Northern Territory schools would be compulsorily conducted in English for the first four hours of the school day. That is like your culture – that of your family and your community – being sent to the back of the school bus. In the drive to close the performance gap, the separation of the school from the family and communal environment is widened, which in turn dampens performance.

As expressed by Gulumbu Yunupingu, a school council member of Yirrkala Primary School:

> We [are]... saddened by such an approach because our language comes from within the very essence of our being. It makes us who we are. That essence is sacred... Just like the English feel about their language. We Yolngu don't know how they think and they don't

know how we think about our language and our stories and our very beings. So you see the language comes from within, it's alive, we are still living, we are not dead yet. (Whitmont 2009)

I should make it abundantly clear – if there could be any doubt – that I support the objective of Indigenous children reaching national standards in reading, writing and numeracy. There should be no soft standards. In Australia, competency in English is essential. Regular attendance at school is essential. Progression to tertiary study, training and employment is the common goal. The real question is about the most effective, sustainable way to achieve these results.

To me, the answer is found in the root meaning of 'education'. The word derives from the combination of the Latin words *e* and *ducare,* meaning to lead out – to draw forth. The concentration on education as a systemic means of delivering instruction, teaching and assessing functional skills and core competencies, together with the provision of the necessary infrastructure and hardware, has obscured this fundamental meaning. This has particular significance for the education of Indigenous children. The notion of 'closing a gap' very easily slides unintentionally into the idea of compensatory schooling – that there is a deficit in our children that must be made up. Or that the languages and cultures of our peoples are part of the problem.

Our starting point must be to envisage children with intelligence, imagination, culture and values, desires and expectations for their lives. And our task is to move from that point – to lead out, draw forth and expand all those human qualities and potential. Education must first affirm who we are, before presenting the potential of who we may be. Schooling must start through building an understanding and connection with the social and cultural context into which Indigenous children are born. It must have meaning in terms of their experience, creating a confluence between their culture and experience, validating identity, building self-confidence and expanding expectations.

There are impressive signs of progress in adopting this approach. I see and hear of schools across our country – like the Majura Primary School – taking on this critical element of education, innovating and excelling in it. Majura School has Indigenous culture and history woven throughout the fabric of the school and the curriculum. There's a gallery including Indigenous art, the Horton map of Indigenous Australia and the Aboriginal and Torres Strait Islander flags are all prominently displayed. These things say to the 20 Indigenous students at the school: 'Your cultures, history and past experiences and identity are recognised and valued here. You are valued here.' Equally important, they say to the non-Indigenous students that Indigenous history, cultures, experiences and peoples are valued and worth learning about.

In rural and remote areas of Australia, things can be a lot more difficult than in the suburbs of Canberra and in other urban settings. Indigenous communities have chronic and acute housing needs; there is an endemic lack of access to standard health services, communications and other vital infrastructure. School facilities are at best basic. The turnover of teachers in remote Aboriginal communities is often measured in months rather than years. There are problems with violence, alcohol and drug abuse, child abuse and neglect, unemployment, underemployment. Serious community malaise and aimlessness.

Just as education is fundamental to improving every aspect of the lives of Indigenous children – from their health and life expectancy to their participation in the workplace – so their wellbeing in every other aspect of life impacts on their education. Tackling health, housing, violence and substance abuse across Indigenous communities – through family education and the promotion of positive parenting skills – must be linked to a shift in our approach to schooling. The school house must be repositioned to place it at the centre of Indigenous communities, inviting participation on a basis of encouragement and trust. Parents are the first teachers of their children. Their role must be recognised, respected and incorporated in the governance of schools and the delivery of education.

Community buses to collect children from home, breakfast and lunch programs run by parents, elders teaching language and culture – all promote connection. Life-long learning activities for parents, family centres, access to early childhood development and other children's services, co-located with the community school, create an environment where the formal education of Indigenous children becomes part of a wider capacity-building process.

Progress across all the fronts necessary to achieve better educational outcomes in these circumstances will be hard fought. I do not need to tell you that to speak of the problems we face as 'challenges' is to place a bit of spin on them. It is difficult to get traction on these challenges. And this difficulty gives rise to frustration and impatience. In Australia I see this impatience expressed in the linkage of welfare payments to school attendance and top-down decisions about the place of Indigenous languages – together with other approaches that attempt to shift behavioural problems and to improve educational outcomes by pre-emptive measures.

In my view, such measures will not drive the necessary changes. They do not build positive, responsible behaviour; in fact they remove responsibility, increase a sense of helplessness, stigmatise and reinforce negative self-images. They compromise human rights and do not foster the human dynamics and capacity building that will drive change. Approaches primarily shaped by a concentration on objective targets and performance measurement become, insidiously, a form of management and regulation that is both destructive of Indigenous culture and the rights of our peoples. While performance indicators are an essential part of achieving and monitoring improvements in the education of our children, there is a coincident, complimentary need to construct and monitor Indigenous educational practice within a framework of rights.

In this respect I believe Australia should look to South Africa. While our countries have commonly ratified all relevant major human rights instruments, in Australia we have no express constitutional guarantee of the enjoyment of the fundamental right to education or of ancillary cultural rights affecting Indigenous education. Chapter 2 of the South African Constitution articulates a Bill of Rights. Section 29 (1) provides everyone with a right to basic education, including adult education. Section 29 (2) specifies a citizen's right to receive education in the official language or languages of their choice, where it is reasonably practicable.

I do not wish to pose as an expert on the South African Constitution. Or advocate its wholesale adoption. Its provisions are adapted to the circumstances of South Africa. South Africa has 11 official languages that reflect the various cultural backgrounds of the major population groups. Indigenous Australians comprise only 2.5 per cent of our national population and, in small numbers, we speak many languages. Moreover, I am acutely aware that the mere articulation of a right does not guarantee its exercise and enjoyment in practice. But when I look at the further provisions in Section 29 (2), which deal with the effective implementation of the right to education in an official language, the section directs the state to take into account: (a) equity, (b) practicability and (c) the need to redress the results of past racially discriminatory laws and practices. The constitutional prescription of these factors throws a framework of values over any approach to the state's delivery of education. It recalls the historical context of this enterprise and clearly identifies the impact of the past as a living factor that must be directly addressed.

A framework of rights not only constrains and guides the state; it speaks directly to citizens – to the people who hold those rights. It takes us down to the community level where the real work of improving the education of our children must take place. It insists on respect for the human rights and the humanity, the cultures and values, the historical and contemporary experiences of the parents and children that must be at the heart of improvements in Indigenous education. It takes us to the human scale and reminds us that we must always start with the engagement of young children, born into the residue of the past, but with full creative capacity to transcend it and to excel. Our greatest opportunity lies in those young children, in their energy and their aspirations. Our greatest challenge is not to fail another generation of Indigenous children.

References

Craven, R G; Parente, A. 2003. 'Unlocking Indigenous educational disadvantage: Indigenous community members' perceptions of self-concept research as a potent potential key'. Paper presented at New Zealand Association for Research in Education (NZARE)/Australian Association for Research in Education (AARE) Conference, Auckland, New Zealand, November 2003. Accessed 19 January 2009. Available from: http://www.aare.edu.au/03pap/par03762.pdf.

Singham, M. 1998. 'The canary in the mine. The achievement gap between black and white students'. *The Phi Delta Kappan* 80, 1 (September): 8–15.

Whitmont, D. 2009. 'Going back to Lajamanu'. *Four Corners*, Australian Broadcasting Commission, 14 September. Accessed 19 January 2010. Available from: www.abc.net.au/4corners/content/2009/s2683288.htm.

My Story Should Not Be Unusual
The Education of an Australian Aboriginal Girl

Inala Cooper
Department of Planning and Community Development, Victoria
Indigenous Advisory Council, Monash University

In Australia it is customary to acknowledge the traditional owners of the land on which we meet. In doing so, we recognise and pay respect to them, their elders and their land. I'd like to acknowledge the people who belong to this land we meet on today, and I pay my respects to them.

My story is important. I was born in 1978, in Melbourne. According to statistics at that time, it was not expected that I would live past 60 years of age compared to 75 years of age for a non-Aboriginal baby born in the same year. So there I was, a baby. When I was three, I went to kinder. When I was four, I went to school. When I was 17, I went to university. When I was 20, I had my degree.

'You're so lucky,' they said, 'to have had that opportunity, to have graduated from university'. But luck should have had nothing to do with it. You see, it was not expected that I would obtain a university degree. In the 1990s, only three per cent of Indigenous people were enrolled in higher education in Australia. Current figures have risen slightly, but still nation-wide only two per cent of Indigenous people have a tertiary qualification, compared to 12.8 per cent of all Australians.

My experience of school and uni was a good one. I liked school and had a lot of support. No, they didn't expect I would fail because I was Aboriginal. It was expected that I excel, because I was the only Aboriginal child there. That was my challenge. 'Do your people proud', they said. 'You're lucky you don't live *out there*, with *them*. You're different.'

But being different should have nothing to do with it. Why shouldn't *those who live out there* have the right to go to school, be supported and excel? What they meant when they referred to *those out there* was the Aboriginal kids. But I'm an Aboriginal kid. Yes, but, you know, the ones that live on the outskirts of town. The ones who play truant, drink alcohol, take drugs and get pregnant at 15; the ones whose parents never know where they are. These are not reasons to deny someone access to education. These are not reasons to presume someone is incapable of academic success.

In Australia only 33 per cent of Aboriginal children complete their schooling, compared to a national average of 77 per cent. I am an example of someone in that 33 per cent. Is this a result of luck, attitude, government policy, money, or a combination of these things? Of the 67 per cent of Aboriginal children who don't complete school, most leave in their last two years. Too many do not take on work or further study. Too many also become involved with the justice system, which establishes another barrier to achieving at school or in higher education and getting a job. Today's young people will set the economic futures for the next generation. This is about making generational change.

As I mentioned before, I was born in Melbourne, in the state of Victoria, which is in the south-east of our country. Aboriginal people have continuously occupied south-eastern Australia for over 40,000 years. Thirty-eight distinct groups shared the land now called Victoria, each speaking a different language. Today, six per cent of Australia's Indigenous populations live in Victoria. Aboriginal cultures in Victoria are vibrant and evolving. Today's Aboriginal Victorians reflect a wide range of backgrounds, cultures and experiences.

Melbourne is my home; it's where I live. The spiritual home of my family is in the town of Broome, in Western Australia, which is a long way away from Melbourne. It's about a seven-and-a-half-hour flight. Geographically, it's about the same distance as from here [South Africa] to Sudan – some 3000 kilometres.

There are many Aboriginal Victorians who, like me, are not living in the spiritual lands of their ancestors. There are many reasons for this, one being the forcible removal and displacement of Aboriginal people by the government. Land is central and of overriding importance to Aboriginal people. The land has physical, emotional and spiritual significance. When people are removed from their land the effects can be catastrophic – on culture, ways of life, law, learning and identity.

Aboriginal social and cultural knowledge is traditionally passed on to younger generations through song, stories, art and dance. The education of the young was, and still is, a shared responsibility – the roles of parents and extended family members have equal importance. Throughout my schooling and into adulthood, my parents and extended family have been my greatest influence. Being surrounded by people who believed in me enabled me to understand that I had the right to be educated.

There are those who don't have people around them to believe in them, push them, nurture them and guide them through their schooling. Remember *those out there*? So what about them? Who will believe in the 67 per cent of Aboriginal kids who are not attending school? A change needs to be made. Not only to get these kids to school but, again, we're talking here about generational change, where attending school is expected and truancy is not tolerated. Where those who can't attend school, for whatever reason, are individually supported by their communities and the education system.

Young people are motivated when they believe there is a genuine interest in them and expectations of them. So, how do we increase the number of Aboriginal students graduating from school and university? Do we go in at the final year of secondary school and encourage all Aboriginal students to 'Choose Monash!'? Perhaps we do. But think about when it first occurred to you that university was even an option. It's not necessarily an idea that pops up in your final year of secondary school. It starts much earlier than that. Exposure to the idea that university is an option needs to begin in the first year of secondary school, when students are 11, 12, 13 years old.

Raising the aspirations of Aboriginal students needs to start early, by enabling them to experience the economy. Conversations about university and work need to begin early. Many young Aboriginal people have little exposure to work, either through their own experience or that of their family, and don't make a connection between learning and working. Young Aboriginal people should be encouraged and given opportunities to experience work while they are at school, regardless of their family or socioeconomic situation (SES).

The link between SES and academic achievement has long been debated and researched. Theories are many, including the belief that students from a low-SES household are disadvantaged at school because they lack an academic home environment. How governments interpret this debate influences education policies designed to ameliorate the educational disadvantage of Indigenous people.

The Australian Government has made a commitment to close the gap in life expectancy between Indigenous and non-Indigenous people. Today, Indigenous people in Australia – that's me – are expected to die 17 years earlier than non-Indigenous people.

Currently I work for the Ministerial Taskforce on Aboriginal Affairs in Victoria, which is chaired by our Deputy Premier. The taskforce was established in 2006 and is responsible for implementing the Victorian Indigenous Affairs Framework. The primary goal of the framework is to improve life expectancy and the quality of life for Indigenous Victorians. Education is a critical component of this framework and within it are six strategic areas for action, including to improve literacy and numeracy, increase the number of Year 12 completions or equivalent qualifications, and develop pathways to employment for Aboriginal people.

Some very successful initiatives already implemented by the government include better access to maternal and child health services for Aboriginal mothers and children, free kindergarten for three- and four-year-old Aboriginal children and an education strategy for Aboriginal students. This strategy highlights the importance of things like culturally inclusive learning environments, intensive literacy and numeracy programs for students achieving below expected levels, and developing an individual education plan for each Aboriginal student.

Government cannot achieve these things alone. The responsibility must be shared. Involvement by parents is crucial. Our parents are our first role models and it is they, together with our extended families and our communities, who have a responsibility to support young people through their education.

Role models and mentors for students have a huge influence, on both individuals and peer groups. To have someone to guide you and who believes in you makes all the difference to a young person. Role models for young people come in many forms – pop stars, athletes, models. Exposure of young people to academic role models is of incredible importance, as is celebrities promoting the importance of gaining an education. Leveraging your alumni, providing leadership and mentoring opportunities to Aboriginal kids will empower them to succeed.

In addition, scholarships for Aboriginal students can have an enormous impact on engagement with and desire to complete their education. Scholarships for high-achieving students in their final years of secondary school and into university are certainly of huge value – but imagine the impact on a 12- or 13-year-old student, in her first year of secondary school, being awarded a scholarship by a university. This is simple. Take, for example, a new laptop, or some money for school books. And then imagine that child – proud, beaming, excited: 'A university believes in me. A university believes that it is possible for me to finish school.' Imagine the impact on that child's identity and sense of self.

In Australia we are struggling to get Aboriginal kids to Year 9, let alone Year 10. The challenge to get Aboriginal kids to Year 12 and to complete secondary school or equivalent is a great one – but not impossible. Investment in these kids needs to begin early. When I completed year 12, one of my teachers remarked that in all her career and the history of the school, I was the first Aboriginal student she had seen graduate.

It should not be unusual to have the school completion rate of Aboriginal students the same or higher than mainstream Australia's. I want to live in an Australia where it is not strange to see an Aboriginal doctor, dentist or lawyer. Where it is not weird to see an Aboriginal judge, professor or scientist. Where it is not extraordinary to expect our country to one day be led by an Aboriginal prime minister or president. I want to live in an Australia where my story is not unusual.

Bridging the Gap in South African Education

Graeme Bloch
Development Bank of Southern Africa

Ordinary South Africans feel troubled by the state of crisis in their education system. More than that, as shown in the recent round of Development Bank of Southern Africa (DBSA) Education Conversations held around the country, people are looking for solutions and want to make a difference. My hope for the conference held at Monash South Africa in November 2009 was that we could learn from differences and similarities in the experience of marginalisation, exclusion and the many barriers to development within the participating societies – Australia, South Africa and New Zealand.

I want to praise the recent round of apologies in Australia. There is often reason to be cynical or questioning. However, I don't think one can overestimate the importance of publicly and symbolically confronting head-on a deep social problem, acknowledging openly its human impact and cruelty, and finding it in oneself to accept responsibility. In South Africa, four young men at Free State University – who treated adult workers old enough to be their mothers in an abysmal and humiliating way – learned in a national debate that there can be no forgiveness without apology.

This chapter is about education and the reproduction of a deep state of inequality and underperformance in South African schools. These inequalities threaten the very cohesion of South Africa's new democracy. In their racial dimensions, education and schooling specifically reproduce inequalities from the past. This bifurcated education system ensures that the children of the poor will not find a way into quality education as a sure and tested route to confront their poverty. There is, however, a growing 'policy space' where South Africans are confronting the reality of poor performance in education and its developmental implications. The potential exists for broad, multi-stakeholder alliances involving communities and citizens, NGOs and business, to confront the education problem, led by a renewed and listening government.

But let the young speak. There was a short lad, part of a guard of honour at a semi-rural school in the Vaal, who greeted me on arrival at Michael Rua School recently. 'I like you', I said, 'you are about the same size I was when I was in grade 6'. 'My name is Gift', he replied. 'I may be small, but I am big in here', and he pointed his fingers to his head.

Yet, for most students, schools in South Africa are a disaster zone.[1] Instead of being places of academic achievement and excellence, where students can develop their talents and shoot for the stars, schools have become zones of exclusion for learners, with poor outcomes, where many students feel unsafe from bullying or violence, and where the skills, attitudes and behaviours for employment and a democratic future are not being nurtured.

Outcomes are poor, so that South Africa does not produce the engineers, doctors, accountants, teachers or managers who can help to imagine a future that has not yet been lived, who can develop plans for it and implement the means to get the society there. Worse, these poor outcomes take a racial dimension in a society where all children rightfully expect the best. Inequalities are reproduced in ways that are neither fair nor sustainable.

There are plenty of facts to show that – despite vast resources and a high budget for education – South Africa s just not getting value for its spend. In Europe, 75 per cent of children can do what only South Africa's top 10 per cent can, yet all have to compete in a cut-throat globalised world. More than half of South African children, mostly black, drop out before Matric. They routinely come last or near the bottom for all international tests on literacy and numeracy, with only some 35 per cent of students reading or counting at appropriate levels and only 18 per cent able to do both. Where half of white matriculants go on to university, less than 12 per cent of blacks do; where 62.5 per cent of Grade 3 students in ex-model C schools could do maths in 2003, only 0.1 of a per cent of township kids could! Neither university nor vocational skills systems have found their measure. South Africa's kids are not getting it. The country is failing generation after generation of young people.

Last year's DBSA-coordinated Education Roadmap – itself a stakeholder process involving teacher unions, government, officials, NGOs, academics and others – identified the interplay of complex factors in the 'toxic mix' that makes education change enormously difficult.

The first factor is historical and real – Dr Verwoerd's[2] refusal to allow blacks to be shown 'the green pastures where they will not be allowed to graze' or to study maths 'when they would not be allowed to use it' has left a poor educational heritage and a shallow layer of maths skills among teachers. Such deficits cannot disappear overnight, despite the best plans. Hiring Zimbabwean teachers or putting Indian experts in deep rural schools – as some propose – may at best be short-term fixes. What future black mathematics graduate will choose teaching over accountancy, business or politics?

Similarly, students are often hungry, suffer from worms, have lost parents to HIV/AIDS, and learn in schools without laboratories, libraries, computers or sports fields and sometimes even electricity. These historical legacies have been compounded by serious policy mistakes in post-democratic South Africa – from inexplicable teacher retrenchments to closure of teacher colleges to the over-optimistic ideals and regressive impacts of outcomes-based education (OBE).

The three levels that interact to hold schools back are:

1. In-class: teachers are not prepared, nor disciplined, nor have content knowledge to teach effectively. Unions have become locked in confrontational labour relations mode in continuous war with education departments. Teaching is the only profession with no agreed supervision. Year after year the South African Democratic Teachers' Union (SADTU), the main teacher union, complains about results in poor schools, but is seldom seen to mobilise its members who are in those poor schools. A culture of victimhood prevails. So Ronald Nyathi, an official of SADTU Gauteng, can threaten students with 'extreme violence' in one strike; say, 'We love our principals; we don't want to see any dead ones' in another strike; complain that naming and shaming child abusers would be unfair, impacting on their careers in yet another. The one hope is that his union is finally beginning to draw a line; even, on occasion, in public.

2. Support to school: there are limited management skills among the 27,000 principals and inadequate support from government and education districts – compliance and forms substitute for pedagogical, social and administrative support that helps teachers get on with the job of teaching. Officials struggle to build real partnerships.

3. Societal: whether it be infrastructure backlogs, gangs, hunger, low parent involvement or a society that fails to value educational aspiration and achievement, education has not found its accepted place as the

tried and tested route out of poverty. Recent plans to make education 'priority number one', led by President Zuma, do give hope.

I am amazed at how successful 'gang' schools are: somehow, in the hidden underworld, the gangs are able to train and nurture young people to achieve their aims of focused, lawless behaviour. This shows how children are able to apply themselves if given opportunities – for young people are out and about at all hours, consistently and with discipline. They can quickly dismantle the latest burglar-alarm technology. They steal to order. They have an income, a steady job and, if they work hard, they have respect in the gang community and enough money to even fund community events. Why can secret criminal schools do what society's schools fail to achieve – provide jobs, skills, respect and a sense of belonging? Why is there no clear social vision of achievement and excellence to challenge the attraction of the gang leaders?

More than that – in the first place, crime and violence in schools reproduce the violence and bullying of the wider society and are carried into schools from that society. Then, violence within schools impacts on all three levels essential to schooling. In the classroom students are disruptive, ill-disciplined and engage in over-sexualised and inappropriate behaviour that threatens learning. In the playground the routine, administration and order of the school day are threatened as gangsters roam across the school grounds and into classrooms. Principals are shot dead by union rivals, as happened recently in KwaZulu-Natal province. And in society students are attracted away from schools by the 'bling' of gang life, are raped and threatened, and the soul of their communities is eaten away.

So a 'toxic mix' conspires to make it difficult and complex to change education outcomes. Very few countries in recent times have succeeded. Yet South Africa expects better and to be different, as it creaks under the unchanged weight of its apartheid past. In-class and teacher-based issues, poor technical, administrative and political support around the school, and limitations of society – from gangs to lack of books in the home – all combine to reinforce the past; to encourage division and mediocrity. Instead of a learning nation going forward, a deep mix of history and sociology, of bad choice and unsatisfactory delivery, institutional failure and social deficit all hold back the country and stop schools from doing what they should do. In particular, poor black, rural and township children are at the receiving end of the 'toxic mix' that holds them back.

Much has been done in 15 years. But the task should not be underestimated. It took enormous effort to unify education departments. There is the logistical achievement of a single national Matric exam and high levels of budgetary allocation to education, realigning spend to pro-poor norms. We have a raft of praiseworthy programs that aim to improve teaching and conditions of learning. Measures support teacher training and bursaries, school nutrition, infrastructure improvement, scholar transport and school safety initiatives, and acknowledge the need for learning strategies around basic literacy and numeracy. Where there were only 1200 black matriculants nationally in 1976, now more than 600,000 students write Matric, two-thirds of whom are black.

Much is also being done on the ground to make a difference. Many schools and communities – from Colesburg in the Hantam, to Bitou/Plettenburg Bay to Soweto to deep-rural Limpopo and historic church schools – daily face their issues and come up with action-plans. They draw down maths support, sports possibilities such as Dreamfields, or NGOs that make a difference from extra-murals to citizenship classes. Even in the poorest circumstances, there are well-managed schools that get results. Graduates from poorer schools 'plough back' to provide networks and assistance to disadvantaged children; corporates have adjusted funding models to encourage better partnerships and contribute skills such as management and resources within a longer term, more hands-on approach.

Government too deserves praise. OBE and some teacher burdens have been removed. Post-Polokwane [ANC conference held in 2007], there is indeed a listening government and there are signals of a new seriousness within a genuine 'policy space'. The President regularly speaks about education, reaffirms the strength of ordinary people as the country's most important asset, and speaks to the role of achievement and excellence as the one sure route out of poverty.

There is much to give hope. Yet without a massive change in mindset, an agreed vision and a clear plan with priorities and targets – unless the whole society mobilises around education as priority number one – South Africa will continue to fail generation after generation of young people. There is nothing wrong with its youth – South Africa's young people made sacrifices at Soweto in 1976 and again and again in the struggle for liberation. They rightfully expect the opportunities and possibilities that quality education can bring.[3]

There is a brief window of opportunity, a 'policy space', in which all are called to come forward, to put shoulders to the wheel and take responsibility together, urgently and with commitment, to renew education, to bridge the country's gaps, and to help the nation's children shoot for the stars.

Endnotes

1. All references can be found in Bloch, G. 2009. *The Toxic Mix: What's Wrong with South Africa's Schools and How to Fix It*. Cape Town: Tafelberg.
2. Dr Verwoerd was the architect of Bantu Education, introduced for blacks in 1953.
3. There are two theoretical questions this chapter does not confront. Why has poverty in South Africa continued and to what extent? Why and how does a dualistic education system reinforce the experience of South Africa's poor and marginalised majority in the country's second economy? Some views would look to the nature of the post-democratic transition, and suggest either an elite transition resulted from a negotiated transition or the conscious 'class project' of local black elites in alliance with globalised neoliberalism. Continued poor education would then have been a simple continuation of an exploitative relation by a parasitic political and economic class. Other views would perhaps be more sociological and look to the difficulties of transformation. In not consciously confronting the role education plays in society, in taking poor policy decisions with a highly limited civil service, the previous structures of inequality were bound to continue or be reinforced. Another, more 'organisational' or institutional, focus would suggest that in the absence of leadership, in the face of inattention and negligence, with 'political symbolism' substituting for a plan and clear agenda, inequalities were bound to be reproduced. This is marginalisation through negligence. Another view would stress the problems and limitations of mobilised civil society and perhaps take a less statist and more empowering view. I think some of these under-researched areas will provide fascinating insights into aspects of the South African transition, itself a deeply under-theorised area served with very little robust literature.

Scholastic Heritage and Success in School Mathematics

Implications for Remote Aboriginal Learners

Robyn Jorgensen
Griffith University

Peter Sullivan
Monash University

In this chapter we draw on our collective experience across two diverse Aboriginal contexts. The first is our research in the Kimberley region, where we have been working on a four-year Australian Research Council-funded project with six communities in the Fitzroy River valley. The second is our research in the Central Desert region of Australia that crosses into three states in Central Australia. These experiences highlight the similarities and differences between Aboriginal communities. For our purposes here, we draw on these experiences to argue the ways in which the practices of school mathematics exemplify the structuring of unequal access to education for many Aboriginal learners. To frame the chapter, we draw on the work of Pierre Bourdieu, to understand how practices function to exclude Aboriginal learners. We use Bourdieu's ideas to identify particular theoretical constructs through which we are able to frame particular practices that contribute to 'scholastic mortality' among Aboriginal learners. However, we then argue that by gaining a better understanding of how such practices work in the reification of educational disadvantage, we are better able to understand structural inequality and propose ways to address it.

Social heritage and success

For Aboriginal[1] learners, school represents a new social world where the rules of engagement are different from those of the community and home. For example, Anangu children from Central Australia are very strong in their cultural histories and are encouraged from an early age to be independent and make their own choices – which includes whether or not they come to school. Anangu learners speak their home language of Pitjantjatjara in their homes and communities, so the school represents a foreign-language environment – yet all instruction and concepts are based in a language and culture that are unfamiliar to them. Indeed, the Northern Territory Government recently announced the cessation of bilingual programs in that territory for Aboriginal learners. This is despite the considerable research into bilingual education that supports a transitory period from the home language to Standard Australian English (SAE). In contrast, schools in the Kimberley recently took the opposite approach and introduced home language in the early years of schooling to enable successful transition into school. Much of the pedagogic relay used in schools is so foreign to Anangu learners that learning anything through the instructional mode of classrooms is an alien process. When such factors are considered, the limits to success for Anangu learners become obvious. We have observed similar differences for Kimberley students, who may not be as strong in their original Aboriginal language or culture and now speak a Kriol. However, this Kriol shapes their language and their world view, posing particular challenges to engaging with the discourse of school mathematics and SAE.

To better understand the processes by which the home language of Aboriginal students clashes with and constrains their access to school mathematics, we use the work of Bourdieu to theorise the symbolic violations that occur when the discord between school and Aboriginal learners is foregrounded. While his focus was on social class, Bourdieu explains that educators need to understand the processes around the conversion of social and cultural backgrounds into school success. He argues that:

> To fully understand how students from different social backgrounds relate to the world of culture, and more precisely, to the institution of schooling, we need to recapture the logic through which the conversion of social heritage into scholastic heritage operates in different class situations. (Bourdieu et al. 1994, 53)

The notion of social heritage thus becomes a central variable in understanding differential success in school mathematics. Using a Bourdieuian framework, the lack of success for some social groups becomes a non-random event, where it is a product of institutionalised practices of which participants may be totally ignorant. In this case, participants are more likely to be those entrenched in the school system rather than the Anangu learners. In the remote contexts of Central Desert communities of Australia, the clash between the culture of school and the culture of Anangu learners contributes significantly to the success, or lack thereof, for Aboriginal learners. We have also observed these clashes in the Kimberley region.

School mathematics represents a particular and powerful example of how social heritage converts to academic success. Language is an integral part of the social heritage that is brought into school mathematics to become reified as an innate ability that facilitates, or not, success in coming to learn the discipline knowledge within the field of school mathematics. We do not subscribe to this view of innate ability, but 'ability' is an entrenched and naïve belief within the field (Zevenbergen 2005). The language, in very broad terms, not only conveys particular concepts but also provides a medium through which those concepts are conveyed. It is therefore important to consider not only the concepts, but also the medium of instruction.

When assuming a Bourdieuian perspective, success in school mathematics is less to do with innate ability and more to do with the relationships between the culture of school mathematics and the culture that the learner brings to the school context. The greater the synergy between the habitus of the student and school mathematics, the greater the probability of success. In Bourdieu's terms, the habitus thus becomes a form of capital that can be exchanged, within the field of school mathematics, for forms of recognition and validation that convert to symbolic forms of power. Such manifestations of this conversion can be seen in grades, awards, scholarships and other forms of accolade. For Aboriginal students, coming to learn school mathematics requires much more than coming to learn mathematics. Coming to learn mathematics requires a significant cultural and linguistic shift. In the following sections we provide some examples of how this may occur. Variables around language and patterns of interactions must be foregrounded.

Taking the communities of Central Desert lands, a common language among learners is Pitjantjatjara. In Pitjantjatjara there are only six prepositions, whereas English has 64, so one can only imagine how learners make sense of the differences between terms such as near, next to, beside, adjacent, left or right when talking about the relationship between two objects placed alongside each other. Similarly, Pitjantjatjara does not have language for comparisons, so terms such as larger, smaller, taller and tallest are not present in the home language. Whorfian theory (Chandler 1995) would suggest that the language and context shape the need for particular terms. As such, Pitjantjatjara learners not only have to learn the language of prepositions and comparisons, but also the deeply embedded concepts associated with such terminology. This is often difficult for those who have grown up with a language and have accepted the terms and concepts as a normal part of that language and culture. In this context, coming to learn the new concepts requires a reconstruction of fundamental learnings. For Bourdieu, this would require a reconstruction of the habitus. In his theory, the habitus is the internalisation of culture and provides a medium through which people interpret their worlds. The complexity of these relationships can be better understood when considering how difficult it would be for those living in temperate zones to imagine 32 different linguistic terms for the concept of snow. Yet, such challenges are what are imposed on Aboriginal learners as they enter mathematics (and other disciplines) in classroom settings.

The ways of interacting and communicating also need to be considered. One of the major aspects of classroom interactions is questioning. In western schooling the role of questioning is significant, but it violates the everyday use of questioning. Teachers use questions to elicit responses from students, even though they may know the answer. In everyday life the function of questions is to elicit responses for an unsolved problem. From a Bourdieuian perspective, the notion of 'game' becomes useful to theorise the role of questioning in classrooms. Bourdieu has employed the metaphor of a game to theorise how social practices enable some participants to be winners and others to be losers. The game metaphor is an apt one, as it offers a theorisation of how the practices within the teaching of mathematics enable some students greater access to mathematical knowledge while excluding others. Bourdieu (1990, 67) explains it in the following way:

> The earlier a player enters the game and the less he is aware of the associated learning, the greater his ignorance of all that is tacitly granted through his investment in the field and his interest in its very existence and perpetuation and in everything that is played for it, and his unawareness of the unthought presuppositions the game produces and endlessly reproduces, thereby reproducing the conditions of its own existence.

The game, which in this case is questioning, often revolves around the students having to guess what the teacher wants or what is in the teacher's head. The purpose of the question is not to find out an unknown piece of information, so when the teacher poses a question such as, 'What is the sum of 16 and 35?', the game being played is not one where the answer is unknown, but rather one in which the teacher elicits responses to identify which students have grasped the concept, which students may be experiencing difficulties with this type of addition, or which students have been able to transpose learning from one addition process to another. However, what happens in many Aboriginal classrooms is that the students appear to engage in a different game. Their game is one where they are seeking to please the teacher by offering responses, or offering responses to help the teacher work out the response, since clearly the initial (correct) response was incorrect, as she kept seeking other responses. We have observed this game in the Cape and Strait schools of far north Queensland in our Kimberley project and in the project located in the Central Desert area of Northern Territory. We suggest that in these contexts the mode for eliciting responses has been misinterpreted by the students. We contend that the students have engaged in a parallel game – not the game in which the teachers intended them to engage. The students' responses are counter to the teacher's goal and as such can be misinterpreted.

From these examples it begins to emerge that the social background of the students shapes their ways of seeing and interacting in the social world of the classroom. In other words, the habitus of the students provides a lens for seeing, interpreting and interacting in the classroom. However, for many Aboriginal learners that habitus is not aligned with the field of school or school mathematics. In conceptualising this observation within Bourdieu's framework, what can be seen is that the social heritage of the students is in combat with the implicit rules of the classroom, thus making success in mathematics challenging. The (in)ability to morph from the habitus of the Aboriginal student to that of a learner of school mathematics demands significant reconceptualisation of the social background of the learner. Not only learning the language of English, with all of its nuances, and of mathematical concepts and processes, the Aboriginal learner must also come to understand, participate in and be successful with the dialogic interactions of the classroom banter. These are not insignificant challenges.

The fundamental assumption that underpins this chapter is that the social heritage of learners is a critical factor in their success. Where that social heritage becomes a strong feature of the habitus, which remains impermeable to change, there is a greater risk of failure within the school setting for students whose habitus is not aligned to the field. Using this as a principle, a significant challenge to views about innate ability and its relationship to success in school mathematics, or schooling in general, emerges. We contend that Aboriginal learners are highly intelligent and that their lack of success in schooling is not due to innate inability, but rather a clash between the practices of schooling and the social heritage of the students.

Scholastic mortality

So far we have highlighted the processes through which the field of school mathematics constructs and constrains access for particular learners. These processes are very subtle and often remain hidden to both learners and teachers, who have come to see school mathematics as an apolitical practice. However, this is the exact process through which hegemony is realised. For Aboriginal learners (along with other marginalised learners), the field of school mathematics remains relatively impermeable. This is not due to the innate abilities of learners, but manifests as a form of social marginalisation whereby the social heritage of the learner is at loggerheads with the objective and subjective structuring practices of the field. Consider the Aboriginal learners who come to school without the comparative signifiers and signifieds in their home language. The instructional discourse of the early years, where comparisons are an integral part of that discourse, are nonsensical: 'Which number is bigger than…?' 'How many more is four than five?' and so on. These types of questions fail to make sense to those whose home language does not have such comparative terms.

Some Aboriginal scholars and activists, such as Sarra (2007) and Pearson (2009), have strong views about the ways in which education needs to be provided for Aboriginal (and Torres Strait Islander) students. These align with the views in this volume expressed by Chris Sarra and Mick Dodson. We concur with the importance they attribute to having high expectations of students (and teachers) and placing the best teachers with Aboriginal students. However, we suggest that even with high expectations and great teachers, what is missing is the understanding of the symbolic violence that Aboriginal learners can experience when educators are not cognisant of the cultural norms and language nuances impacting on learning. What we have attempted to argue here is how coercive this process can be. Educators need to be astutely aware of how culture is implicated in learning and how this can be addressed to reduce the possibility of scholastic mortality among

Aboriginal and Torres Strait learners. In the following sections we show how, in a practical sense, the practices of schooling manifest scholastic mortality for Aboriginal learners.

Scholastic mortality and NAPLAN testing

Within the Australian context, a national testing regime has been implemented. Since the mid-1990s, tests have been administered across most Australian schools. The test items have been challenged (Zevenbergen 2005) and shown to have a language and cultural bias. This bias significantly disadvantages Aboriginal learners, but particularly those who live in remote areas. Not only does the language and sociology of the testing process violate the students' cultural and linguistic norms, but the items also fail to account for the contexts of these students. Imagine the ludicrousness of asking questions about inline skates to students who live in Central Desert regions, or conversions between English and Brunei currencies – yet such examples appeared in the 2008 tests. These may be challenging for urban students due to their context, but would be even more profoundly so for English-as-Foreign-Language learners such as the students in the Kimberley or Central Desert regions.

Funding models and reporting schemes, such as those included on the Australian Curriculum, Assessment and Reporting Authority (ACARA 2010) site, show schools' results for the NAPLAN tests. The normalising processes associated with this 'objective' and standardised testing scheme are highly problematic. It is well documented that students from economically disadvantaged families, students living in rural or remote regions, students whose first language is not SAE and first Australians are the most at risk for poor performance on these tests. When Aboriginal students from Central Australian or Kimberley regions are considered, their levels of educational disadvantage are multiplied. Testing students does not make them smarter, but appropriate intervention can help to address the gross inequalities in education in this nation.

The structuring practices of school mathematics

In this section we draw on some practical examples from our work across Aboriginal contexts to highlight the problematic nature of school mathematics for Aboriginal learners, particularly those in remote areas of Australia. These are the students who are at most risk of scholastic mortality and who are the scapegoats for much current educational policy, especially the national testing regimes of Australia. Bourdieu differentiates between objective and subjective structuring practices. Zevenbergen (2005) has drawn on this framing for understanding the processes of streaming in mainstream schools. This same streaming is currently endemic in Aboriginal schools, where the 'cream' of the remote schools is being sent away to elite boarding schools in major urban areas. Despite decades of research into streaming, the highest achieving Aboriginal (and Torres Strait Islander) students are being sent to out-of-country sites to learn western ways of being. Aside from pragmatic issues around support for students out of country who are immersed in upper-class value systems, there remains the challenge of the circumstances for those who remain behind, as well as what happens to those students who leave country and acquire a taste of western life. This 'brain drain' from Aboriginal communities represents a challenge to those who remain in-country[2] in so many ways.

Such objective structuring practices also need to be considered alongside subjective practices. Practices such as streaming produce effects on learners, who come to see themselves as successful (or not). In doing this, they internalise the outcomes in an insidious way, so that they are unquestioned and the internalisation of success or failure becomes the lens through which the learners see themselves. This subjective structuring practice now shapes how learners interact with mathematics – for example, as engaged or disengaged learners – which comes to influence how they interact with mathematics and education.

The status quo: Doing maths as it has always been done

In terms of curriculum, available text and other resources, assessment and system monitoring tools, and even learning programs, there is an implicit assumption by governments that mathematics will be taught the same way in Indigenous schools as in other schools. Indeed, there have been pushes for school curriculum to remain as it has always been and that anything less is an impoverished curriculum. However, there have been excellent examples of 'two-way strong' curriculum that include rigorous western knowledge systems but also embed traditional modes of learning and knowledge so that students get the best of both worlds (Harris 1990). A curriculum focused only on western values fails to recognise the obvious disconnect between 'the culture of school mathematics and that which the learner brings to the school context' (Jorgensen [Zevenbergen] in press), and that the chances of learning the conventional curriculum are limited by 'linguistic, social and cultural habitus' (5). It also fails to recognise and celebrate the strengths of the Indigenous culture of the groups. In this way the death of Aboriginal culture is almost certain. It should not be an either-or curriculum but one with high expectations of learning in and about both cultures.

In exploring the habitus of teachers and how they have framed mathematics learning, we asked teachers at Nyangatjatjara College to reflect on the challenges they are experiencing in teaching mathematics to Anangu learners, particularly in attempting to teach the students mathematical concepts and processes. They said that students:

- tend to see mathematics learning as memorisation, and doing mathematics as remembering rather than reasoning
- give up quickly when confronted with ideas with which they are not familiar
- are unfamiliar with many fundamental concepts, even those that have practical significance such as comparative measurements and names and properties of plane shapes
- experienced a curriculum that was not age appropriate and spent much time being taught material that they have previously encountered but not necessarily mastered
- had difficulty in transferring skills learned in one context to another context
- found it difficult to work with large numbers and more abstract ideas such as fractions and decimals.

While such difficulties are by no means unique to Indigenous learners, program designers seeking to engage Indigenous learners with school mathematics need to find ways to connect the mathematics to be learnt to the students' social, cultural and linguistic backgrounds. The comments made by the teachers were framed in deficit models of thinking and failed to account for the differences between the two cultural systems. What remains clear to us is the need to work with teachers to move away from deficit models towards two-way models.

As a further exploration of the disjunction between students' habitus and the curriculum with which they are expected to engage, we examined the assessment items on the Year 7 calculator-free 2008 Australian numeracy assessment, based on the context of money. It is noted that the government uses the results of this assessment to report on educational progress, and various compliance mechanisms are in place to ensure schools prioritise the content assessed by these tests.

There were four items on money. The first asked: 'What is $10 as a percentage of $40?' offering students four choices. Even though adults would more frequently find a given percentage of a money amount, this is a reasonable question. The second question presented drawings of a pair of inline roller skates, a cricket bat and a tennis racquet, labelled respectively at $42, $26 and $98. The question asked: 'What is the best way to estimate the total cost of these three objects?' and presented four choices, the correct one being '$40 + $30 + $100'. Even ignoring the unrealistic prices for these objects, the items seem a somewhat unusual collection for a national assessment that is presumably intended to be inclusive. Further, the form of the question is dependent on students having had experience with the notion of rounding as a way of progressively estimating money totals. The third item presented a two-way table of data, three rows by three columns, related to mobile phone costs, with a question that required reading and synthesising data from two columns. To answer the question, students needed to interpret text involving over 50 words and symbols, but the mathematical demand was that they merely add 12 and 28. The question assumes familiarity with mobile phone bills, tabulated data and sorting relevant from superfluous information. The fourth question required students to interpret two straight-line graphs and convert British pounds to Brunei dollars. There was a similar complexity to the text of the question and, for those students not familiar with the notion of three-way currency conversions, they would have to infer what the task was asking them to do.

The latter three of these items can hardly be considered culturally inclusive, and the reliance of the items on school content rather than realistic situations is an obvious example of how the social heritage of Aboriginal students is not considered in the design of the questions, thus creating greater opportunities for scholastic mortality. Imagine a question that was embedded in desert knowledge – the backlash from city and non-Aboriginal educators, parents and communities would have been forthcoming – but when the situation is reversed, there is silence as if there is no real educational challenge at all. It is also worth noting that the assessments not only communicate to students that school knowledge is not connected to what they know, but also reinforces to them that they are failing. Thus the objective and subjective structuring practices become obvious.

Finding ways to connect mathematics learning and student experience

In this concluding section, we suggest possible ways forward for teachers working in remote communities. To consider what the characteristics of a relevant curriculum might comprise, what follows draws on a series of teaching explorations at an Indigenous Community School in a remote region of Western Australia, which was part of the Maths in the Kimberley (2010) research project, conducted at the invitation of the Association of Independent Schools of Western Australia.

There are two main dimensions to connecting prospective learning with retrospective experience: the first is to identify ideas with which students are familiar and build on those; the second is to create connections between ideas that are fundamental to a modern mathematics curriculum and students' prior experience. In exploring the former, it is possible to examine Indigenous languages to check mathematical ideas that are present in the culture. For example, in a publication that is both a language guide and dictionary for the Nyikina language (Jarlmadangah Burru Aboriginal Community 2003), one of the languages in the Kimberley region, there is a developed lexicon for place and direction words. For example, there are 18 different words for describing location, as well as four different expressions for each of the four compass directions, making a total of 34 distinct terms that can be used. It would be possible to use this language as a starting point for an exploration of modern mathematical concepts associated with location, direction, map reading, networks, and possibly even co-ordinate geometry.

In considering the latter dimension, it seems that both traditionally, as reflected in the language, and currently, in terms of the limited use of quantities in their everyday lives, number activities all tend to be remote from students' experience. To overcome this, we are exploring ways of building connections between money, with which the students have some familiarity, and more abstract number ideas. This has its own challenges.

One of the products of this project is a set of recommendations to teachers that addresses both planning and pedagogy, and that encourages them to accommodate cultural, social and linguistic backgrounds of the students. We are conscious that inexperienced teachers sometimes err by underestimating the potential of the students and set expectations that are too low. Indeed, some structured programs also seem to adopt a deficit approach. Our perspective is that students benefit when teachers set high expectations and expect them to engage in the full range of mathematical actions such as understanding, problem solving and reasoning, not just fluency. On this point we concur with many Aboriginal educators, that having expectations of students (and teachers) is paramount to success in Aboriginal (and Torres Strait) education. In summary, our recommendations to teachers are:

- Identify big ideas that underpin the concepts you are seeking to teach, and communicate to students that these are the goals of the teaching.
- Build on what the students know, both mathematically and experientially, including creating and connecting students with stories that both contextualise and establish a rationale for the learning.
- Engage students by utilising a variety of rich and challenging tasks, which allow students opportunities to make decisions and which use a variety of forms of representation.
- Interact with students while they engage in the experiences; encourage them to interact with each other, including asking and answering questions; and specifically plan to support students who need help and challenge those who are ready.
- Adopt pedagogies that foster communication and mutual responsibilities, and encourage students to work in small groups, where they can speak in home languages when communicating with each other, and use students' reporting to the class as a learning opportunity.

Each of these recommendations is further elaborated for teachers. To see how they might apply, consider the following activity, adapted from the well-known and well-publicised work of the Shell Centre in the UK.

The task involves a set of cards containing a number of rows like the following (which address subtraction), with each row comprising four ways of representing a particular operation.

I collect groceries worth $17.85 at the store and give the sales person $20. How much change do I expect to get?	Subtract 17.85 from 20	20.00 − 17.85	$2.15

The task involves connecting representations and being able to see that the mathematics needed to solve the problem in the first box is represented on the other cards. The activity addresses an important mathematical idea, it uses the notion of story, it is a variation on the conventional pen-and-paper form of representation, it is challenging, and it provides content that can form the basis of later reporting back by students.

There is a variety of ways in which the cards can be used. The teacher, for example, can invite students to discuss similarities and differences in the cards, sort them into groups, arrange them into order of difficulty, and so on. Certainly it is intended that students be given opportunities to make their own decisions. There are, though, still substantial challenges in using such a task.

Even though the task is designed to connect to a shopping context, with which it is hoped the students would be familiar, it can be anticipated that specific actions would be needed by the teacher to ensure that the task can be connected to the students' social, cultural and linguistic backgrounds. For example, it might be necessary for the teachers to do what the National Accelerated Literacy program (Department of Education and Training Northern Territory 2009) terms as 'putting the language through their system', or what Munro (2003) calls 'getting knowledge ready'. This might involve role plays of shopping, including giving change, or particular strategies such as chunking the key phrases in the text and deciding which phrases make a difference to the task and which are irrelevant to the mathematics, and searching for the words that identify the mathematical operation. This means that, after the activity, the reviews not only focus on revising such ideas, but also on the similarities and differences in the mathematical cards, the connections between the cards, and the ways of performing the operations on the cards.

Our experience with the Maths in the Kimberley project indicates that students at all levels can engage effectively with tasks such as these, as long as the teachers anticipate pedagogical pitfalls, and that with appropriate choice of task and pedagogical support, such tasks help form the bridge between the habitus of the students and the demands of school mathematics. By acknowledging the social heritage of the students, realising that this shapes their knowledge and ways of thinking and learning that they bring to the formal school context, and that *all* students can learn mathematics if they are provided with the right learning environments, then scholastic mortality will be reduced and, we would hope, eradicated. But much of this will depend on reshaping the habitus of teachers working in these regions.

Endnotes

1. As we are drawing on experiences from the Central Desert and the Kimberley regions, we are concerned with Aboriginal learners. We do not address issues around Torres Strait Islander people, but recognise their rights and ties to Australia and indigeneity in Australia.
2. Country is very strong to Aboriginal learners. Taking students out of country often creates new issues for learners, as they want to return to their country.

References

ACARA (Australian Curriculum, Assessment and Reporting Authority). 2010. ACARA is responsible for a national curriculum (K–12), a national assessment program, national data collection and reporting. Accessed 10 April 2010. Available from: www.acara.edu.au/.

Bourdieu, P. 1990. *The Logic of Practice*. Trans. Nice, R. London: Polity Press.

Bourdieu, P. 1991. *Language and Symbolic Power*. Trans. Raymond, G A M. Cambridge: Polity Press.

Bourdieu, P; Passeron, J C; de Saint Martin, M. 1994. *Academic Discourse: Linguistic Misunderstanding and Professorial Power*. Trans. Teese, R. Palo Alto: Stanford University Press.

Chandler, D. 1995. 'The Sapir-Whorf hypothesis'. Accessed 14 April 2010. Available from: www.aber.ac.uk/media/Documents/short/whorf.html.

Department of Education and Training Northern Territory. 2009. *National Accelerated Literacy Program* (NALP). Accessed 29 February 2010. Available from: http://www.nalp.edu.au/.

Harris, S. 1990. *Two Way Aboriginal Schooling*. Canberra: Aboriginal Studies Press.

Jarlmadangah Burru Aboriginal Community. 2003. 'Jarlmadangah Burru'. Accessed 10 May 2010. Available from: http://www.jarlmadangah.com/.

Jorgensen [Zevenbergen] 'Exploring scholastic mortality among working-class and Indigenous students'. In *Equity and Discourse Conference*, edited by Choppin, J; Herzelmen, B; Wagner, D. Rochester, New York.

Maths in the Kimberley. 2010. 'Maths in the Kimberley: Connecting remote schools'. Accessed 10 May 2010. Available at: http://kimberleymaths.org/index.php.

Munro, J. 2003. 'Fostering literacy learning across the curriculum'. *International Journal of Learning* 10. Accessed 10 May 2010. Available from: http://ijl.cgpublisher.com/.

Pearson, N. 2009. 'Radical hope: Education and equality in Australia'. *Quarterly Essay* 35: 1–49.

Sarra, C. 2007. 'Engaging with aboriginal communities to address social disadvantage'. *Developing Practice: The Child, Youth and Family Work Journal* 19 (1): 9–11.

Zevenbergen, R. 2005. 'The construction of a mathematical habitus: Implications of ability grouping in the middle years'. *Journal of Curriculum Studies* 37 (5): 607–619.

Section 2:
The structure and entrenchment of disadvantage

Old Gaps are Closing, New Gaps are Opening

Education, Ethnicity and Gender in New Zealand, 1986–2006

Richard Bedford
University of Waikato

Paul Callister
Victoria University of Wellington

James Newell
Monitoring and Evaluation Research Associates NZ

Context for a debate about 'gaps'

In a thought-provoking examination of the prospects for 'closing the gaps' in socioeconomic outcomes for Indigenous Australians, Altman et al. (2008, 1) have suggested that: 'The origins of the term "closing the gaps" can probably be traced to the special programs of governments in New Zealand in the 1990s that sought to target Maori and Pacific Islander disadvantaged groups with assistance'. In the early years of the three Labour governments led by Helen Clark between 1999 and 2008, extensive use was made of the closing gaps metaphor and several reports addressed progress towards closing economic and social gaps between Maori and non-Maori populations (eg Te Puni Kokiri 2000).

The language of 'gap closing' was criticised by Maori, among others, for several reasons, not the least of which was because it encouraged 'deficit thinking' – Maori were always behind the group that was being used to define the standards or levels that everyone was being measured against. The group used to define the standard was either 'European' – if several ethnic groups were being compared – or 'non-Maori' – everyone who did not identify themselves as Maori. As Altman et al. (2008, 4) have noted with regard to the measurement of socioeconomic gaps in Australia, 'the social indicators that are drawn from census questions reflect the social norms of the dominant mainstream society. Arguably, a number of social indicators that we use mean different things to Indigenous and non-Indigenous Australians'.

In New Zealand, Te Puni Kokiri (the Ministry of Maori Development) has emphasised what it calls a strengths-based approach; one that emphasises potentials of people rather than persistent deficits or gaps between measures of Maori and non-Maori performance and participation in education, the labour market, health and other dimensions of social and economic wellbeing. This approach resonates closely with Chris Sarra's (2009) 'stronger smarter philosophy' as a means by which Indigenous Australians embrace a positive sense of identity and leadership in schools and communities and have high expectations of positive outcomes.

Both Te Puni Kokiri's strengths-based approach and Sarra's stronger smarter philosophy emphasise that achievement in education comes from empowerment and confidence in institutional settings that value diversity in identities and languages, differences in perspectives and objectives, and do not always see disparities in outcomes as signs of failure. Maori performance and achievement in education has been assisted by the development of a distinctive set of institutions offering pre-school, primary, secondary and tertiary education. In some of these institutions the curriculum is taught entirely in *te reo* (the Maori language), while others use bilingual approaches. All have been embedded in *tikanga* Maori (Maori customary approaches and perspectives). Education of Maori is also being impacted by an innovative program of professional development for teachers – Te Kotahitanga – developed by Russell Bishop and his colleagues at the University of Waikato. Te Kotahitanga, which is discussed briefly later in the chapter, is seeking to improve educational performance and outcomes for Maori in the 'mainstream' state-funded school system.

There has been considerable progress over the past 25 to 30 years in Maori educational achievement in New Zealand. This progress is an important component of the Maori renaissance that has accompanied the Waitangi Tribunal process, which acknowledges, and seeks compensation for, injustices relating to land and other resources acquired by European colonists and their attempts to assimilate Maori into a European-dominated economy, society and culture. Maori in the early twenty-first century are in a very different position from the one in the early 1970s when major protests over loss of land, language and livelihoods led to the establishment of the Waitangi Tribunal and the beginnings of a period of sustained Maori resistance, empowerment and renaissance (eg Fleras and Spoonley 1999; Spoonley 2009).

Measuring progress in Maori educational attainment

In New Zealand there remains a concern among policy makers to document progress made in reducing disparities in a range of measures of social and economic participation and achievement. In the case of education, which is compulsory for children aged between five and 15 years, participation rates are frequently used to assess progress towards desired educational outcomes. Investment by the state in education in New Zealand is influenced by performance of different groups in the primary, secondary and tertiary components of the system. There has been a move in recent years to measure performance in a variety of ways, including statistical indicators that are used for comparative purposes internationally (eg participation rates) as well as via group-specific measures that are sensitive to different value systems and priorities (eg Te Kotahitanga).

In this chapter we review changes between 1986 and 2006 in a range of simple measures of participation and attainment in education for four ethnic components in New Zealand's population – Maori, Pacific, Asian and European/other. Much of the data that are used here were compiled for a project that addresses disparities between males and females in different ethnic, age and relationship groups: the 'Education capital formation, employment, migration, gender, work-life balance and missing men' project led by Associate Professor Paul Callister from the Institute of Policy Studies, Victoria University of Wellington, and funded by the Foundation for Research Science and Technology. The database was compiled by James Newell, a population statistician who directs Monitoring and Evaluation Research Associates (MERA) in Wellington. A detailed report that addresses several important methodological issues relating to the analysis of New Zealand census data over time by ethnic group is available at MERA's website (Newell 2009a). We do not review these issues at length in this chapter, although some caveats that need to be kept in mind when interpreting the data are provided in different places.

In order to situate the discussion of some simple measures of participation and achievement in education by Maori, evidence from recent surveys of social wellbeing, living standards, employment and education are reviewed in the next section. The discussion then turns to data relating to the four major ethnic populations in 1986 and 2006. Changes over the 20 years are compared for the four ethnic populations aged 15 years and over, and then for males and females in the Maori and non-Maori populations. The chapter concludes with some observations on two key findings from the analysis. The first of these is the ongoing lag among Maori in the statistics on achievement in the basic secondary school qualification – National Certificate of Educational Achievement (NCEA) Level 2. The second is the gender disparities in participation and achievement in education among both Maori and non-Maori – another dimension of what has become known in New Zealand and Australia as the 'missing men' or 'man drought' problem (eg Salt 2008).

Setting the scene

New Zealand's population in June 2006 was estimated to be just under 4.2 million – less than the population of Sydney and about half the number living in Johannesburg. When adjusted for under-enumeration in the 2006 census, the number of Maori estimated to be resident in New Zealand in June 2006 was 624,300, just under 15 per cent of the total population. In addition to the New Zealand-resident Maori, there were estimated to be around 150,000 Maori living overseas – about 110,000 in Australia and a further 40,000 in other countries, mainly the United Kingdom, Europe and North America, and an increasing number in countries in Asia (Bedford et al. 2005; Hamer 2007; 2009; Newell 2009a). Unlike indigenous peoples in some other parts of the world – such as the Australian Aborigines, the Canadian First Nations peoples, and some of South Africa's indigenous groups – Maori are an integral part of a very extensive diaspora of New Zealand's population (Bedford and Pool 2004).

Maori and non-Maori also have quite similar population distributions within New Zealand, with around 85 per cent of both living in urban areas. There are some differences in distribution within urban areas, but Maori and non-Maori are not separated spatially or in terms of social and economic interaction from the rest of the population to anywhere near the extent that Australian Aboriginal peoples and Canadian First Nations peoples are. Like the Aborigines and First Nations peoples, Maori lost most of their lands, forests and fisheries to European colonial governments and settlers in the nineteenth century, but they were never confined to reservations or denied participation in civil society to the extent many other colonised indigenous peoples were. Maori were exploited, discriminated against and subjected to massive pressure to 'assimilate' by abandoning their language, culture and traditions. However, from the early 1970s they have fought back to retain the latter and to regain some of their resources through a major renaissance, which has given birth to some quite distinctive resolutions of grievances with the Crown (Treaty settlements), some innovative education institutions (*kohanga reo*, *kura* and *wananga*) and a new political power base (the Maori Party).

Maori in the early twenty-first century are not a depressed and repressed minority. They comprise the community that provides many of the defining features of New Zealand's identity internationally: the symbols used on its national airline (the *koro*) and many of its export products; the war dance (*haka*) that initiates all its international rugby games; central concepts that underpin its marketing as a 'safe clean green country' (*whanaungatanga, manakitanga, kaitiakitanga*). Maori define and epitomise New Zealand in ways that none of the indigenous peoples of Canada, the United States, Australia and South Africa define and epitomise their countries. Notwithstanding this position of comparative strength, Maori still remain prominent in many of the country's negative social and economic statistics. It is to the mixed evidence of Maori achievement in some of these statistics that the discussion now turns.

Taking stock: Three recent assessments of social and economic wellbeing

Late in October 2009, Statistics New Zealand released the preliminary results of its first New Zealand General Social Survey, which sought a wide range of information on the attitudes and perceptions of a sample of 8721 of New Zealand's residents, with particular reference to their living conditions between April 2008 and March 2009 (Statistics New Zealand 2009). The survey found a rather surprising convergence in some of the indicators of socioeconomic wellbeing. For example, over 80 per cent of those interviewed in the major ethnic components of the population were satisfied or very satisfied with their lives (Table 5.1). Higher proportions of Maori than any other ethnic group also felt safe or very safe in their neighbourhoods.

Table 5.1: Indicators of wellbeing, New Zealand Social Statistics Survey, October 2009, in percentages

Indicator	Maori	Pacific	Asian	European
Satisfied/very satisfied with life	81.5	80.2	84.1	87.1
Safe/very safe in neighbourhood	56.1	52.7	45.6	52.6
Not enough money for everyday life	25.3	31.3	20.3	11.5
Problems with house/neighbourhood	62.4	62.1	56	49.3
Discriminated against in previous 12 months	16.0	14.1	23.2	7.9

Source: Statistics New Zealand (2009).

Despite this general satisfaction with life, there were also indications that Maori were lagging behind other groups, especially the Europeans, on indicators such as the extent to which their incomes met their everyday needs, the extent to which they faced problems with their current housing or in their residential neighbourhoods, and the extent to which they had experienced forms of discrimination during the previous 12 months (Table 5.1). Maori were not always the group with the worst statistics on these measures, but they were generally not as well placed as the European population.

The New Zealand Living Standards Survey, last conducted in 2004, has consistently found Maori disproportionately concentrated in the population with 'severe or significant hardship' as measured on a multidimensional living standards scale (Ministry of Social Development 2006). Comparisons of the share of Maori households in the sample population covered by this survey, and their share of households deemed to be experiencing 'severe or significant hardship' and to be having 'good' living standards (the most favourable living standards category), are shown in Table 5.2.

Table 5.2: Indicators of living standards, 2004, in percentages*

Indicator	Maori	Pacific	Other	European
Share of survey population	15	8	12	74
Share experiencing severe/significant hardship	29	23	12	50
Share with good living standards	8	2	11	84

* Because some people belong to more than one ethnic group, the totals for the four ethnic components do not sum to 100 per cent.

Source: Ministry of Social Development (2006).

Maori households were almost twice as likely to be in the severe/significant hardship category (29 per cent) than their share of the national population (15 per cent), while European households were under-represented in this category (50 per cent) by quite a large margin compared with their share of all households surveyed (74 per cent). In the case of households with 'good' living standards, only eight per cent of Maori households were in this category, while 84 per cent of the European households were deemed to have 'good' living standards – much higher than their share of the survey population. The Pacific households were also represented much more prominently in the category with poor living standards outcomes than their share of the survey population merited (Table 5.2).

This socioeconomic disadvantage for Maori in terms of living standards is deeply entrenched; it is not a recent phenomenon. However, it is not a static situation – as indicated earlier, Maori themselves, with support from successive recent governments, have taken major steps to break cycles of intergenerational disadvantage. This can be seen in some recent statistics relating to Maori participation in pre-school, secondary and tertiary education, even though Maori still 'disappear' from the mainstream formal education system in larger proportions than non-Maori.

The development of alternative education provision for Maori through institutions that do all or a significant part of their teaching in *te reo* Maori at the pre-school (*kohanga reo*), primary and secondary school systems (*kura kaupapa* Maori) and tertiary (*wananga*) levels has played an important role in improving education and Maori language outcomes for increasing numbers of Maori. However, the great majority of Maori attend 'mainstream' schools, and it is in this predominantly English-speaking education environment that the Te Kotahitanga program is seeking to improve Maori performance and outcomes. Te Kotahitanga is a professional development program that assists teachers to create a learning environment in the classroom where Maori pupils are able to feel connected to their teachers, and to other pupils, through a shared understanding of and vision for what constitutes excellence in educational outcomes. The program was piloted in 2001 and 2002, and is now being used in schools throughout New Zealand. Bishop situates Te Kotahitanga in a wider context of Maori education in his chapter in this book. A critique of the program can be found in Openshaw (2009).

In its annual *Social Report*, the Ministry of Social Development publishes several indicators of educational performance and achievement for the major ethnic groups. Four of the indicators of progress towards higher levels of social wellbeing that relate to education are summarised in Table 5.3 with reference to 2006. These are national figures, drawn from institutions across the education sector. It can be seen that with regard to participation in early childhood education, 90 per cent of Maori children aged three and four years were registered at a pre-school (including the Maori language medium *kohanga reo*). This is close to the levels of pre-school participation for Europeans and Asians, and slightly ahead of that for Pacific peoples living in New Zealand.

At the secondary school level, Maori had much lower levels of achievement among school leavers during 2006. Only 37 per cent completed either the first or second levels of the National Certificate for Educational Achievement, compared with 65 per cent of Europeans and 82 per cent of Asians. In this case, Pacific school leavers had a better completion rate than Maori. The Ministry of Social Development cautioned that there are significant variations at the level of the school according to the socioeconomic status of the populations they serve. Whereas 60 per cent of New Zealand's school leavers in 2006 left with NCEA Level 2 (what you would expect to get at around age 15 or 16), only 43 per cent of those leaving schools in areas in the lower three deciles of socioeconomic status – the decile 1–3 schools – had NCEA Level 2 in 2006. Of those leaving decile 4–7 level schools, 57 per cent had NCEA Level 2, while those leaving decile 8–10 schools had 74 per cent with this level of educational attainment. It can be seen from Table 5.3 that Maori leaving school in 2006 had a lower proportion with Level 2 NCEA (37 per cent) than

Table 5.3: Indicators of educational achievement, 2006, in percentages

Indicator	Maori	Pacific	Asian	European
Participation in early childhood education (3–4 years)	90	84	96	98
School leavers with NCEA Level 2	37	50	82	65
Participation in tertiary education (15+)	20	15	18	12
Educational achievement total population 15+				
a) upper secondary school	61	54	84	80
b) tertiary qualification	9	7	20	39

Source: Ministry of Social Development (2008).

the average for all decile 1–3 schools (43 per cent). This is arguably the most entrenched of the disparities between Maori and non-Maori in education – a disparity that has profound implications for subsequent educational participation and achievement. It is this disparity that Russell Bishop's Te Kotahitanga program is aiming to address.

At the tertiary level, the position was reversed in the 2006 statistics – Maori had the highest level of participation in 2006 (note this is not completion) among the population aged 15 years and over (20 per cent), reflecting a significant drive within the community to gain qualifications. The lowest percentage for actual participation in 2006 was found for the European population (12 per cent) – a population that has a much longer tradition of seeking tertiary education. This can be seen in the final row in Table 5.3, which shows that 39 per cent of the adult European population had already attained a tertiary qualification by 2006, compared with nine per cent of Maori.

Towards convergence in educational achievement?

While differences in educational achievement are frequently highlighted, there are also some important indications of convergence towards aggregate measures of attainment across the major ethnic groups. In illustrating these tendencies, evidence is drawn from analysis by Paul Callister and James

Newell (Callister 2009; Callister and Newell 2008; Callister et al. 2008; Newell 2009b; 2009c). The data come from New Zealand's quinquennial Census of Population and Dwellings between 1986 and 2006. The ethnic groups used in these tables relate to the populations identifying with one or more of the four major ethnic groupings used in the population census.

When assessing aggregate levels of educational attainment, as this can be identified in national census enumerations for different ethnic populations, it is important to keep in mind that these populations have quite different age structures. The Maori and Pacific populations are much younger, with more than 34 per cent aged under 14 years, compared with around 20 per cent for the Asian and European populations (Table 5.4). The percentages in the tables here have not been standardised in order to take account of these age structural differences.

Levels of change

In 1986 almost 70 per cent of the Maori population aged 15 and over had left school without a qualification, by far the largest share of any of the major ethnic populations (Table 5.4). Twenty years later the share with no qualifications of any kind had fallen to just under 40 per cent, and the percentage change between the two censuses (22 per cent) was the largest for any of the major ethnic groups. The gap between Maori and Europeans in terms of proportions aged over 15 with no educational qualifications had narrowed – in 1986 it was 24 per cent but by 2006 if was just under 16 per cent. Some of this change is due to the fact that the Maori population has a more youthful age structure than the European one; it is not just due to improvements in educational performance.

As far as performance at the first four levels of the National Certificates of Educational Achievement (NCEA) is concerned, the gap in proportions of Maori and European whose highest qualification was the equivalent of NCEA Levels 1–4 had also fallen, suggesting, again, a trend towards convergence (Table 5.4). In 1986, 22 per cent of Maori aged 15 years and over had achieved NCEA Levels 1–4, compared with 29 per cent of Europeans – a difference of seven per cent. Twenty years later, the difference between Maori and Europeans had shrunk to two per cent, and Maori had one of the largest percentage changes (10 per cent) compared with just over five per cent for Europeans.

With regard to degree qualifications, the differences between Maori and Europeans aged 15 and over had widened, not shrunk (Table 5.4). In 1986 only six per cent of the European population aged 15 and over had degree

Table 5.4: Changes in measures of educational achievement for the population aged 15 years and over, 1986–2006, in percentages

Measure	Maori	Pacific	Asian	Euro/other
Population structure 2006				
0-14 years	34.5	36.6	20.7	20.1
15-24 years	18.6	18.8	22.2	12.2
25 years +	46.9	44.6	57.2	64.3
No qualifications				
1986	69.9	56.4	31.8	37.9
2006	39.9	35.3	12.3	24.7
Change	-22.0	-21.1	-19.5	-13.2
NCEA Levels 1-4				
1986	22.2	27.9	34.5	28.8
2006	32.2	43.0	35.0	34.2
Change	10.0	15.1	0.5	5.4
Degree qualifications				
1986	1.2	1.3	16.7	5.9
2006	7.1	5.6	29.2	15.6
Change	5.9	4.3	12.5	9.7
Other post-school qualifications.				
1986	14.7	14.4	17.0	27.4
2006	20.9	16.2	15.5	25.5
Change	6.2	1.8	-1.5	-1.9

Source: 'Missing men' project, Victoria University of Wellington.

qualifications, compared with just over one per cent of Maori – a difference of five per cent. By 2006 the percentage with degree qualifications had increased to just under 16 per cent for Europeans and seven per cent for Maori – a difference of nine per cent. The European component had experienced almost a 10 percentage-point increase in number of degree completions, compared with six percentage points for Maori. Maori had made better progress in terms of increasing the share of the population aged 15 years and over with a degree than the Pacific population in New Zealand, and by 2006 Maori no longer had the smallest percentage of completions (Table 5.4).

Finally, with regard to other post-school qualifications (certificates, diplomas, trade certificates etc), there was actually a smaller number of Europeans with these qualifications in the 2006 census population aged 15 years and over than there had been in 1986 (Table 5.4). Newell and Perry (2006) assign this change to the inclusion of certain types of non-vocational training and 'other not specified' post-secondary codings in the 1986 and 1991 census definitions but not in earlier and later census counts. This is also complicated by the impact that international migration has on the mix of people with different qualification and skill sets at the time of the census. Notwithstanding this complexity, there has been a tendency to prioritise degree completions over certificates obtained for completing trades qualifications, for example, especially among the European and Asian populations. For the Maori and Pacific populations, however, numbers gaining these qualifications had increased – by over six percentage points for Maori over the 20 years, followed by a much smaller increase for the Pacific peoples in New Zealand (Table 5.4).

The evidence relating to changes in the shares of people in the different ethnic groups who have reached particular levels of educational achievement suggests that there has been some convergence of Maori with the other clusters of ethnicities. However, it is important to keep in mind that differences in age structure also have an impact on the observed changes. Another way of looking at change over the 20 years 1986–2006, as well as the most recent intercensal period, 2001–2006, is with reference to index numbers for specific ethnic groups. These give a better indication of the comparative rates of change in the numbers reaching different levels of educational achievement.

Rates of change

In Table 5.5, changes in the numbers aged 15 years and over at the different levels of educational achievement in the 20-year and the five-year periods are shown for Maori and non-Maori (a composite population comprising the Pacific, Asian, European and other ethnic groups). The index number for the population attaining each of the qualification levels in 1986 and 2001 is 100. The numbers for 2006 show the comparative index numbers for the populations, working from comparable bases of 100 in 1986 and 2001.

Over the 20-year period, the most dramatic change for Maori was in the numbers taking out degrees. Maori aged 15 and over with degrees increased more than eight times – from 2778 to 23,070 – compared with an increase of 3.4 times for the non-Maori population. In both the school qualification and other post-school qualification categories Maori numbers doubled, while non-Maori numbers increased more slowly (Table 5.5). In all cases the pace

Table 5.5: Changes in numbers of Maori and non-Maori aged 15 years and over attaining qualifications at the specified levels, 1986–2006 and 2001–2006

Group	Qualification			
	None	School	Degree	Post-school
1986–2006 (1986=100)				
Maori	92	207	830	203
Non-Maori	72	129	343	130
Difference (Maori - NM)	20	78	487	73
2001–2006 (2001=100)				
Maori	106	106	173	147
Non-Maori	103	98	152	133
Difference (Maori - NM)	3	8	21	14

Source: 'Missing men' project, Victoria University of Wellington.

of change had been faster among Maori, in part reflecting the small numbers with qualifications, especially degrees, at the time of the 1986 census in a population with a youthful age structure that was growing more rapidly than the non-Maori population throughout the period.

Over the most recent intercensal period the changes have been much more modest, but in all cases Maori numbers have increased more rapidly than those for non-Maori. This is reflected in the higher index numbers for Maori across all of the qualifications shown in Table 5.5 Again, the largest increase was for degree qualifications, followed by post-school qualifications. There was little change in the numbers with no qualifications or with a school qualification.

While evidence from this preliminary analysis of changes in levels of educational achievement is rather mixed, it is clear that there has been some considerable progress among Maori since 1986, especially in tertiary education. Analysis of the secondary-school performance data produced less convincing evidence of significant improvement in attainment of qualifications, but it should be kept in mind that these data pre-date the development of te Kotahitanga. The 2011 Census of Population and Dwellings will be the first to capture one dimension of the impact of this professional development experiment.

On the basis of the evidence presented so far, it can be argued that gaps between Maori and the European ethnic populations are being closed. There is less evidence that this has happened as much for the Pacific migrants and their descendants who have entered New Zealand in large numbers since the 1960s. On several of the indicators used in this analysis, the Pacific population, which includes a large number of people of mixed Pacific-Maori ethnicities, is the most disadvantaged. In common with the initiatives taken by Maori from the 1970s to protect their language and culture from further disintegration, and to win back resources to enable much more investment in education for their children, some Pacific communities are seeking to gain greater recognition of Pacific ways of knowing and learning in the classroom. Maori successes have stimulated other groups to play more active roles in education in their communities.

The gender gap
There is one disparity in New Zealand's education statistics that is beginning to attract more attention from researchers and policy advisers. This is the gap in achievement between males and females. There is considerable interest in the 'missing men' – men who have vanished from the statistics, including the census population, without dying or migrating (Callister et al. 2006; 2007). This is a complex problem from a statistical point of view and this is not the place for a major analysis of the 'missing men' problem. It is appropriate, however, to conclude this discussion of gaps with a brief comment on the disparities in educational achievement between males and females in the census statistics that were used in the previous section.

When index numbers are used to show the magnitude of the changes in numbers at different qualification levels for both 1986 and 2006, rates of change for females are almost always faster, with numbers of women obtaining degree qualifications increasing at more than three times the level for men over the 20-year period (Table 5.6). Indeed by 2006 there were more females (239,238) taking out degrees than males (208,542). This compares with a very different situation at the time of the census in 1986, when there were 79,614 males and 42,145 females recording they had degrees.

It is evident from Table 5.6 that there were much greater relative increases in degree attainment by females, both Maori and non-Maori, than males. Again this reflects, in part, the very small numbers of Maori women with degrees in 1986 – 1077 compared with 14,150 in 2006. The rate of change between 1986 and 2006, as reflected in an index number for Maori females of 1351 (13.5 times more than the respective number in 1986), compared with 488 (4.9 times) for non-Maori females, gives a clear indication of the magnitude of the change in degree attainment over the 20 years (Table 5.6).

Table 5.6: Changes in numbers of males and females aged 15 years and over attaining qualifications at the specified levels, 1986–2006 (1986=100)

Group	Qualification			
	None	School	Degree	Post-school
Males				
Maori	96	201	501	158
Non-Maori	77	121	257	104
Total	80	127	262	107
Females				
Maori	88	213	1351	269
Non-Maori	67	136	488	118
Total	70	143	507	126
Differences (females and males)				
Maori	-8	12	850	111
Non-Maori	-10	15	231	9
Total	-10	16	245	19
Differences (Maori and non-Maori)				
Male	19	80	244	54
Female	21	77	863	151

Source: 'Missing men' project, Victoria University of Wellington.

By 2006 there were just under 6000 more Maori women with degrees than men – the gender disparity was much greater and growing much faster among Maori than in the non-Maori population.

A concluding comment

Gaps in educational achievement in New Zealand between major ethnic groups persist, especially when the standards for attainment used are those for the majority European population. However, there is evidence in the aggregate statistics that can be derived from quinquennial censuses that these gaps are narrowing, except in the case of those between males and females, where they may be widening in favour of women, especially among Maori.

Persisting disparities between Maori and non-Maori in both participation and attainment in education remain a concern for policy makers in the Ministry of Education, but for many Maori the critical issue is not so much about closing gaps but about the way students are empowered to learn in the mainstream classroom setting. Recognising and tapping the potential for learning among diverse groups of students in the classroom is at the heart of innovative programs, such as te Kotahitanga, that aim to ensure better outcomes from education for all students in New Zealand, and especially Maori students. Monitoring the effects of these programs will be critically important for evaluating changes in educational participation and performance in the next two decades.

Acknowledgment

The research that underpins this chapter has been funded by the Foundation for Research, Science and Technology (FRST) through the program 'Education capital formation, employment, migration, gender, work-life balance and missing men', led by Associate Professor Paul Callister, Institute of Policy Studies, Victoria University of Wellington. We acknowledge with gratitude this support from FRST.

References

Altman, J C; Biddle, N; Hunter, B H. 2008. 'How realistic are the prospects for "closing the gaps" in socioeconomic outcomes for indigenous Australians?' CAEPR Discussion Paper No. 287/2008. Canberra: ANU College of Arts and Social Sciences, Australian National University.

Bedford, R D; Didham, R; Ho, E S; Hugo, G. 2005. 'Maori internal and international migration at the turn of the century: An Australasian perspective'. *New Zealand Population Review* 30 (1 & 2): 131–141.

Bedford, R D; Pool, I. 2004. 'Flirting with Zelinsky in Aotearoa/New Zealand. A Maori mobility transition'. In *Population Mobility and Indigenous Peoples in Australasia and North America*, edited by Taylor, J; Bell, M. London: Routledge: 44–74.

Callister, P. 2009. 'Which tertiary institutions are educating young, low-skill Maori men? A research note'. Institute of Policy Studies Working Paper No. 09/07. Wellington: Victoria University of Wellington.

Callister, P; Didham, R; Bedford, R D. 2006. 'Globalisation, gendered migration and labour markets'. Department of Labour Working Paper. Wellington: Department of Labour.

Callister, P; Didham, R; Bedford, R D. 2007. 'Changing sex ratios in New Zealand: Real change or a statistical problem?' *New Zealand Population Review* 32 (1): 117–129.

Callister, P; Leather, F; Holt, J. 2008. 'Gender and tertiary education. Is it useful to talk about male disadvantage?' Institute of Policy Studies Working Paper No. 08/05. Wellington: Victoria University of Wellington.

Callister, P; Newell, J. 2008. 'Gender and tertiary education enrolments and completions: A review of trends 1994–2006'. Institute of Policy Studies Working Paper No. 08/05. Wellington: Victoria University of Wellington.

Fleras, A; Spoonley, P. 1999. *Recalling Aotearoa. Indigenous Politics and Ethnic Relations in New Zealand*. Auckland: Oxford University Press.

Hamer, P. 2007. *Maori in Australia: Ngā Maori i Te Ao Moemoeā*. Wellington: Te Puni Kōkiri.

Hamer, P. 2009. 'One in six? The rapid growth of the Maori population in Australia'. *New Zealand Population Review* 33 & 34: 153–176.

Ministry of Social Development. 2006. *New Zealand Living Standards 2004*. Wellington: Ministry of Social Development.

Ministry of Social Development. 2008. *The Social Report, 2007*. Wellington: Ministry of Social Development.

Newell, J. 2009a. 'Progress towards a high skill society? Trends in the accumulation of educational capital in New Zealand – a 2006 update'. MERA Working Paper No. 2009/01. Wellington: Monitoring and Evaluation Research Associates.

Newell, J. 2009b. 'A comparison of New Zealand and Australian labour markets: Current similarities and long-term trends'. MERA Working Paper No. 2009/02. Wellington: Monitoring and Evaluation Research Associates. Accessed 1 February 2010. Available from: http://www.mera.co.nz/.

Newell, J. 2009c. 'Converging and diverging strands in the evolution of gendered New Zealand occupational pathways, 1981–1996'. MERA Working Paper No. 2009/03. Wellington: Monitoring and Evaluation Research Associates.

Newell, J; Perry, M. 2006. *Trends in the Contribution of Tertiary Education to the Accumulation of Educational Capital in New Zealand*. Wellington: Ministry of Education.

Openshaw, R. 2009. 'Solution or problem? Te Kotahitanga as cultural politics'. In *The Politics of Conformity in New Zealand*, edited by Openshaw, R; Rata, E. Auckland: Pearson: 135–153.

Salt, B. 2008. *Man Drought and Other Social Issues of the New Century*. Sydney: Hardie Grant Books.

Sarra, C. 2009 'The stronger, smarter philosophy'. A paper presented at the Closing the Gap in Education: Improving Outcomes in Southern World Societies Conference. 25–27 November; Monash South Africa, Johannesburg.

Spoonley, P. 2009. *Mata Toa. The Life and Times of Ranginui Walker*. Auckland: Penguin.

Statistics New Zealand. 2009. New Zealand General Social Survey: 2008, Hot off the Press, 29 October 2009. Wellington: Statistics New Zealand.

Te Puni Kokiri. 2000. *Progress Towards Closing Social and Economic Gaps Between Maori and Non-Maori: A Report to the Minister of Maori Affairs*. Wellington: Te Puni Kokiri.

The Structure and Entrenchment of Disadvantage in South Africa

Thobeka Mda
Human Sciences Research Council, South Africa

The structure

The origins and structure of the South African inequalities lie in the previous law of apartheid, meaning separation or, literally, aparthood. The separation was characterised by inequality and prejudice against one race, while privileging the other. The philosophy or ideology of apartheid was implemented through laws such as the Population Registration Act and the Group Areas Act.

The Population Registration Act of 1950 'required that all inhabitants of South Africa be classified in accordance with their *racial characteristics* as part of the system of apartheid. Social rights, political rights, educational opportunities and economic status were largely determined by which group an individual belonged to' (Wikipedia 2010).

The Population Registration Act in turn determined the implementation of other racially based laws such as the Group Areas Act (EconomicExpert.com 2010), which mandated each racial group to reside in an area exclusively designated for the group, with amenities and services all within the area. These included schools, hospitals, stadiums, administrative offices and universities, if any. Universities were further classified by ethnicity and language, so there were universities for white Afrikaner, white English, Indian, coloured, Xhosa, Zulu, Sotho, Tswana, Shangaan and Venda.

A government department called Bantu Affairs, and later Own Affairs, for instance, was established to administer all 'home affairs' (births, deaths, identification, movement and residence) of black people. In addition to these, and in support of this law, homelands – rural, urban and self-governing areas – were established for the various geographical locations of black people. This was done under the guise of 'separate development', which was promoted by the apartheid government as 'separate but equal' – of course, a lie. Through this separate development ideology, South Africa ended up with 18 departments of education for the different racial groups (African, coloured, Indian, white); the different provinces (Cape, Natal, Orange Free State and Transvaal); the 'independent states' (Transkei, Venda, Bophuthatswana, Ciskei); self-governing homelands (KwaZulu, KwaNdebele, Lebowakgomo, Qwaqwa, Gazankulu, KaNgwane); and the black people in the cities (ie urban).

The language laws and policies

A cornerstone of the apartheid ideology became 'language'. Language-based homelands were created and African-language speakers were then allocated to the various homelands according to the languages they spoke, even if they had never been to those regions. Even universities were classified according to language; hence the various universities for specific language groups (eg the University of Zululand for amaZulu, and Fort Hare for amaXhosa). Teachers were trained in teacher colleges for their own language groups, and in the urban areas, where there were multiple ethnic groups, schools were classified according to language. Two languages were declared official languages and neither of them was one of the African languages spoken by the majority of South Africans. Otherwise, there were nine recognised local African languages, under which homeland areas, schools and universities were classified.

Separate development

As already mentioned, separate development meant inequalities and disadvantage for one group. There was unequal provision for schools in terms of money, buildings, teacher training and curricula. Most black teachers and university students had no background in natural sciences, having taken the 'General' curriculum (ie excluding maths and science), majoring in African languages (which was highly promoted among the Africans) and biblical studies and/or history and/or education. This was a natural progression from matriculation subjects, since most would have taken at matriculation an African language, English, Afrikaans and three or four subjects chosen from history, biblical studies, geography, biology, and some commercial subjects such as economics or mercantile law. As a result of these Language Laws, the black students at university and the teachers in black schools increasingly had very limited access to and competence in English or Afrikaans, the white people's languages.

Universities for the African people (universities of Zululand, Fort Hare and Turfloop) were built in rural areas and had very limited resources compared with urban and white universities. These African universities had narrow curricula and very few esteemed academics. During apartheid, they were almost exclusively staffed by Afrikaner lecturers who blatantly promoted the Nationalist Government ideology. The managers of these universities, who seemed to have been chosen on the basis of being apologists for South African Government policies, ran the universities as police states. The black universities were not typically, or expected to be, Liberal Arts universities that would teach and promote independent, critical thinking. Neither were they universities of technology that would produce engineers and technologists, since few students had been prepared for such careers before Matriculation and/or excelled in natural science subjects.

The education of the black people provided limited career choices. For instance, those students who were good in physics, chemistry and mathematics became medical doctors or pharmacists, while others obtained BSc degrees and went on to work in pharmaceutical companies or went on to teach natural science subjects at high school. The wide choices and advanced careers in the natural sciences only became open to black people late in the 1980s.

Despite the discouragement of critical and independent thinking, the condition of being oppressed and discriminated against, the oppressive laws in the country and the universities, and all the limitations generally placed on a black person's path to success led to high student political activism in all black (African, coloured and Indian) universities. The strikes and protests that were very common in black universities always resulted in big numbers of students, and sometimes lecturers, being expelled from the universities. Since there was no freedom of expression, but suppression of dissent, a culture of protests and boycotts (sometimes very aggressive) to make one's voice heard developed, and became the only way of communication between authorities and students in these universities.

Closing the gap

In 1994, a new democratically elected government came into power and, for the first time since settlers arrived in South Africa in the seventeenth century, the country was governed by the majority. Apartheid was officially abolished. As a result of the new era South Africa had a new constitution, the Constitution of the Republic of South Africa, 1996. Through the constitution, 11 languages were declared official and racism was declared unconstitutional. South Africans now had the right to equality (section 9); freedom of association (section 18); citizenship (section 20); freedom of movement and residence (section 21); freedom of trade, occupation and profession (section 22); and property (section 25).

All the education departments were integrated into one national department and nine provincial sub-departments. This meant that matriculants of all races, ethnicities and languages sat for the same examinations. Teachers were now employed by one employer, and educators could exercise their rights and became highly unionised. New education policies came into being: a series of white papers in the education field resulted in the 1996 South African Schools Act and the 1997 Higher Education Act. Access was made possible to all by removing discriminatory and exclusionary measures.

Schools and universities could no longer be classified according to race but, in motivated cases, according to language.

Money was injected into poor schools, including rewards for schools and universities admitting many black or poor learners. The new Language in Education Policy (LiEP) for schools was announced in 1997 and for higher education the new Language Policy in Higher Education (LPHE) was developed. For schools, a new curriculum, Curriculum 2005 and later the National Curriculum Statement, was introduced to address irrelevant education.

Entrenched disadvantage

One national education department, however, just like one nation, does not address inequalities and differences. Just as South Africa has two nations (haves and have-nots/rich and poor), so is the education system divided into two. Inequality remains between provinces: Gauteng and the Western Cape are the privileged and rich provinces, with better schools, more resources and better school results. Moreover, the gap between the rural areas and the urban areas is growing wider.

The historically advantaged universities, often with an international reputation – for example, the University of Cape Town and the University of Witwatersrand – are the universities of first choice to both the acclaimed scholars and the best Matriculation students. These historically advantaged universities attract high-calibre scholars from abroad and locally, who are able and continue to conduct ground-breaking research. They are full-time lecturers able to participate in academic exchange and sabbatical leave abroad. Poor rural black universities, on the other hand, are unable to attract high-calibre scholars to spend sabbatical leave in them or to exchange places with scholars from the advantaged universities. The rural black universities are characterised by very big classes and very little research output. Often there is no research culture in these universities. Since they do not have rated scientists and do not publish much, they do not attract funds to conduct research and are not contracted to do so. This then becomes a vicious cycle.

Furthermore, these black universities reputedly have no niche areas, since historically they had to cater for all ethnic students assigned to them. For example, the University of Zululand had to cater for all Zulu-speaking students, meet the aspirations of this population of students from any province, in all fields, and the needs of the region where this university is located.

Universities have remained bilingual – English and Afrikaans are the languages of tuition in all South African universities. Multilingual tuition programs are few and far between; for example, the requirement for all students in certain disciplines to take a course in the African languages. For most black students, English and Afrikaans are their second and third languages, especially English, which most black students choose as a language of learning. As these languages are inaccessible to many, it makes it difficult to do well in university studies, but this consequence is often pooh-poohed, ignored or minimised by commentators and analysts. Further, university fees remain too high for many students. This is one of the causes of the high dropout rate among black students, together with high levels of unpreparedness for higher education (Cosser and Letseka 2009).

Tables 6.1 and 6.2 illustrate the graduation and non-completion rates of students from the seven universities studied by the authors (see Bhorat et al. 2009).

Racism in universities is reportedly alive and kicking among academics, management, students and the institutional culture. This is mostly illuminated by occasional flare-ups of racist or racial incidents, especially in former white universities, and even more so in former Afrikaans universities.

South Africa has no programs like the United States' 'first-generation college-goers', a redress measure for supporting historically disadvantaged students to succeed. It could be that South Africa, emerging from years of classifying and categorising people by race and ethnicity, is not ready for class descriptions that emphasise 'haves' and 'have-nots', even though this would be fair discrimination.

The study by Bhorat et al. (2009) reports that it is harder for African graduates to secure employment and they earn less than other race groups – the white graduates' unemployment rate is 14 per cent and that of African graduates is 24 per cent; the total unemployment rate of Africans from historically white institutions is lower than that of Africans from historically disadvantaged/black institutions; and African graduates wait longer for work.

Most productive researchers are mainly in their 60s and are white males. Most research is done in Afrikaans and English universities, for example, Stellenbosch University, University of Cape Town, University of Pretoria, and University of KwaZulu-Natal. The result is that the black universities, especially the African universities, do not attract black students into academia because they have very limited role models, if any. The black universities also have the reputation for paying low salaries for academics.

South African universities on the whole produce very low numbers (and quality) of research degree graduates. The need to increase throughput rates in research degrees has been identified as a national imperative. Institutions of higher learning, as well as funding agencies, including the National Research Foundation, have developed and implemented a variety of interventions to help institutions and individuals to improve their throughput and the graduation of students with research degrees. This is meant to increase the number of researchers, to change the profile of researchers and improve

Table 6.1: Distribution of graduates and non-completers, by race (frequencies and percentage shares)

	African Female	African Male	Coloured Female	Coloured Male	Indian Female	Indian Male	White Female	White Male	Total
Graduates	3 787	3 154	795	613	249	242	2 671	2 264	13 775
	34.32	49.17	49.35	42.60	60.88	54.38	75.62	57.83	47.24
Graduates: Total	6 941		1 408		491		4 935		13 775
	39.78		46.16		57.49		66.27		47.24
Non-completers	7 246	3 260	816	826	160	203	861	1 651	15 023
	65.68	50.83	50.65	57.40	39.12	45.62	24.38	42.17	52.76
Non-completers: Total	10 506		1 642		363		2 512		15 023
	60.22		53.84		42.51		33.73		52.76
Sample size	17 447		3 050		854		7 447		28 798
Share of total	60.58		10.59		2.97		25.86		100.00

Source: Bhorat et al. 2009.

Table 6.2: Distribution of graduates and non-completers, by institution and race (percentage shares)

	African			Coloured			Indian			White		
	NC	G	Total	NC	G	Total	NC	G	Total	NC	G	Total
University Of Fort Hare	7.5	2.1	9.5	-	-	-	-	-	-	-	-	-
Stellenbosch University	0.2	1.0	1.1	3.7	6.3	9.9	-	1.3	1.3	7.7	32.4	40.1
University of the North	14.5	2.5	17.0	-	-	-	-	0.4	0.4	-	-	-
University of the Western Cape	3.1	3.9	6.9	27.3	16.4	43.7	1.9	9.5	11.4	-	-	0.1
University of the Witwatersrand	4.9	5.1	10.0	1.8	0.9	2.7	33.0	41.8	74.8	2.8	13.2	16.0
Peninsula Technikon	6.8	6.1	12.9	18.2	21.4	39.6	0.6	0.2	0.8	0.1	0.3	0.3
Pretoria Technikon	24.0	18.3	42.5	2.8	1.2	4.1	7.0	4.3	11.4	23.1	20.4	43.5
Total	61.0	39.0	100.0	53.8	46.2	100.0	42.5	57.5	100.0	33.7	66.3	100.0
Apartheid classification of institution												
HBI	31.8	14.6	46.4	45.5	37.8	83.3	2.5	10.1	12.5	0.1	0.3	0.4
HWI	29.2	24.4	53.6	8.3	8.4	16.7	40.0	47.4	87.5	33.6	66.0	99.6
Total	61.0	39.0	100.0	53.8	46.2	100.0	42.5	57.5	100.0	33.7	66.3	100.0

Notes: NC = non-completers, G = graduates.

Estimates corrected for by person weights.

In this table - indicates missing values where no sample was present or where the sample size was too small to construct an estimate or confidence intervals.

Source: Bhorat et al. 2009.

the quality of knowledge production in the country. Interventions include increasing the numbers of students in postgraduate degrees and rewarding supervisors for their supervisees who complete masters and doctoral research degrees. However, graduation rates in these programs indicate that many of the admitted students either spend many years in the programs or drop out before graduation. Even more shocking are the negligible numbers of students from the historically disadvantaged groups who get admitted to the senior degree programs, particularly at PhD level, and those who actually graduate with a research degree.

While a number of South African analysts refute this, South Africa's apartheid history has contributed greatly to this poor performance and low output of previously disadvantaged groups in higher education. Apartheid created inequalities among races, offered unequal education to races and, therefore, the quality of teaching and education has always been very uneven among races. Lamberti, referring to the poor state of most black schools in South Africa, states: 'Apartheid's most devastating and enduring legacy was that it destroyed the human capital of our nation' (Kane-Berman 2007, 1). According to Bloch (2007), South Africa has not succeeded in providing quality education and ensuring equality in education. He says, 'If there is one phrase that summarises the failings of the education system, it is poor quality. In failing to achieve quality delivery, the education system is working only for a proportion of the learners who are able to access the relevant institutions' (Bloch 2007, 6). Bloch ascribes this failure to the quality of teaching and teacher support. I fully support Lamberti's and Bloch's views.

The result of the poor quality in education that Bloch laments (2007, 4) is that, '[South Africa] is not able to meet national goals, either around provision of adequate skills for growth, nor in terms of providing access to quality education that would enable equitable sharing of opportunities'. He argues how this affects the country's economy negatively, as the quality of education influences individuals towards improving their personal efficacy, productivity and incomes. 'Accordingly, the quality of education makes a significant difference to the prospects of achieving a wide range of individual and development goals' (UNESCO–Education for All, cited in Bloch 2007, 3).

The scarcity of skilled researchers needed to fill senior research and management positions across a variety of government and non-governmental sectors in South Africa and the African continent has been well documented. This need is particularly acute among populations that historically were prevented from gaining access to, or participating fully and equitably in, the research enterprise. In South Africa the inequalities have manifested themselves in a range of ways. There is uneven access to higher education opportunities which offer white students a greater chance than black South Africans (Waghid 2002). Historically, South Africa has trained from five to 10 times more white postgraduates than black postgraduates in the scientific fields (MRC 2006). Inadequate financial resources have been identified as one of the barriers for entry into postgraduate training programs for young black graduates (MRC 2006). Research, as a career, is not an obvious choice for black school leavers and graduates (MRC 2006). The success rates of students, in terms of outputs of historically privileged institutions, were significantly better than those of other groupings (Waghid 2002; Bhorat et al. 2009) and in a recent study (Bhorat et al. 2009), in terms of race, 66 per cent of whites graduate, while 39 per cent of Africans graduate in South African higher education institutions.

In the period spanning 1990 to 2000, the percentage of scientific publications by authors in the 50 and above age group increased from 20 per cent to 47 per cent, while the number of articles authored by the 30 to 49 age group declined from 75 per cent to 52 per cent. In addition, in the year 2000, 92 per cent of scientific publications were authored by white authors while black (Africans, coloured and Indian) researchers authored only 1.1 per cent, 2.6 per cent, and 4.4 per cent of the articles respectively (HSRC 2007). There are unequal employment opportunities (Waghid 2002), under-representation of women and black people in certain professional programs (Waghid 2002) and unequal staffing resources in terms of student–lecturer ratios (Waghid 2002).

According to the HSRC's 2003 Human Resource Development Review, it was established that there was a shortage of academics in South African higher education institutions, given the vacancies at many institutions and the increased reliance on foreign nationals and a shortage of PhDs among staff in tertiary institutions (Woolard, Kneebone and Lee 2003). There is a serious general scarcity of suitably qualified African candidates, in particular, to take up scientific leadership positions in the social and human sciences. At the same time, there is an apparent failure to attract and develop a new generation of African researchers as suggested by the scientific publication outputs of researchers in South Africa.

As a result of the shortage of skills in academic and research fields, initiatives have been introduced over the past 15 years, since the formal end of apartheid. These have included institutional funding and individual bursaries towards increasing the number of students who enter higher education, and those who proceed to postgraduate studies; improving the participation of previously disadvantaged groups in higher education and science studies; and creation of mentoring and internship opportunities for the previously disadvantaged, especially in higher education and research institutions. These initiatives have, in the main, been designed for science, engineering, technology, innovation, and research and development, and are linked to the South African National

Skills Development Strategy 2005–2010, which was established with the intention of radically transforming education and training in South Africa by improving both the quality and quantity of the training of students (DST 2007).

Incidents of gate-keeping in terms of who gets published in which journals are cited by many. This keeps the rate of research outputs low – limited to a few individuals and groups – and the profile of researchers or contributors to this output unchanging. The accused in this regard are editors and journal reviewers who may be a clique belonging to an 'Old Boys' Club'.

What is noticeable these days is the politicisation and yet non-democratic culture in all areas of the South African university: management, appointments, teaching, autonomy and independence of groups in the university, as well as in the university as a body. Critical thinking and debate were suppressed during apartheid and now are condemned or viewed as politically incorrect because vice-chancellors are black and therefore supposed to be free of bias and discrimination, especially because a number of them have 'struggle' credentials. The result is the same: there is no room for criticism.

Bridging the gaps by focusing on structure

While the focus of this chapter is higher education, and the problems discussed here those of higher education institutions, most of the problems in higher education would be significantly reduced if more attention were paid to good foundation education and schools. Higher education would benefit significantly from a system that ensures a set of minimum standards in all South African schools regarding safety and security, facilities, teacher competence, and a culture of learning and teaching, so that one may be able to say any South African school, anywhere in the land, has got these. This, then, would go a long distance in levelling the field for all learners in the school system and later in higher education.

There is a need to prioritise demonstration of political vision and will as criteria when appointing officials (often politicians) tasked with implementation of the new education system for redress and transformation. In addition to these criteria, high standards must be set for education officials appointed in district, local, provincial and national offices, as well as for university vice-chancellors, and all these officials must be held accountable for non-implementation.

African languages must be elevated in all spheres of South African life so that they play a significant role – manufacturers, bottlers, packaging people must be forced to include African languages in labelling products such as tea, cleaning products and so on. It is crucial for the users to understand the directions on medication boxes and bottles, and so people's languages must be accommodated in these as a matter of urgency and safety. Just as English and Afrikaans continue to be used in labelling and instructions, the languages could be English and Sesotho, English and TshiVenda or Afrikaans and IsiZulu. Big supermarkets, such as Pick and Pay, could be forced to have aisles with signs in African languages instead of alternating English with Afrikaans, as if all people speak both or either and will therefore be comfortable in any aisle. African languages must be used in signs at the banks and at the airport too. Using all 11 official languages at the same time is not the idea, because it is not practical, but alternating them is possible. Otherwise, what is the point of having 11 official languages if only two or even one is to be used exclusively? African-language-speaking teachers must be deployed in suburban schools – many qualified in these languages and may not be teaching anymore. African language teachers might be shared by a cluster of suburban schools the same way French and German teachers often are in South Africa.

There is a need to create a department or office of Diversity Education by the education departments to ensure incorporation of all histories and heroes in the curriculum; recognition of all histories and heroes as well as observation of holidays pertaining to all South African past heroes; and to assist schools and institutions of higher learning (if necessary) with culture change, integration and dealing with diversity. Such an office and its functioning was observed in Nova Scotia Province in Canada.

Most importantly, in South Africa there is an urgent need to depoliticise appointments in education governance, management and provision/suppliers. Political appointments have crept in since 1994 and seem to be settling in and need to be squashed urgently. Being an African National Congress (the current ruling party) cadre should *not* be the criterion for appointing a minister of education, but especially a director general or a university principal.

While racial redress and sensitivity to race will remain important factors in South African society, race, just like politics, should not be the sole or ultimate criterion when making appointments in education governance, management and provision/suppliers. Being black does not automatically sensitise one to issues of equity, inequality and redress. Black and white candidates must be able to demonstrate understanding of, and commitment to, ensuring implementation of the issues discussed above in order to be appointed into senior positions. Recruitment and appointment of key personnel must therefore be deracialised.

In conclusion, despite the impatience about the lack of implementation, I strongly believe that these changes can still be implemented. With a little pressure on the powers that be to demonstrate will, there is no doubt that they are achievable.

Acknowledgment

Thank you to HSRC Press Cape Town South Africa for permission to reprint two tables from *Student Retention and Graduate Destination*, edited by Moeketsi, Cosser, Breier and Visser, and published in 2009.

References

Bhorat, H; Visser, M; Mayet, N. 2009. 'Student graduation, labour market destinations and employment earnings'. In *Student Retention and Graduate Destination*, edited by Moeketsi, L; Cosser, M; Breier, M; Visser, M. Cape Town: HSRC Press: 97–124. Accessed 1 May 2010. Available from: http://www.hsrcpress.ac.za/product.php?productid=2272&freedownload=1&js=n.

Bloch, G. 2007. 'The persistence of inequality in education: Policy and implementation priorities'. Paper for *Knowledge Week* 20–22 November 2007. Development Bank of Southern Africa.

Cosser, M; Letseka, M. 2009. 'Introduction'. In *Student Retention and Graduate Destination*, edited by Moeketsi, L; Cosser, M; Breier, M; Visser, M. Cape Town: HSRC Press: 1–9.

DST (Department of Science and Technology). 2007. 'South Africa invests in young graduates'. Accessed 28 January 2010. Available from: http://www.dst.gov.za/media-room/press-releases/south-africa-invests-in-young-graduates.

EconomicExpert.com. 2010. 'Population Registration Act'. Accessed 28 January 2010. Available from: http://www.economicexpert.com/a/Population:Registration:Act.html.

HSRC (Human Science Research Council). 2007. 'Business plan for the Human Sciences Research Council, 2007/2008'. Pretoria: HSRC Press.

Kane-Berman, J. 2007. 'The skills deficit looks permanent'. *Fast Facts* 12. December 2007. Johannesburg: South African Institute of Race Relations.

MRC (Medical Research Council). 2006. 'Policy: Post-graduate research training internship programme'. Accessed 28 January 2010. Available from: http://www.mrc.ac.za/researchdevelopment/internship.pdf.

Waghid, Y. 2002. 'Knowledge production and higher education transformation in South Africa: Towards reflexivity in university teaching, research and community service'. *Higher Education* 43: 457–488.

Wikipedia. 2010. 'Population Registration Act'. Accessed 3 January 2010. Available from: http://en.wikipedia.org/wiki/Population_Registration_Act.

Woolard, I; Kneebone, P; Lee, D. 2003. 'Forecasting the demand for scarce skills, 2001–2006'. *Human Resources Development Review 2003: Education, Employment and Skills in South Africa.* Cape Town: HSRC Press.

Gendered Violence and Pedagogical 'Resources for Hope'

Mothers' and Daughters' Stories From the Fringe of an Australian City

Jane Kenway, Lindsay Fitzclarence & Johannah Fahey
Monash University

Violence is a major social problem of our times. It occurs on many scales and takes many forms. It is always ugly and always leaves scars. Addressing violence is a big issue for education. Schools can be violent places and many students have experienced some form of violence in their lives within and outside of schools – sometimes in the family. Thus violence should be seen as one of the major issues in current debates about education. Not just in terms of the many gaps that need to be closed in educational achievements and outcomes, but also in terms of educational practices, cultures and school–family relationships and students' experiences of these. We cannot improve school experiences or outcomes unless we understand the complex problems of violence in students' lives. Also, of course, such understandings must lead to a range of anti-violence pedagogies, practices and policies.

Violence is expressed in many ways that include rape, domestic violence, childhood sexual abuse, sexual assault and harassment, homophobia, racial vilification, emotional abuse, self-harm and other forms of verbal and physical harassment and, on a different scale, war and genocide. It thus can be seen as variously configured with regard to scale and time. It is not a phenomenon restricted to particular races or social groupings, as various reports indicate (Sokoloff and Dupont 2005; Sokoloff with Pratt 2006). That said, it may have particular spatial inflections to it (Weldon 2002). Violence also occurs along a continuum of practices that shade into one another; this involves physical, sexual, verbal and emotional abuses of power at individual, group and social structural levels (Kelly 1987). As Iris Marion Young argues, it is one of 'five faces of oppression'; the others are exploitation, marginalisation, powerlessness and cultural imperialism (Young 1990; 1992). But of course these are all related to each other. Many forms of violence have a common character. Social, cultural and psychic power relations between and within the genders are central to this common character.[1]

Our particular focus in this chapter is on girls and women who have been physically, sexually, verbally and emotionally abused. Their stories illustrate the continuum of practices just mentioned. The first part of this chapter arises from a cross-generational study in Australia of the lives of educationally, economically and culturally marginalised girls, young women and their mothers.[2] The girls are seen as at risk of leaving high school early. The young women did leave early and, like their mothers, many are now young mothers too.

Experiencing various forms of violence is a recurring theme in a significant number of these girls' and women's lives. For example, some of the young women/young mothers who had recently left school reported experiencing sexual abuse, molestation and rape. They also discussed their disrupted family patterns, frequent changes of school and mental and physical illness. The experiences of two of these post-school young women stand out as examples. Kara is 26 and left school when she was 15. She identified a number of key turning points in her life that occurred prior to her leaving school. These include being molested by a babysitter when she was in primary school, losing her virginity at age 11, terminating a pregnancy at age 13 and leaving home at 15. Sandra is 23 and left school at 15. Prior to leaving school she reports taking drugs at age 10, child prostitution, which she quit at age 13, and anorexia. She was diagnosed manic-depressive at age 16. The schoolgirls talked about harassment and verbal abuse at school, fraught family relationships, family breakdown (nearly all of the participants' parents had separated) and wanting to move out of home.

From a number of possible mother–daughter narratives we have chosen to tell two in detail: the story of Sally and her daughter Kirsty, and that of Louise and her daughter Anna. Then we discuss the implications for anti-violence pedagogies in schools, drawing on an earlier project that examined the relationships between masculinity and violence and explored the potential of narrative pedagogy. In telling these stories, we deploy a process of circling back to consider various ways of understanding them and their implications.

Loss, anger and melancholia

Research on women's and girls' experiences of sexual violence often documents a sense of loss, which has many dimensions, including the loss of control, loss of a sense of safety and security; loss of self-worth and self-esteem, of sexual desire and trust; and even a loss of self (eg Fortune 2005; Schwartz 1997). However, the grief that victims experience may also be expressed through feelings of anger and outrage (Brison 2002), which may not necessarily be directed at the victim's attacker but towards others, including family and friends, and towards themselves, including such things as self-harm and suicide attempts.

We theorise this archive of emotion (ie feelings of loss and anger) in terms of melancholia. We propose that theories about different manifestations of melancholia have the potential to enrich understandings of the complex reproduction and disruption of gender, violence and family turmoil across generations of women. And, as we will show, when coupled with the idea of narrative pedagogy, these theories have the potential to assist us to develop powerful possibilities for anti-violence pedagogies for women and girls.

Most discussions of melancholia start with Freud's early work, *Mourning and Melancholia* (1957 [1917]), and the fundamental distinction he makes between mourning and melancholia: 'Mourning is regularly the reaction to the loss of a loved person, or the loss of some abstraction... such as one's country, liberty, an ideal and so on' (1957, 243). In other words, mourning is about letting go of 'lost objects'. It involves the eventual detachment of the mourner from the lost object. The mourner acknowledges that the lost object is dead, and is then able to move on and find new objects to invest in psychologically.

Melancholia, in contrast, is the enduring attachment of the ego to the lost object. It is a continuous mourning; a mourning that never ends. The melancholic cannot let go of the lost object and as a result cannot resolve her grief. In other words, the melancholic has a sustained devotion to the lost object. Freud states: 'in grief the world becomes poor and empty, in melancholia it is the ego itself' that becomes poor and empty (1957, 246). In sum, mourning is viewed as a 'successful' resolution of loss, while melancholia is seen as a failure to resolve loss.

Certain feminist critiques of Freudian theory offer understandings of the relationship between gender and melancholia. Although critically engaging Freud's ideas, like Freud they also theorise melancholia as a fundamentally deficient psychic state. However, unlike Freud they claim that it is not just a deficient abnormal state that is detrimental to the ego, but that for women melancholia has much deeper significance, psychically as well as culturally. As we proceed, we mention the arguments of Irigaray (1985) and Silverman (1988) as they relate to the narratives.[3] Despite the differences between Irigaray and Silverman, both see the mother as a central figure representing lack and ambivalence.

Different manifestations of melancholic mothering

Narrative one: Loss, lack, emptiness and insufficiency

Sally and her baby brother were removed from their parents and placed in a home when she was two years old. Her father was working away from home and her mother had suffered a nervous breakdown. Her parents were both 17 at the time. At age four, Sally's paternal grandparents adopted her and her brother. She describes life with them as very difficult. It was an authoritarian and unloving household. Her grandmother was full of anger. School was as loathsome as home, but Sally was not afraid to rebel there. By 16 she had moved out of home to live with her future husband. By the time she was 20, her daughter Kirsty had been born.

Sally's life has been frequently touched by violence and tragedy – a close friend of 18 years died from a drug overdose, and her first boyfriend and her grandfather both committed suicide. Sally subsequently had a nervous breakdown. More recently, she has become estranged from her grandmother, brother, and aunts and uncles on her father's side. Kirsty accused her father of bashing her. Sally did not believe this, but her extended family did and this led to the rift.

Sally feels an intense sense of longing for an idyllic family life. Like her grandmother, she is 'strict' about limiting Kirsty's social life to activities appropriate for a 13-year-old girl. But in addition she yearns to provide Kirsty with an idealised version of girlhood: a 'girly' girlhood. Kirsty is unpopular and isolated and cannot/will not be this sort of girl.

Sally's demeanour is dejected, her speech halting but insistent. It is clear from her story that absence and emotional deprivation were features of her childhood. In her early years, neither her father nor her mother were significant presences and she rejected both her grandparent/parent figures. She believes that in effect they brought about the loss of her childhood. Sally says: 'Our family was absolutely weird. I'm still shocked. And I keep thinking to myself, I'm not going to bloody bring Kirsty up like I was brought up'.

In Freudian terms, Sally has been unable to resolve her grief and to mourn this loss. Indeed, it seems she cannot turn from the lost object to the ego, and so cannot find her self. She has later compensated for the emptiness invoked by the absences and losses in her life with fantasies of an idealised childhood and family and has not been able to let go of these abstractions. Arguably, this has resulted in her adoption of a form of melancholic motherhood.

She tries to create a present and future in terms of a lost past that she never had – hence the 'girly' symbolic economy that she tries to create for her daughter. This symbolic economy certainly links to the representational gender order in the traditional and restrictive terms that Irigaray discusses. But it is her intense investment in this fantasy family that prevents Sally from more realistically and productively representing herself to herself as a mother.

This fantasy idyllic family also seems to screen from view what is really going on in Kirsty's life. There are mournful echoes here of Sally's own childhood experiences. Further, it may mean that she has become unwittingly and unwillingly complicit in the loss of her daughter's childhood:

> I said, 'You effing little c'. Sometimes I will say that to scare her, and I think, 'What am I doing?'... I can remember when I got married my grandmother turned around and goes 'Would you shut up! I've got better things to think about than your wedding', and I hated her. I still hate her for that. That's how she spoke to me.

In spite of Sally's attempts to provide a happy life for her daughter, Kirsty is deeply unhappy. This is manifest in anger and violence at home and school; aerosol abuse; self-harm, including chronic vomiting at school; and a suicide attempt. She has been hospitalised and medicated for depression. Sally attributes Kirsty's depression to a 17-year-old boy 'taking sexual advantage of her', but other accounts suggest that she suffers from the violence of her father. She finds it hard to tell her mother about the bad things that happen because then Sally yells at her.

Kirsty exhibits melancholic symptoms of self-loathing and expresses her devalued sense of self by cutting herself and attempting suicide – acts that seem to support Silverman's argument that women consider themselves 'inferior, insufficient, and unworthy of love' and ultimately torment themselves.

Further, Kirsty finds it hard to speak, and perhaps this is best interpreted via Irigaray's discussions of the problems of cultural representation for women. As Irigaray (1985, 68) might suggest: 'It is really a question for her of a loss that radically escapes representation... hence the impossibility of mourning that loss'. She has no way to represent and engage her loss other than through anger and self-harm.

Narrative two: Melancholic agency

Louise left home when she was 12 and lived for a time in various state institutions and halfway houses. Her stepfather raped her when she was nine. Louise describes her stepfather as a time-waster, a drunk and a gambler who repeatedly kicked her out of home, but told her mother she had run away. She left school permanently at 15 and lived on the streets in Sydney. Louise married her partner at 17 and had a number of miscarriages before Anna was born when Louise was 19.

Two years ago Anna was sexually assaulted by her uncle and has since tried to commit suicide. The same year, two bus drivers raped Louise. There is tension between mother and daughter because Louise insisted that Anna go through a court case but did not report the rape by the bus drivers.

Louise has a history of embodied loss through sexual violence. She has lost her family of origin and, like Sally, her childhood. When speaking of this loss, Louise says, 'I hit depression, I suppose, not deep depression but lost, you know. It was like there was something missing. It's just total emptiness and you don't want to look at yourself. Why bother?'

Louise can be seen as suffering from 'the complex of melancholia', which Freud describes as behaving 'like an open wound emptying the ego until it is totally impoverished' (Freud 1957, 253). And yet, despite her classically negative melancholic symptoms, Louise has activated and confronted her grief through an adamant refusal of closure. This does not mean that she lives in the past and is overburdened by it in the present. Rather, by speaking of a silenced past, she empowers herself and sets herself apart from her own mother and the weight of an unspoken but not unspeakable history. For Louise, speaking about her loss is an integral part of her process of recovery. She says her mother:

> is from the old generation so you just don't talk about it. If you don't talk about it, it's going to go away. But if you *don't* talk about it, it *eats* you away. It eats you and not just you as in part of a person, but you as a whole person. You withdraw from yourself; everything about you changes and eventually you'll start to go crazy [her emphasis].

Furthermore, as she deliberately engages her mother in a dialogue about her sexual abuse, she not only speaks about the unspeakable, but also succeeds in representing what had hitherto been unrepresentable. She states:

> At 22 I cracked up and said [to my mother], 'Would you like to explain to me *how* a nine-year-old sleeps with a man that is in his forties? It does not work'. And after that I earned her respect. How I don't know, but [laughing] probably from *throwing realisation at her* [her emphasis].

Although Louise suffers from melancholia, it is not, as Silverman might maintain, precipitated by her identification with and punishment of her mother. Louise's status as a melancholic subject does not place her in an 'inferior, unworthy' position; rather, it has become a source of agency for her.

Irigaray claims that women have no way to express or politicise their feelings of loss within a male-signifying economy. But it might be argued that feminism has assisted women to 'coin the signifiers' of loss and, more broadly, to develop a signifying economy that challenges phallocentric constructions of women as deficient. Indeed, this is precisely the approach Louise takes when speaking about her experiences of loss through sexual violence. She says:

> I won't put up with crap from males. That part of me has gotten stronger because I know that I'm not beneath them, any more. I never was; I put myself beneath them because I allowed them to control me. It shouldn't happen. I had to teach myself that: 'Hey, you're worth something; you can give back and you can take'.

Significantly, Louise's ability to articulate her feelings about men and about sexual violence using feminist discourse has also translated into an equally 'feminist' awareness in her daughter, Anna. When commenting on men's ways of thinking about girls, Anna says, 'Most guys have got really, really bad attitudes'. Neither Louise nor Anna accepts the inferior status imposed upon women within the phallocentric order. Rather, they vocally challenge these norms, revalue themselves as women and in the process politicise their feelings of loss.

In terms of these narratives, it is clear that neither of the mothers has severed her attachment to her history of loss, and thus both can be described in Freud's terms as melancholic subjects and in our terms as melancholic mothers. While they are both constantly haunted by burning images from the past, each nonetheless engages in a different manifestation of melancholic mothering.

Considering the remains of loss

In their edited book called *Loss*, Eng and Kazanjian (2003) seek to depathologise melancholia, make visible its social bases, and draw attention to its creative, unpredictable and political aspects. They argue that 'the politics and ethics of loss lie in the interpretation of what remains' (ix). They draw on Benjamin's discussions of the history of Left melancholia to consider how 'loss has been animated for hopeful and hopeless politics' (2).

They characterise melancholia's active and open relationship with the remains of the past as a 'hopeful politics'. They see a potentially creative quality in examining what remains after loss, as the mourners may see things that they haven't been able to see before. In contrast, they view the fixing of the remains of the past as a 'hopeless politics'. To mourn the remains of the past hopelessly is to become buried under the weight of the past, to become overburdened and immobilised by the past, ultimately disempowered by the past in the present.

For Eng and Kazanjian, 'as soon as the question "What is lost?" is posed, it invariably slips into the question "What remains?" That is, loss is inseparable from what remains, for what is lost is known only by what remains of it, by how these remains are produced, read, and sustained' (Eng and Kazanjian 2003, 2). These women's and girls' stories can be read through Eng and Kazanjian's understanding of melancholia, particularly in terms of their notion of 'hopeless' and 'hopeful' politics.

Narrative one again: Hopeless politics?

Sally's history of loss relates in general to her loss of persons, of relationships, of parents; a loss through violence – through the suicides of people she loved. For Sally, what remains of loss is expressed emotively in the present as a devastating rage that she has inherited from her grandmother. When speaking about her grandmother, Sally (2002) says:

> She would be the one yelling and screaming and carrying on… I can see Nana's traits coming out in me, especially the anger. I scream and yell especially at the kids. But I *hate* the grandmother side. I absolutely hate it and I can't snap out of it. It was an angry house, like there was *never* much laughter, most of the time it was just negative, very negative. Nothing was ever good [her emphasis].

Sadly, as Sally now directs this anger towards her daughter, it has become her daughter's inheritance. When speaking about her mother, Kirsty (2002) says:

> Every time I tell her something she'll get angry at me. When I get into trouble she'll yell at me… If people look at me the wrong way I will go off at them. Some people really annoy me and then I will get up and start swearing and yelling at them.

Sally also sees the conflicts of her own school life – the remembered feelings of hate, anger and rebellion – in her daughter. Fourteen-year-old Kirsty is now in Year 8 and, like her mother, she loathes school. Sally advises Kirsty on how to deal with conflict at school: 'I've taught her, if anyone harasses her, don't you back down. Don't let anyone walk over you. If someone does something to you, do whatever you have to… Look, let 'em have it and they'll leave you alone'. Kirsty has been suspended twice for physical and verbal abuse. She describes herself as more likely to bully than to be bullied, by teachers or students.

For Sally (and her daughter) the remains of the past have become a 'constricting force'. She is burdened by the weight of the past and as a result is left feeling disempowered, discouraged and depressed in the present. Sally's attachment to loss might lead us to describe it as a 'hopeless politics', based on the fact that she cannot move beyond her loss and seems to have little agency with regard to it. Let us leave this as an open statement for the moment.

Narrative two again: Hopeful politics

Louise has taught her kids to walk away and cool down when they are angry, as she does not want them to feel that they can use violence to deal with problems. 'I've always taught my kids, if you're going to get that upset and that angry that you feel like you're going to hit someone, well walk. Don't stay there. It's the best thing to do'. She also believes strongly in listening to what her children have to say in building trust, so that they feel safe in talking to her about their problems. Louise points out that the 'messed-up' relationship she had with her own mother helped her figure out what kind of parent she wanted to be for her children. She feels that her most important role as a mother is to be friends with her children, so they feel safe to talk about anything and everything. Louise has been able to mobilise the remains of loss as an affirmative force in both her own and her daughter's life.

At the same time, Louise does acknowledge the traces of anger that remain as a result of her daughter's loss. However, in this context it is possible to characterise the anger as a kind of strength or form of empowerment by which Anna becomes a force to be reckoned with. When talking about her daughter, Louise says, 'She's built with anger. And when you're built with anger, nothing stops you. You don't look at people as if to think, "Well, he's a guy, I can't beat him". You look at it as if he's a male that's it'.

Although Louise's melancholia is a result of violence and her consequential feelings of loss, by re-articulating and rewriting her past she is able to re-imagine this violence in the present moment. In this moment, she is able to reinvent herself not as an object but as a subject, a melancholic subject, a melancholic agent. Louise and Anna might therefore be seen as having adopted a 'hopeful politics' characterised by a sense of empowerment expressed as a capacity to articulate feelings of loss and exercise a form of affirmative rage that challenges male dominance.

Of course as educators we cannot afford to think in terms of hopelessness. To quote Raymond Williams (1989), we have a responsibility to provide 'resources of hope'. But what and how? This question raises an important pedagogic, theoretical and political issue. The challenge is to establish a bridge between 'hopeless' and 'hopeful' politics. It is necessary to find ways to avoid a dualism that consolidates and reproduces many current contradictions and distinctions. Without such a strategy, there is a danger that certain individuals and groups will be labelled and stereotyped as 'hopeless', while others will be characterised as 'hopeful'. In other words, existing cultures of violence will be normalised and reproduced. For a counter politics of violent practices, a pedagogy of transformation is necessary. This will require a focus on 'education' as a generic category that is applicable in many life situations and is focused on progressive and liberating change. Once this happens, it will be possible to identify the implications for transformative education within the context of schooling. With this caveat in mind, we now move outside the mainstream educational literature in order to examine approaches that have been valuable and useful in other professional practices where 'education', used in the generic sense, has occurred.

Anti-violence education

Violence is a psychosocial phenomenon and many social institutions and cultural forms are implicated in its various causes, expressions and prevention. One such institution is the school. However, accounts of gender, schooling and violence, and accounts of programs that address the issues that arise, seldom benefit from the insights of psychoanalytic theory. In this section, we seek to build on the psychoanalytic perspective we have developed in the first section by drawing on the work of Alice Miller. We are aware that she is not critical of Freud's theorising about mourning and melancholia specifically, but rather his notion of the 'Oedipus complex' and 'infantile sexuality' (Miller 1984). But this critique is of relevance here as, in her opinion, Freud's drive theory is a device that blames the child for the abusive sexual behaviour of adults and therefore protects the parents. For Miller, perpetuating this untruth is the basis of illness and depression. In her work she refers to this as 'poisonous pedagogy' and discusses the therapeutic work of the narrative therapist Michael White. We draw on this thinking in order to offer a tentative account of the ways in which educators might benefit pedagogically from our earlier accounts of gender, violence and melancholy.

A big question for schools is not just how they can create cultures of respectful relationships, but how they might develop pedagogical interventions in the cycles of voice that these mothers' and daughters' stories represent. It is clear from these stories and the broader research on violence that anti-violence pedagogies are likely to touch deep and quite different psychic sensitivities and investments for victims, survivors and perpetrators and for those who are complicit. Schools are deeply embedded in existing practices of violence. The first task is to acknowledge this fact in the process of developing alternative and transformative practices.

Many theories about effective learning and associated 'sound' teaching practices are supported by assumptions of relative helplessness, 'innocence' and ignorance of human infants and young children. Evidence of such is readily available in many theories of early childhood development. In certain ways these ideas provide the raison d'être for many accepted practices in the early years of parenting, pre-school and primary school. They also produce a warrant for control and 'hands-on' management of children, lest these characteristics lead them astray. Miller, formerly a psychoanalyst but now a writer, has come to a different conclusion (1987a; 1987b; 1990). Drawing on her extensive experience over many decades, Miller has challenged these so-called self-evident truths of childhood development. Offering the label of 'poisonous pedagogy', Miller has argued that these dominant ideas and practices have opened the way for wide-ranging abuse of young children by older children and adults. In practical terms the label is used to describe the types of teaching and management required to eradicate 'dangerous' and 'wild' characteristics that children are 'typically' born with. It is an idea, and a term, carried over from the very earliest days of mass schooling. As re-interpreted and critiqued by Miller and others, it signifies a process of controlling, manipulative and abusive patterns of teaching/learning and then, at a later time, repeating cycles of abuse (Miller 2010).

Miller has argued that emotions from early childhood normally cannot be consciously acknowledged and understood and are carried forward into the future without conscious recognition. When strong feelings are embedded in abusive experiences that cannot be remembered, they become disassociated from the original cause and often produce reactions of anger, helplessness and despair. If such feelings continue without clear expression or acknowledgment they can result in destructive acts against the self and/or others (Miller 1990, 168). This seems a plausible explanation of what has happened with Sally, as expressed within her problematic relationship with Kirsty and their ongoing struggles with abusive behaviour. On the other hand, Louise's story of being able to find acknowledgment of her experiences via dialogue with her mother has helped to bring early experiences involving conflict into an active state of consciousness.

Miller's analysis of poisonous pedagogy has opened the way for counter practices. Sustained trust, security and empathy provide the foundations of a non-violent identity. Given the world we are living in, for such practices to be sustained, a child needs an 'enlightened' witness who can help break the more dominant patterns of fear, anxiety and destructive emotions. On this matter, Miller is worth quoting directly when she asserts: 'Here lies the great opportunity for relatives, social workers, therapists, teachers, doctors, psychiatrists, officials and nurses to support the child and to believe in her or him' (Miller 1990, 169). The challenge here is to work constructively with these insights and to explore fields of inquiry and practice that may help us to do this. Narrative therapy is one such field with the potential to break the orthodoxy, oppression and violence of poisonous pedagogy.

Narrative therapy, developed by Michael White in conjunction with David Epston (1990; 1992), is conducted at the intersection of the psychic and the social. White uses the 'story' metaphor to explore the perpetual process of identity construction through meaning making (2007). According to White (1992, 123), people live and shape their lives by stories. These stories, he argues, 'have real, not imagined effects'; they 'provide the structure of life'.

White's 'pedagogic'[4] strategies provide opportunity for participants to express ideas, seek meaning, share experiences and remake understanding. As a first-order strategy, White is interested in the importance of 'externalising' ideas, thoughts, beliefs, feelings and fears. Unlike those who hold onto the ancient belief that some individuals are born 'bad' and continue to be so throughout their life, White's assumption is that knowledge, mores and values exist outside the person and are progressively internalised through daily practices and interactions. In this process there are constant choices to be made and problems to be resolved. This is part of the ongoing process of developing and sustaining an identity and it becomes manifest or visible in such matters as appearance, speech and ways of interacting with others. Significantly, this also suggests that change and transformation are constant possibilities.

The narrative method, as pedagogy, is very much a social process. Identities are formed and sustained in concert with others. Constant negotiation and readjustment occur as the influences of the wider culture percolate into and saturate communal contexts. It is within the process of sharing narratives that important educational and re-learning opportunities occur. To be consciously educative, these moments that might begin as serendipitous events need to be managed strategically and formally. White uses the term 'definitional ceremonies' (White 1995, 184) to describe the formalisation of this social activity. Where the sharing process has been open and empathetic, there are important chances to recognise critical or significant opportunities in one's narration. White has described these moments as 'unique outcomes', a term used to depict the disruption in the normal flow of a person's experiences in which alternative possibilities become apparent and possible.

It is clear that in terms of the hopeful politics of Louise and Anna they have, in a sense, gone through this process. Louise identifies male power over women, poor communication between mother and daughter and generational attitudes as among the dominant story lines that she has been subjected to and confronted. Her 'unique outcome' has been to deploy feminist insights to help her to read and rearticulate her own and Anna's circumstances, and anger management strategies to enable them to avoid physical confrontation. However, there have been no such 'unique outcomes' for Sally and Kirsty.

The dominant story lines that have shaped Sally's and Kirsty's lives are manifold. While Sally can articulate the effect of her emotionally deprived childhood on her later behaviour, she has not been able to or had the opportunity to externalise this or to identify and articulate alternative story lines. The alternative story lines of the perfect family and the girly symbolic economy are both dependent on stereotypes, which are oppressive for them both. But neither does she seem to have access to alternative sociocultural story lines that are empowering, or an aspect of her own story that resists the dominant narratives. While her situation may thus seem hopeless, narrative therapy would suggest otherwise.

For educators there are a number of important ideas in White's analysis. Given the social and group nature of mainstream schooling, narrative pedagogy involves a process of two-way understanding of one's relationships. Using the idea of a definitional ceremony, an educator will take the chance to form a group, allow the sharing of narratives and facilitate feedback in the process of providing alternative accounts. This approach offers a formal collaboration designed to provide new ways of thinking and behaving. In turn, this becomes a process of shaping new and alternative story lines through which to rebuild identity and relationships.

There are several advantages to using narrative therapy ideas to address the problems of violence in schools. Firstly, storying is a key feature of schooling and of students' and teachers' ways of making meaning about their place in schools. Secondly, the indeterminate nature of storytelling suggests that collective and individual stories and identities are fluid and can therefore be rewritten or retold – albeit not easily. For both perpetrators and victims of violence, alternative stories point to the possibility of changing direction. A third advantage of the narrative approach is that it enables people's experiences to be considered within wider frameworks of meaning. It encourages them to consider the impact on their lives and relationships of wider cultural and social power relations. For example, a personal story can be linked to a more general cultural story. This helps to develop an appreciation of the ways in which people are situated within the dominant story lines of a culture or a society.

But, of course, unlike narrative therapy, narrative pedagogy in schools is not one-on-one; it does not have the benefits of time that therapy provides; it must compete with the demands of the school curriculum and contend with the limits of preservice training and professional development programs for teachers. The possibility of adaptations of narrative therapy for use in schools is recognised in the work of David Denborough (1996), a professional counsellor well skilled in the uses of narrative therapy. His practices show that in the hands of a skilled therapist, narrative therapy can become narrative pedagogy. The following example is taken from a program in which Denborough worked with male students in a single-sex class program designed to address problems in junior secondary schools. Specifically, the program addressed issues of sexual harassment or violence and by implication power relations and contested identities. It then assisted students to find some positive counter-narratives, to draw out and upon alternative sources of strength and status and to build new communities of support for alternative ways of being male. The following summary, derived from Denborough's work, is provided in order to clarify how narrative therapy can become a pedagogic process. Key features of the method involve:

- establishing *basic ground rules* of interaction that are characterised by respect and support rather than blaming and shaming
- *sharing personal experiences* as a means of *mapping* the extent of violence in participants' lives
- *naming the dominant plots* of those issues that are clearly embedded in the dynamics of society more generally, including identifying the gendered nature of violence

- *mapping the effects* of this dominant plot on different social groupings
- *articulation of the need for change*
- *finding exceptions* to the dominant plot; identifying critical moments that tell a different story – what White describes as 'unique outcomes'
- *identifying a counter-plot* or an alternative story line, thereby assisting students to find some positive counter-narratives
- *broadening the responsibility* by exploring how suggestions could be supported, in their new narrative form, by staff, the school, families and the local community.

The approach outlined is part of a layered pedagogy. This involves discussions at a number of different levels in the school and includes parents and community members.

One obvious question is: Can such a narrative pedagogy approach also be used with girls and women who have been subjected to and indeed meted out various forms of violence?[5] We believe so. This would include adapting some of Denborough's ideas to the situations faced by girls and women in families and in relationships between and within the genders and generations and in connection to their cultures and communities outside of and within schools. Around the world, there is a considerable body of literature on women's and girls' experiences of violence in different circumstances, locations and cultures, and numerous policies and practices have been developed to address their experiences. But for teachers to be effective in this regard they would need to study this material and carefully explore its implications for narrative pedagogy. They would also need to become educated and accomplished in adapting narrative therapy to the different demands of narrative pedagogy in the school setting. Clearly, there is a role here for ongoing professional development programs designed to facilitate the development of appropriate knowledge and skills. As the narratives we have shared indicate, violence can have a lasting impact in the form of identity and health problems, family conflict, breakdown and loss, educational failure, withdrawal and much more. 'Closing the gap' in education means taking the matter of violence very seriously and developing pedagogical 'resources for hope'.

Acknowledgment

This paper draws on Kenway and Fitzclarence (1997) and Kenway and Fahey (2008). Both were published in the journal *Gender and Education*. We express our appreciation for permission to re-use sections of these papers.

Endnotes

1. As we have argued elsewhere, particular forms of masculinity are a feature. We point out that the males who are most likely to resort to serious physical violence against females subscribe to traditional and patriarchal views of male power and supremacy, traditional gender roles and to the view that violence is an acceptable way of resolving conflict (Kenway and Fitzclarence 1997).

2. This paper arises from the Australian Research Council Discovery Grant (2002–2004) 'Young women negotiating from the margins of education and work: Towards gender justice in educational and youth policies and programs', awarded to Jane Kenway (Monash University) and Alison Mackinnon (University of South Australia) and Julie McLeod and Andrea Allard (Deakin University). It also draws on a Deakin University faculty grant for the project 'Violence in schools: A cross disciplinary inquiry', awarded to Lindsay Fitzclarence and Jane Kenway.

3. In Kenway and Fahey (2008) we have developed these ideas at greater length than we are able to do here.

4. This is our term. We are not aware of White using the concept in the way it is frequently employed in education.

5. Artz (1998) is very useful with regard to schoolgirls and violence.

References

Artz, S. 1998. *Sex and the Violent School Girl*. New York. Teachers College Press.
Brison, S. 2002. *Aftermath: Violence and the Remaking of a Self*. Princeton, New Jersey: Princeton University Press.
Denborough, D. 1996. 'Step by step: Developing respectful and effective ways of working with young men to reduce violence'. In *Men's Ways of Being*, edited by McLean, C; Carey, M; White, C. Denver: Westview Press: 91–117.
Eng, D L; Kazanjian, D, eds. 2003. *Loss*. Berkeley: University of California Press.
Fortune, M M. 2005. *Sexual Violence: The Sin Revisited*. Cleveland, Ohio: Pilgrim Press.
Freud, S. 1957 [1917]. 'Mourning and melancholia'. In *The Standard Edition of the Complete Psychological Works of Sigmund Freud*, vol. 14, edited and translated by Strachey, J. London: Hogarth Press.
Irigaray, L. 1985. *The Speculum of the Other Women*. Trans. Gill, G C. Ithaca: Cornell University Press.
Kelly, L. 1987. 'The continuum of sexual violence'. In *Women, Violence and Social Control*, edited by Hanmer, J; Maynard, M. London: McMillan: 46–61.
Kenway, J; Fitzclarence, L. 1997. 'Masculinity, violence and schooling: Challenging "poisonous pedagogies"'. Special issue of *Gender and Education*, on boys' education, 9 (1): 117–133.
Kenway J; Fahey J. 2008. 'Melancholic mothering: Mothers, daughters and family violence'. *Gender and Education* 20 (6): 639–654.
Miller, A. 1984. *Thou Shalt Not Be Aware*. New York: Farrar, Straus and Giroux.
Miller, A. 1987a. *The Drama of Being a Child*. London: Virago Press.
Miller, A. 1987b. *For Your Own Good: The Roots of Violence in Child-rearing*. London: Virago Press.
Miller, A. 1990. *The Untouched Key: Tracing Childhood Trauma in Creativity and Destructiveness*. London: Virago Press.
Miller, A. 2010. Thisisawar.com. Accessed 15 May 2010. Available from: http://www.thisisawar.com/AuthorsAlice.htm.

Schwartz, M D, ed. 1997. *Researching Sexual Violence Against Women: Methodological and Personal Perspectives.* Thousand Oaks, California: Sage Publications.

Silverman, K. 1988. *The Acoustic Mirror: The Female Voice in Psychoanalysis and Cinema.* Bloomington: Indiana University Press.

Sokoloff, N J; Dupont, I. 2005. 'Domestic violence at the intersections of race, class and gender'. *Violence Against Women* 11 (1): 38–64.

Sokoloff, N J; Pratt, C, eds. 2006. *Domestic Violence at the Margins: Readings on Race, Class, Gender and Culture.* Piscataway, New Jersey: Rutgers University Press.

Weldon, S L. 2002. *Protest, Policy, and the Problem of Violence Against Women: A Cross-national Comparison.* Pittsburg: University of Pittsburg Press.

White, M; Epston, D. 1990. *Narrative Means to Therapeutic Ends.* New York and London: W.W. Norton & Company.

White, M. 1992. 'Deconstruction and therapy'. In *Experience Contradiction Narrative and Imagination: Selected Papers of David Epston & Michael White, 1989–1991.* Adelaide: Dulwich Centre Publications: 109–152.

White, M. 1995. *Re-Authoring Lives: Interviews and Essays.* Adelaide: Dulwich Centre Publications.

White, M. 2007. *Maps of Narrative Practice.* New York and London: W.W. Norton & Company.

Williams, R. 1989. *Resources of Hope: Culture, Democracy, Socialism.* London: Verso.

Young, I M. 1990. *Justice and the Politics of Difference.* Princeton: Princeton University Press.

Young, I M. 1992. 'Five faces of oppression'. In *Rethinking Power,* edited by Wartenberg, T. Albany, New York: SUNY Press: 174–195.

Two Orientations to Education System Reform

Australian and South African Politics of Remaking 'the Social'

Terri Seddon
Monash University

The conference at Monash South Africa in November 2009 addressed the gap in social and educational outcomes between different social groups in three southern worlds – South Africa, Australia and New Zealand. The evidence indicates that in all three white settler societies there are socioeconomic gaps, which tend to be particularly acute between Indigenous and non-Indigenous groups. However, the patterns of inequality are complex, rooted in history and influenced by the politics of policy, which reflect the effects of minority and majority white settlement across the three countries. It is notable that progress in 'closing the gap' appears to be most advanced in New Zealand, where population numbers of Maori and Pakeha are more equal than in either South Africa with a white minority, or Australia with a white majority.

This patterning of the gaps in the three southern worlds indicates that inequalities are deeply embedded in the 'social': the way in which patterns and experiences of social life have been made in each nation state (Smith 1999). The social is constituted within particular spaces and times through the social and cultural practices that form and are anchored in the histories of nation-states, their social relations and governing-state regimes. Understanding the gap between Indigenous and non-Indigenous Australia requires a consideration of the 'local spaces' that contribute to Australia's national history and also the way these locales of everyday life, their customs and myths, are tensioned by 'travelling ideas' that flow globally through policies, transactions and processes of mobility (Jones 2001). Closing the gap in socioeconomic inequality depends on interventions in this stream of history, which necessarily entail the mobilisation of power and authority.

My chapter considers the contribution of national education systems to closing the gap in social and educational inequalities. It is part of a larger research program, which has examined the changing relations between schooling, states and societies and the implications of these sociopolitical contextual changes for education (Seddon 1993; forthcoming). This work, embedded in the tradition of cultural historical sociology (Abrams 1982; Bonnell and Hunt 1999) and informed by notions of path dependency (Mahoney 2000) and policy feedback (Pierson 1993), is necessarily a global sociology. I argue that the institutionalisation of education as a system is a political achievement that is negotiated as a means of making the social within nation-states (Centre for Contemporary Cultural Studies 1981; Williams 1976). It is formed as an instrument of government, with particular purposes and priorities within prevailing spatialised relations of power. These relations were once uncompromisingly national in focus. Now policies and practices framed by national histories and traditions are tensioned by imperatives arising in the global economy and its cultural consequences associated with intensified global interconnectedness and mobility. This contradictory national–global context and its systemic achievements are realised in processes that make the social through the occupational agency of the education workforce. I call this occupational agency, which is constituted by the ordering of the education system and its limits, 'educational work' (Seddon forthcoming).

The failure to close the gap in social and educational outcomes is, I suggest, a consequence of the way the terms, conditions and practices of educational work are institutionalised as a system of endorsed and unendorsed educational agency. I develop this argument by considering the shifting patterns of educational work through two steps. First, I look at the trajectory of Australian education policy in relation to Indigenous education, historically and in our contemporary contradictory national–global context, to show how system reform has reconfigured ways of doing educational work. The visibility and resourcing of innovative practices of educational work that address national–global contradictions is a political outcome that is framed by the political culture in Australia and has developed on the basis of Indigenous–non-Indigenous relations of power. Next, I consider ways in which educational work might be mobilised to address the gap in socioeconomic inequalities by looking to South Africa. I note a different political culture, which appears to support a more overt dialogue about reform of education policy and practice.

I then analyse the inaugural speech in 2009 by Jonathan K. Jansen as Rector of the University of the Free State. This speech offers a different mode of thinking about the ways institutionalised educational work might contribute to closing the gap in socioeconomic inequalities. It is a contribution that targets the processes of making the social by addressing both the imperatives of globalising times and social divisions that anchor inequalities and are underpinned by persistent institutional biases in national education systems.

This cross-national methodological process does not claim to be comparative analysis. My comments on South Africa represent insights grasped through my first short visit to that country, based on observations, conversations and subsequent reading. They are, at best, the glimpses of an outsider. However, even as glimpses, they are helpful in disturbing my local Australian understandings of education systems, and the politics of policy and practice that constitute educational work. It is a strategy that offers distance on what is familiar and taken for granted in my southern world, Australia. I conclude the chapter by drawing out the features of educational work that help to remake the social in the light of contemporary national–global contradictions.

Unpacking the 'gap' in social and educational outcomes

The gap in social and educational outcomes between Indigenous and non-Indigenous Australians is well documented (see the other chapters in this volume). Disparities exist on a wide range of indicators relating to longevity, health, housing and employment as well as education. But unlike other disadvantaged groups in Australia, Indigenous Australians have a particular history of invisibility.

The cultural myth that the British settled an empty land when they put up their flag in Sydney Cove in 1788 provided the foundation for Indigenous dispossession. This view was formalised in the legal principle of *terra nullius*, which rendered any pre-existing rights of Indigenous Australians invisible within legal frameworks. Indigenous traditions and patterns of governance and decision making were obscured and marginalised in the formation of Australia and its patterns of citizenship. The 1990 Wik judgment in the Australian High Court, which overturned the principle of *terra nullius* and affirmed the existence of Indigenous land rights, has led to some legal and socio-attitudinal change, as commitments to reconciliation between Indigenous and non-Indigenous Australians have gained greater public affirmation. Until recently the imported Australian democracy has not been required to enter into any compact with its Indigenous population. By contrast, in New Zealand the Maoris retained a political presence through the negotiated 1840 Treaty of Waitangi. In South Africa the compact between racial groups was formalised in its multi-racial constitution that marked the end of apartheid in 1993.

Over time, Australia's social and cultural practices took on persistent institutional biases because of these racialised social relations. While the developing Australian welfare state has gradually offered equity to migrants, its blindness to Indigenous Australians (who were not landholders) lingered into the late twentieth century. Until the 1970s these Indigenous 'non-citizens' were managed as a dependent population of state wards through a system of state- or church-administered reserves, and many did not gain the right to vote in Commonwealth elections until 1967.

Institutional biases persist in education, evident as differences in attainment, participation and practices. These biases rest on contradictory politics, where policies specify the importance of Indigenous education and achievement, but where dominant Anglo-Australian cultural expectations and norms are conveyed through the everyday work of teachers. Mostly, these teachers are non-Indigenous and have very limited opportunity to learn about Indigenous Australia. Everyday cultural dissonances between established education identities in schools, TAFE institutes and universities on one hand and Indigenous learners on the other compound the structural disjunctures between Indigenous and non-Indigenous worlds.

Indigenous educator Chris Sarra draws attention to the deep-seated nature of these problems. In an interview on the ABC, he commented about teachers he inherited when he became principal of Cherbourg State School in Queensland. Critical of teachers' apparent acceptance of Indigenous children who couldn't read, he recalled asking the staff about this:

> Their response was, oh, well, the Department doesn't support us, or, there's many social complexities. And I sat in this room here… and said, look, what I believe, what the elders in our community believe, is that our children can leave here with academic outcomes that are just as good as any other school in Queensland. And that they can leave here with a very strong and very positive sense of what it means to be Aboriginal. And if you don't believe it, then it's time for you to go. And half the teaching staff got up and left. (ABC 2004)

Of course, the problem does not just lie with individual teachers or schools, but in the institutional biases built into Australian education. Sarra is critical of particular teachers, but they are not simply individual actors, but institutional artefacts of schooling; a consequence of the way terms, conditions and practices are defined to enable the instrumental mobilisation of educational work for purposes of governing (Lawn and Ozga 1981). Like other educational workers, these teachers act as intermediaries between governments and communities. Their job is to enable learning; their skill lies in the way they make social spaces that support processes of socialisation and education that are mixed to suit particular learners and yield learning. Hamilton (1989, 13) clarifies the distinctions between these processes that support learning, noting:

> 'Socialization'… is a relatively diffuse process; it generates learning that is 'picked up' or 'rubbed off' in the course of human interaction. By comparison, 'education' is a 'stronger' and more visible process; it yields learning that has been deliberately promoted through 'teaching'.

These teachers use their occupational expertise to enable learning but, in particular, they use workplace terms and conditions defined by the institutionalisation of 'schooling'. Such schooling is a more socially visible sub-set of these processes of learning because it entails practices that produce 'learning that, in its turn, has been shaped by formalized and institutionalized modes of teaching' (Hamilton 1989, 13). It means that some capacities for teaching are formalised and systematised through policy and industrial processes that determine the purposes and priorities towards which educational work is directed as schooling. This nationally defined orientation of schooling orders educational work, the exercise of occupational agency and its capacities to act, in and beyond the boundaries of formalised schooling. It also orders the way teachers mix socialisation and education in local spaces to prioritise particular learning outcomes in the light of community needs and government expectations. These processes of governing through educational work make the social in local spaces at every scale, but in everyday ways that tend to remake persistent social divisions and inequalities over time.

The character of Australian schooling as a system is anchored in Australia's social and symbolic history and its transforming welfare-state regime. This education system, and those who inhabit or are affected by it, is framed by the state's authorisation of institutionalised terms, conditions, practices and purposes of educational work. The form and function of educational work as schooling therefore orders occupational agency in and beyond schooling. These system effects are an outcome of institutional rules, resource allocations and narratives that give meaning and legitimacy to particular configurations of power relations. In this way, some forms of educational work rather than others are realised through the contested agency of government because they are endorsed and authorised as schooling.

Shifting systemic purposes and priorities

Since white settlement, the education system has been used to tackle relations between Indigenous and non-Indigenous Australians. Where Indigenous Australians were long managed through mission schools and as a menial workforce, by the 1970s they were recognised as a 'disadvantaged group'. By the 1980s, the national social justice agenda began to be disrupted by travelling ideas that asserted the benefits of markets over states in human service work, including education (Marginson 1997).

The globalising economy compounded contradictions in government policy making. Lifelong learning reforms were prioritised in pursuit of workforce development and competitive economic advantage. Policy implementation across the Australian education system diversified patterns of educational provision in terms of both programs offered and the types and autonomy of providers (Seddon 2001). Vocational Education and Training (VET) reform, in particular, was a means of increasing Indigenous participation in education and training.

This trajectory of the education system over time indicated growing contradictions in the Australian political regime. Practical politics in everyday life that were framed nationally were exposed to increasing tension due to the global economy and its cultural consequences, which arose from expanded interconnectedness and mobility on a world scale. These practical and lived contradictions between the national and global profoundly disturbed the social, the everyday life, customs and cultural myths that constitute particular space-times, like Australia.

These developments prompted transforming politics at every scale. Since the 1970s, identities, relationships and cultures have been renegotiated in the process of remaking the social in ways that address national–global contradictions in everyday life. Within the education system, the social justice agenda seeking to support those disadvantaged by migration and marginalisation struggled with the economic agenda that stressed the importance of competitive advantage in a global capitalist economy. In local spaces, these large-scale agendas were mediated through educators' occupational agency in mixing socialisation and education to benefit learners, while also meeting government expectations, institutionalised as accountability frameworks. Localised educational work showed that it was possible to do smart schooling that addressed national and global priorities in ways that also supported learners (Sachs 2003).

Slowly these politics moved towards new levels of understanding and action. By the late 1990s, there was a discernable policy shift towards issues of social inclusion (eg Kirby 2000). Notions of community capacity building increasingly mediated the policy agenda around competitive advantage that justified marketisation and privatisation. This was prompted in part by research on participation rates in employment, education and training among different social categories in the 15 to 19 and 20 to 24-year-old age groups (Dusseldorp Skills Forum 1998; 1999). The message was that lifelong learning had increased participation, but there were significant numbers of individuals who were falling between learning and earning. Economic reforms were returning economic benefits to individuals but these benefits were limited for some groups, due to intractable social and cultural constraints. This policy feedback indicated that economic development was contingent not only on the mobilisation of human capital but also on social development.

Policy dialogue began to focus on the human dimensions of innovation and development. In Victoria and Queensland, in particular, there was a proliferation of partnerships between communities and governments, which anchored problem-solving activities in local places and their communities (Smyth et al. 2005). These policy initiatives acknowledged that there were 'wicked problems' that were highly resistant to resolution, cutting across established portfolios and institutional arrangements, and demanding whole-of-government action in collaboration with local communities (APSC 2007). Localised policy making was described as 'an evolving art'. These complex and intractable problems:

> require thinking that is capable of grasping the big picture, including the interrelationships among the full range of causal factors underlying them. They often require broader, more collaborative and innovative approaches. This may result in the occasional failure or need for policy change or adjustment.

Whole-of-government and community problem solving created contexts where different agencies worked together on wicked problems. Small-scale initiatives proliferated as Indigenous and non-Indigenous Australia worked up partnerships oriented towards community capacity building (eg Seddon et al. 2002; Seddon et al. 2008). In these local places, communities and governments were remaking the social in ways that acknowledged contradictory national–global imperatives and their localised everyday practical manifestations. This complex intercultural work has challenged ways of living the social that were framed by racialised power relations embedded in national histories and politics.

Restating the problem

The education policy trajectory since the 1980s has made some inroads into the gap in social and educational outcomes in Australian education. But it also highlights the obdurate character of socioeconomic inequalities. These inequalities, I suggest, are anchored in the history of the national system of education and the institutional biases that have become embedded in human service work, including education, which makes the social. They are disturbed in contradictory ways by globalising changes in economies and cultures and the consequent effects of political problem solving. Yet the national system of education also houses resources that can be mobilised to remake the social for globalising times.

My argument is that the institutionalisation of education as a system is a key instrument in the work of remaking the social. Education systems help to make the social when they order schooling and its capacities for action as an instrument of government. This history of government investment to institutionalise and formalise teaching creates a social technology, made up of particular social spaces, a technological infrastructure and a human capacity, which is realised as educational work. The particular occupational expertise and associated capacities to act that enact educational work are embodied, individually and collectively, in the form of educational workers. The character of this workforce and the nature of its occupational agency are ordered by the politics of welfare-state development that has, until recently, privileged the learning of children and young people rather than adults. In this political regime, Indigenous learning and outcomes have been more or less invisible, relative to national priorities (including addressing marginalisation) among non-Indigenous Australians. Travelling ideas, such as lifelong learning, problematise this ordering and also its major legitimising myths relating to the formation of national identities (Kuhn 2007).

Educational work, the occupational agency of educational workers, is the critical resource that is made available and ordered through education systems. However, the familiar national patterning of this work between the centres and margins of schooling is destabilised by national–global contradictions that demand political solutions. These practical politics shift the locus of action away from familiar, nationally framed places of work and learning, like schools and other public education institutions, towards boundary zones and multi-agency spaces, which also exist as localised places. In these conditions of rapid change, boundaries slide, creating new boundary zones where different agencies come together in new trans-boundary spaces.

In these processes that respatialise schooling, educational work is reterritorialised and recultured (Angus and Seddon 2000; Robertson 2002). 'Between spaces' emerge as territories to be occupied and challenged. Boundaries are crossed, defended and renegotiated. The resulting reconfiguration of educational agency reveals (and also forms) unfamiliar identities engaged in educational work. These educational workers share capacities for intermediary work with those in the heartlands of nationally framed schooling. However, the way they exercise their agency in making the social in specific locales is defined at the nexus where governing is negotiated between different agencies. In this way educational workers' identities, relationships and cultures diversify and come to embody distinctive relational expertise. In and beyond the formalised education system, educational workers exercise this expertise through their occupational agency, making spaces of orientation that yield learning for living the social.

Bringing these elements together focuses the problem of the gap in social and educational outcomes, and also suggests solutions full of new challenges. Remaking the social in globalised times means reconfiguring the education system as an instrument that yields the kind of learning in civil society that will address inequalities embedded in national histories, as well as global imperatives related to workforce development. This policy solution must target institutional biases, built into national schooling, which endorse and constantly remake social divisions through the institutional patterning of socioeconomic inequalities. Such institutional reform requires the mobilisation of occupational agency by intermediaries, including educational workers, who can use their relational expertise in and between national and trans-boundary spaces to address the fundamental problem of political will. As Haug (2010) suggests, this work in and across boundaries is the 'art of politics'. It 'is not about defining the "right" goal and then implementing it… [but] about building connections, about creating a space of orientation which can re-contextualise fragmented struggles'.

The historic contribution of the education system in making the social offers solutions to the problem of the persistent gap between Indigenous and non-Indigenous Australians. The key questions are: What kind of educational work can make a difference for learners? How might we address the problem of institutional bias and political will? My suggestion is that current contradictions between national–global and localised priorities create conditions for educational agency that develop capacities for action in national and trans-boundary spaces. Educational work is a key resource in this regard, offering support to individuals and institutions as they unlearn and relearn ways of living the social interculturally. The next section elaborates this suggestion through reflections on South Africa

Glimpsing other ways of being social

South Africa is a white minority settler society with a visible history of brutal apartheid. Australia is a white majority settler society with an invisible history of dispossession and discrimination. During a short visit to South Africa in late 2009 and in subsequent reading, I was struck by the visibility of political struggle in South Africa and its intercultural forms of political agency. Four features of education and politics in South Africa strike me as different from Australia and also suggestive of ways of remaking the social in globalising times. These relate to ways of working in a democratic culture, an openness to critique oriented to problem solving, active public debate and imaginative rethinking of possibilities. These cross-national observations offer a vantage point on education systems and their contribution to making the social that gives distance and perspective on the Australian education system and its political culture, which underpins persistent institutional biases.

Democratic culture

I found it remarkable that South Africa could produce a Mandela despite its history of apartheid. The story seems to build through a particular kind of mission schooling, indigenous traditions of governance and an experience of racial violence that prompted some people of all races to work together to end apartheid (Mandela 1995). The national constitution crystallises these principles for working within and across racialised social categories and cultures in trans-boundary spaces that had to be occupied to end apartheid. The first two principles affirm human dignity, equality, advancement of human rights and freedoms, and non-racialism and non-sexism. The ways of working in a less racialised social space, which was constituted as a trans-boundary space because participants crossed historically embedded boundaries and social divisions, are suggested in the opening lines of the constitution, which marked the end of apartheid:

We, the people of South Africa,

Recognise the injustices of our past;

Honour those who suffered for justice and freedom in our land;

Respect those who have worked to build and develop our country; and

Believe that South Africa belongs to all who live in it, united in our diversity.

We therefore, through our freely elected representatives, adopt this Constitution as the supreme law of the Republic so as to—

Heal the divisions of the past and establish a society based on democratic values, social justice and fundamental human rights;

Lay the foundations for a democratic and open society in which government is based on the will of the people and every citizen is equally protected by law;

Improve the quality of life of all citizens and free the potential of each person; and

Build a united and democratic South Africa able to take its rightful place as a sovereign state in the family of nations.
(Republic of South Africa 1996)

Overt critique oriented to problem solving

The possibility of realising this way of working depends on people being willing to grapple with wicked problems that are embedded in both national and global relations of power. South Africa, like Australia, faces the challenge of closing the gap in social and educational outcomes (the national problematic), but in conditions that are compounded by global as well as local imperatives. Inevitably, these conflicting priorities and purposes mean that policy making is a contradictory process that yields contradictory policy outcomes.

In South Africa, more than in Australia, there seems to be an honest and open-minded engagement in the complex work of building a democratic post-apartheid regime. There is recognition and overt critique of contradictions in education policy and practice, but there is also a willingness to identify ways forward that address national issues and are also responsive to global lifelong learning policy agenda. Wallace (2009), for instance, highlights the double reform agenda being pursued in South Africa, which addresses the need for information and communication technology (ICT) investment in education to build capacity and compete in the world economy, and the need to redistribute resources to address inequalities from the past. She argues that these contradictory imperatives increase regional inequalities because rich provinces can self-fund development while other provinces 'do not have the time or resources to pursue partnerships oriented towards ICT developments' (1987).

These critiques are significant because they name the political challenges that confront and constrain education reform in South Africa. There appears to be a willingness to call it like it is, between policy and practice, regardless of the authority of the agencies involved. Critique of the state is explicit, not veiled nor marginalised. For instance, McGrath (2009) criticises standardised VET reforms because they tend to 'reflect and reinforce broader domestic power dynamics'. He notes that the lifelong learning settlement has had successes but claims too much in terms of its coherence and responsiveness. The 'move away from state control and towards responsiveness both to market forces and to the wishes of local people' (464) has disruptive effects in terms of state authority and legitimacy. Despite market rhetoric, he suggests, the South African state continues to address 'equity and effectiveness'. It is accepted that 'the market cannot be left to decide on skills or on policy areas more generally'. There are also concerns about 'the State's capacity to deliver' on its development aspirations (465–466).

Active public debate

These features of South African political culture create a space for dialogue that appears more open to imaginative problem solving than in Australia. Initiatives are not just the preserve of policy executives and elites; they can also come from localised places where practitioners grapple with complex problems every day. The perspective of the lowly, like Mandela as law clerk, seems respected. Judgments about the adequacy of these initiatives, as solutions to wicked problems, is not the exclusive responsibility of the state but occurs through wider public scrutiny and dialogue. This context of openness is contested but is also historically embedded; citizens and communities do speak out on public issues rather than seeing such matters as none of their business.

It was these features that distinguished the inaugural lecture by Jonathan Jansen as Rector of the University of the Free State (UFS) from most speeches by Australian vice-chancellors (the equivalent of rectors). Rather than speaking to executive decision makers within government, Jansen's lecture was presented to and received by wider publics. The press mediated this communication but it fuelled substantial public dialogue because communities within South Africa are responsive to active public debate. The speech was undoubtedly controversial, but it ran the gauntlet of public comment, which served to draw out the rationale of the initiative and also educate the public about the shared problems of building a post-apartheid regime.

Imaginative rethinking

This engaged political culture opens up the possibility of imaginative solutions that address the contradictory national–global context of contemporary South Africa. Jansen's speech is a public commentary that makes a case for mobilising educational work to address the wicked problems arising from national history and global competitiveness. The way he unpacks these problems in the local space of UFS recognises the contribution that the occupational agency of educational workers can make and the institutional conditions necessary to enable the exercise of that agency.

I consider Jansen's speech in some detail in the next section for two reasons. First, he offers a perspective on the way educational systems can remake the social in contradiction to national–global conditions, which is relevant to my argument in this chapter. Second, his orientation to educational work is almost unimaginable in the Australian context, particularly at the national scale. There are lots of practical initiatives where localised educational work of the kind described by Jansen is going on in Australia. However, it occurs mostly under the radar of government policy and accountability, and is not endorsed for take-up in large-scale public debates.

A strategy for remaking the social

A case for reform

Jansen's inaugural speech works the contradiction between national traditions and global expectations. He began by acknowledging the achievements of the UFS, its proud traditions and distinguished alumni, but quickly moved to express shame at a racial incident in Reitz, one of the UFS student residences, in which four young white men violated the dignity of five black workers.

Jansen articulated an institutional response to the incident by redefining the problem that needs to be solved. Reflecting on this incident, 'committed on the grounds of an institution of higher learning', he asks, 'What was it within the institution that made it possible for such an atrocity to be committed in the first place?'

In answering this question, Jansen steps outside the prevailing economic problematic that dominates education policy and practice around the world and, instead, highlights the social. He insists that the racial incident must not be understood as a problem of individual pathology. Noting the shameful behaviour of the white students and associated interventions by colleagues and parents to hose down the incident, he states that the problem is not 'four racially troubled students'. Rather, it is a problem of 'institutional complicity', which embeds these students, Reitz and UFS in institutionalised racial relations of power. Seeing the problem this way suggests a solution that moves beyond issues of workforce development that are prioritised in the prevailing frames of economic and prudential lifelong learning policy and practice. As Jansen notes, his historicised and contextualised way of defining the problem 'has important implications for how we move towards healing, forgiveness and social justice on our campus and in our country'.

Defining the problem in institutional terms, he maps the dimensions of this problem of institutional culture. First, he captures the complex moral terrain. Jansen distinguishes the general from the particular as a way of clarifying ethical responsibilities that are embedded in history and tradition. The particular incident involved whites, but it is inappropriate to condemn all whites for the actions of a few. Yet, the hurt to five black workers is a hurt to all black people on campus and in the province, because this hurt arises from the 'long history of exclusion and marginalisation of black people' at UFS. This hurt feeds further hurts experienced by 'white citizens of the university' who were shamed and subjected to over-generalised 'criticism of whites' in the wake of the incident.

This line of argument highlights the obdurate political and cultural character of the problem. The roots of these hurts lie in 'racism and bigotry', which have grown from a failure to reconcile in the nineteenth century, through a history of exclusion that was institutionalised and naturalised through apartheid. Yet the end of apartheid has left South Africa with 'unfinished business'. Jansen continues:

> Who would have thought that barely a decade after the miracle of our transition [from the apartheid regime] we would be talking about 'minorities' in a democracy founded on the principles of non-racialism? Who could have imagined that in Mandela's country human appointments to jobs would be instructed by the calculating phrase, 'the demographics of the country'? And who could have predicted the bare-knuckled violence that kills white farmers on their

lands and foreign nationals on our streets, or that the poorest of black citizens would be felled by the racial anger of an 18-year-old white boy barely out of high school?

Seeing these everyday problems and their trajectory towards violence as a consequence of institutional culture locates the incident within relations of power. The Reitz incident occurred between white and black identities in localised relationships in a particular student residence. These activities entailed and endorsed cultural practices that confirmed I–we and I–other relationships along historical fracture lines of racialised class divisions. These events all occurred locally, in actual places where actual people interacted, although the symbolic effects rippled beyond the four walls of the student residence and the lives of the individuals concerned.

The problem to be addressed is therefore a collective task about how 'we' make the 'social'. When shameful behaviour is part of a seemingly natural order, individual retribution makes limited sense. As Jansen states, the four white students are 'outcomes' of this racialised order of things, which is handed down from the past and enacted through the stewardship of successive generations of adults. In this respect, the Reitz students are 'children of this country, they are youth of the province, and they are students of our university. They are… my students'.

The challenge is to address the institutional design that naturalises such unacceptable behaviour. This means seeing the problem in terms of a collectively owned history of segregation, the naturalisation of racism, and the dualistic mindsets that see moral behaviour differently for white and black citizens.

The solution is to create institutional arrangements that produce: 'compassionate humans, critical citizens and ethical leaders in their disciplines and professions', teaching 'not only how to give of their skills, but how to give of themselves in service to communities' (Jansen 2009). Without this, 'I will still wake up on Monday morning dealing with the same social, cultural and ideological complexities that stand in the way of transformation'.

Yet this shift in mindsets comes up against the established structuring and culturing that has sustained a racialised institutional culture. This agenda confronts established relations of power: not just the students and workers involved, but also wider social forces ordered through the province, the country and the world. Jansen's commitment, 'in humility and determination', is to set in train processes that address the cultural practice that gave rise to the Reitz incident because: 'As a student of institutional cultures, I know that such embedded practices do not change easily. But as a student of educational change, I also know that through decisive action, these negative cultural practices can be steadily eroded'.

Jansen argues that there is a need to tackle 'unfinished business'. These are wicked problems, which are rooted in a minority white settler society and the history of apartheid. However, these problems are compounded by the lifelong learning institutionalisation of schooling for three reasons.

First, this globalised institutional design confirms orientations that privilege individuals. This way of seeing the world fails to acknowledge the social and, hence, the socially and culturally embedded actors whose agency is contingent on institutional rules, resource allocations and socially ordered patterns of recognition and responsibility. It implies that individuals are responsible for actions, rather than recognising the way responsibility is realised through relational practices, ethics and agreements about the forms of mutual coercion that we can agree on.

Second, lifelong learning policy configures the university (and by implication the wider social organisation and ordering of schooling) as a service provider. Educational work is to be restricted to building skills for work, serving the economic human capital and 'inclusion' agenda, which measures success in terms of economic participation, and managing residual and resistant populations. As Jansen (2009) asserts: 'A university is not a welfare organisation. It is not a FET (Further Education and Training) College. It is not a giant compensatory programme for students who crawled over the matric finishing line demanding to study for a degree'.

Finally, this institutional design neglects the contribution that the university (and other organisations of schooling) makes to 'social leadership' necessary to solve wicked problems. Jansen makes this point by recalling the failure of the Bloemfontein Conference – 'a last-ditch effort at reconciliation between what was called "two races". The reconciliation talks failed, [leading to] the Second Boer War'. He attributes this outcome to a profound 'failure of leadership', which 'at *such a crucial time as that* left scars on the South African political psyche to this day' (emphasis in original).

To avoid a similar failure of policy and institutional design today, he sets out an agenda for building skills for social leadership. This looks beyond the question of employability and technical skilling for work. Instead, he focuses on the terms and conditions of learning that will help to remake the social in ways that support social leadership, political participation and intercultural learning at every level of the community. Focusing on the local situation at UFS, he proposes practical reforms, which could be scaled up. Jansen:

1. Reconfirms and uses the institutional division of labour that distinguishes the work of courts from the work of universities. To this end, he indicates that the UFS will withdraw its charges and invite the four students to continue their studies. This was a deeply controversial step in a society that operates on an individualist model and therefore seeks individual retribution.

2. Recognises the institutionalised powers and therefore the rights and responsibilities of the university. To this end, he states that 'in recognition of our institutional complicity in the Reitz saga, and the need for social justice, the University of the Free State will not only pursue forgiveness but will also pay reparations to the workers concerned for damages to their dignity and their self-esteem'.

3. Uses the university as a locus of higher learning that builds capacities for social leadership among all social groups. In other words, Jansen mobilises the powers of educational learning to disrupt socialisation in racially divided society and culture. He does this by endorsing this purpose and prioritising those capacities for educational work that are embedded in UFS to drive and direct student learning in preferred directions. This moral and political agenda seeks to build capacities among all participants at UFS that will help to avoid a repeat failure along the lines of the Bloemfontein Conference. He makes a number of comments about this (Jansen 2009):

    - A university is an institution of higher learning serving the best available talent in the nation and beyond. With this purpose in mind, we will recruit only the best white and the best black students and academics to the University of the Free State.

    - The university will become a place that exemplifies the scholarship and the practice of reconciliation, forgiveness and social justice.

    - The university will move very quickly to become a national and indeed international centre for academic excellence.

    - Scholars and students from around the world will descend on the institution to study and understand the theory and practice of building community across the divides of race but also religion, gender, disability, national origins and, thanks to Athletics South Africa, sexual identity. In this respect the University will soon launch what we hope to call *The Reitz Institute for Studies in Race, Reconciliation and Social Justice*.

In elaborating these university-level policy decisions, Jansen targets key initiatives that he believes will make a difference to these entrenched racial orderings of culture in the student residence, the university and, hence, the country. These include creating learning pathways from communities into UFS to support students who carry the cultural debts of a racist history. He targets gender inequity in staffing by committing to the appointment of 25 senior professors who are 'the smartest and most diverse pool of scholars to this institution'. He identifies the problem of 'troubled knowledge' for immediate attention, through the redesign of curriculum, which offers students the opportunity to engage with 'basic human questions such as who we are and where we come from', while also 'learning how to live and learn together in ways that prepare our youth for leadership in the workplace'. Finally, he addresses the 'sub-cultures of derision' that confirm 'small-mindedness among undergraduates who see the university as an uninterrupted extension of high school with authoritarian rituals learnt elsewhere'. Banning alcohol, initiation practices and patriarchal relations between older and younger students are means of addressing racism, sexism and militarism that have become naturalised in the institutional culture.

These initiatives redesign UFS not just as a context for learning but as a space of orientation that helps to remake the social. In this way, Jansen's speech reminds us that schooling is not just a part of wicked problems but also an institutional instrument that can be turned to their resolution.

Lessons for Australia

Glimpses of South Africa suggest that there are different ways of doing the social. It makes a difference if you are in a settler society with a white majority, like Australia, or a white minority, like South Africa. It means that inequalities, such as those around race, are an artefact arising out of particular spatialised histories. They are a practical outcome arising from the institutionalisation of power relations in the national history and its political culture.

The character and persistence of socioeconomic inequalities in Australia are not inevitable, but closing the gap requires a step change in making the social. Incremental changes in social relations occur over time through ongoing policy debates and implicit as well as overt practical politics, negotiations and conflicts. These processes tend to set up path-dependent social and cultural practices that pattern everyday life in Australia. Revising these terms, conditions, practices and priorities of everyday life requires interventions that reframe not just ways of thinking, but also ways of acting in the world.

The education system is a key instrument in the kind of step change necessary to remake the social in Australia and around the world. Travelling policies over the last 30 years have recognised the power of education systems in shaping everyday life and its path dependencies. There is now significant experience in ways of remaking path-dependent patterns of institutionalisation and driving education systems towards preferred outcomes. For much of this time, the privileged purposes and priorities have been framed economically, focusing on market reforms and workforce development, which tackle challenges in the global economy but, also, consciously or unconsciously, fuel elite formation and suggest that inequality is the natural order of things.

In this chapter I argue that the social can be remade in different ways, depending on the way the education system shapes and constrains the occupational agency of educational workers. The institutionalisation of education does not have to privilege economic outcomes, particularly human capital formation, as the measure of good education. There is also value in recognising the political outcomes of education and designing the political purposes that should be achieved through educational structures and agencies. Addressing these outcomes opens up ways of intervening in the prevailing political culture that locks in social inequalities and confirms the historically institutionalised invisibility of Indigenous Australians. The education system and the occupational agency of educational workers, in and beyond schools, can be mobilised in ways that build individual and collective capacities in using power responsibly to advance localised problem solving, decision making and innovation among all citizens and communities. Mobilising this kind of learning to be a citizen mediates power relations in everyday life. It builds citizens' capacities to not only work together, but also recognise and problem-solve national and global pressures that inflect and disturb local places.

However, appropriate system reform depends on political will. While the social dimensions of human capital formation development agenda are increasingly recognised by policy makers, there has been little acknowledgment of the links between those agenda and the everyday work of educational workers in and beyond schooling. Yet educational work, the occupational agency of educational workers, makes the social in local places, which aggregates at the national scale. The way this work is organised not only returns skills for work and dispositions for employability, but also builds the capacities of citizens and communities to recognise shared problems, work together and use power responsibly in moving towards solutions.

Currently, openness to dialogue about the way the education system makes the social seems unusual in Australia. By contrast, in South Africa there seems to be a more explicit acknowledgment that remaking the social means addressing historically institutionalised structures of political relations. No one is saying that this is easy work, but acknowledging the politics and inequalities does mean there is a shared recognition of problems to be solved. The way educational work is institutionalised within this more open political culture means that imaginative proposals for closing the gap, like Jansen's, can surface and be subject to public scrutiny. It also means that the distinct contribution that educational work can make to national capacity is recognised more accurately.

Education systems are not just means of building skills for work, they also build skills for citizenship, whether or not this is an acknowledged outcome. The way individual and collective capacities for action are developed makes the social and its path dependencies over time. This is because educational work mobilises power to realise cultural achievements (including the formation of education systems) that sit at the heart of political action. It is the mediating practices that enable individual and collective learning, which also constitutes particular political cultures and patterns the way citizens use power in complex problem solving throughout everyday life.

Educational work is the agency, the 'art of politics', that mobilises and enacts education systems. It is a particular governed agency that makes spaces of (re)orientation where processes of socialisation and education are mixed to yield learning that presses the social towards publicly agreed ends. The education system is the means of shaping the exercise of this occupational agency on behalf of the public in democratic societies. Its history of institutional biases is not given, but open to transformation. With appropriate system design, recognition and respect between policy and practice, and delegation of authority, educational work can remake the social in ways that not only tackle the imperatives of globalisation but also address persistent social divisions in ways that can help to close the gap in socioeconomic inequalities.

References

ABC 2004. 'Good morning Mr Sarra'. *Australian Story* program transcript, 4 October. Accessed 29 April 2010. Available from:
http://www.abc.net.au/austory/content/2004/s1212753.htm.

Abrams, P. 1982. *Historical Sociology*. Shepton Mallet, Somerset: Open Books.

Angus, L; Seddon, T. 2000. 'The social and educational renorming of education'. In *Beyond Nostalgia: Reshaping Australian Education*, edited by Angus, L; Seddon, T. Melbourne: Australian Council for Educational Research: 151–169.

APSC (Australian Public Service Commission). 2007. 'Tackling wicked problems: A public policy perspective'. Accessed 2 December 2009. Available from: http://www.apsc.gov.au/publications07/wickedproblems.htm.

Bonnell, V E; Hunt, L. 1999. *Beyond the Cultural Turn: New Directions in the Study of Society and Culture.* Berkeley: University of California Press.

Centre for Contemporary Cultural Studies. 1981. *Unpopular Education: Schooling and Social Democracy in England Since 1944.* London: Hutchinson.

Dusseldorp Skills Forum. 1998. 'Australia's youth: Risk and reality'. Sydney: Dusseldorp Skills Forum.

Dusseldorp Skills Forum. 1999. 'Australia's young adults: The deepening divide'. Sydney: Dusseldorp Skills Forum.

Hamilton, D. 1989. *Towards a Theory of Schooling.* Brighton: Falmer Press.

Haug, F. 2010. 'A politics of working life'. In *Learning and Work and the Politics of Working Life: Global Transformations and Collective Identities in Teaching, Nursing and Social Work.* edited by Seddon, T; Henriksson, L; Niemeyer, B. London: Routledge: 217–225.

Jansen, D J. 2009. 'Inaugural speech of the 13th Rector and Vice-Chancellor of the University of the Free State (UFS)'. Accessed 10 December 2009. Available from: http://www.uovs.ac.za/news/newsarticle.php?NewsID=1533.

Jones, K. 2001. 'Travelling policy/local spaces'. *Education and Social Justice,* 3 (3): 2–9.

Kirby, P.C. 2000. 'Ministerial review of post compulsory education and training pathways in Victoria'. Melbourne: Department of Education, Employment and Training.

Kuhn, M. 2007. *New Society Models for a New Millenium: The Learning Society in Europe and Beyond.* New York: Peter Lang.

Lawn, M; Ozga, J. 1981. 'The educational worker?' *Schools, Teachers and Teaching.* London: Falmer Press.

McGrath, S. 2009. 'Reforming skills development, transforming the nation: South African vocational education and training reforms, 1994–2005'. In *International Handbook of Education for the Changing World of Work,* vol. 2, edited by Maclean, R; Wilson, D. Bonn: UNESCO-UNEVOC and Springer: 453–468.

Mahoney, J. 2000. 'Path dependence in historical sociology'. *Theory and Society* 29 (4): 507–548.

Mandela, N. 1995. *Long Walk to Freedom.* Boston: Little, Brown and Company.

Marginson, S. 1997. *Markets in Education.* Cambridge: Cambridge University Press.

Pierson, P. 1993. 'When effect becomes cause: Policy feedback and political change'. *World Politics* 45: 595–628.

Republic of South Africa. 1996. 'Constitution of the Republic of South Africa, No. 108 of 1996'. Accessed 18 April 2010. Available from: http://www.info.gov.za/documents/constitution/1996/a108-96.pdf.

Robertson, S. 2002. 'The politics of re-territorialisation'. *Curriculo sem Fronteiras* 2 (2): 17–34.

Sachs, J. 2003. *The Activist Teaching Profession.* Buckingham: Open University Press.

Seddon, T. 1993. *Context and Beyond: Reframing the Theory and Practice of Education.* London: Falmer.

Seddon, T. 2001. 'National curriculum in Australia'. *Pedagogy, Culture and Society* 9 (3): 307–331.

Seddon, T. Forthcoming. 'Social innovation and education: Liquid learning, making spaces and the politics of orientation. London: Routledge.

Seddon, T; Billett, S; Clemans, A; Ovens, C; Ferguson, K; Fennessy, K. 2008. *Sustaining Effective Social Partnerships.* Adelaide: NCVER.

Seddon, T; Fischer, J; Clemans, A; Billett, S. 2002. 'Evaluation of local learning and employment networks'. Melbourne: Department of Education and Training.

Smith, D E. 1999. *Writing the Social: Critique, Theory and Investigations*. Toronto: University of Toronto Press.

Smyth, P; Reddel, T; Jones, A. 2005. *Community and Local Governance in Australia*. Sydney: University of NSW Press.

Wallace, T. 2009. 'Education system profile: South Africa'. In *The International Handbook of Education for the Changing World of Work*, vol. 4, edited by Mclean, R; Wilson, D. Bonn: UNESCO-UNEVOC and Springer: 1971–1988.

Williams, R. 1976. *The Long Revolution*. Harmondsworth: Penguin.

Section 3:
The challenges facing Indigenous education

Indigenous Australians as 'No Gaps' Subjects

Education and Development in Remote Australia

Jon Altman & Bill Fogarty
The Australian National University

Introduction

In February 2008 the Australian Prime Minister made an apology to the 'Stolen Generations' on behalf of the nation. Since then, we have witnessed the rapid implementation of a policy framework focused on 'Closing the gap' and an increasingly complex, managerial and technical approach to addressing undeniable Indigenous disadvantage. This approach has been endorsed by the Council of Australian Governments (COAG). As policy has become more monolithic and monopolistic, the state has become less sympathetic to the diversity and difference that is a feature of Indigenous societies, especially in remote Australia.

At one level the goal of current policy is little different from the broad assimilationist aims of the past 50 years, except that the more polite term 'normalisation' is increasingly used. At another level, the nature of the state has changed from Keynesian welfarism to an embrace of neoliberalism that has served Australia well at the macroeconomic level in recent years.

In this chapter we want to problematise the notion that closing the gap in education will improve socioeconomic outcomes. In short, we question whether human capital theory that is so uncritically accepted as an elixir to socioeconomic disadvantage is applicable in all cross- or inter-cultural contexts, or in all territorial spaces.

We base our challenge on some fundamental paradoxes in Australia. While available statistics since 1971 show socioeconomic gaps in all jurisdictions, the focus of the current National Indigenous Reform Agreement (NIRA) is on remote Australia – where only 25 per cent of the Indigenous population lives. This is also the region where Indigenous people predominantly live in small discrete communities, on Aboriginal-owned land. Many of these people are now looking to make a livelihood from their land, using a diversity of approaches. It is unlikely that there will be sufficient standard mainstream employment opportunities in remote Australia to close the gap or that all people will migrate from their land. Hence, making a livelihood will also require participation in the customary, or non-market sector, of the economy.

In our view, education needs to be tailored to serve the livelihood aspirations of Indigenous people participating in a hybrid and intercultural economy. Such an alternative development future is illustrated in this chapter with reference to natural and cultural resource management. Rather than providing mainstream education for futures in the market (sometimes called the 'real') economy, consideration also needs to be given to educational innovation to meet diverse vocational needs in the hybrid economy. In conclusion, we ponder how the current hegemonic focus on closing the gap, in statistical terms only, might be modified to contemplate such a possibility.

Closing the gap as a policy framework

In February 2008 the new Rudd government (Rudd 2008), on the very first day of parliamentary sitting, made a belated national apology to Australia's Indigenous peoples on behalf of the nation. The apology was in two parts. The first very moving and compassionate part focused on the past, reflecting on the mistreatment of those who were Stolen Generations – 'this blemished chapter in our nation's history' – and reminded Australia that such practice continued until the early 1970s.

The second part switched from the symbolic to the practical, from the particularity of the Stolen Generations to the generality of Indigenous Australians and their contemporary socioeconomic marginality, from the past to the present and future. Here the focus was on building a bridge between Indigenous and non-Indigenous Australians – a bridge based on a partnership to 'close the gap between Indigenous and non-Indigenous Australians in life expectancy, educational achievement and employment opportunities'. In aiming to close the gap, the Prime Minister set concrete targets for the future: to *halve* the *widening* gap in literacy, numeracy and employment outcomes, opportunities for Indigenous children and infant mortality rates *within* a decade; and to close the appalling 17-year gap in overall life expectancy *within a generation* [emphasis ours]. It is noteworthy that the extraordinary diversity of Indigenous circumstances barely rated a mention in the apology speech. The Australian Government committed to report annually on progress in meeting these gaps. The apology was widely acclaimed nationally and internationally.

It is the second part of the speech on which we focus. 'Closing the Gap' was quickly adopted by COAG – the key intergovernmental forum in Australia's federal system – as its over-arching reform agenda for the project of improvement for Indigenous Australians. During 2008 and 2009 the Prime Minister's ambitious targets to close the gap between Indigenous and non-Indigenous Australians across urban, rural and remote areas were adopted by all governments, although in four of the six targets (mortality rates for children under five; reading, writing and numeracy levels; Year 12 attainment rates; and employment outcomes) 'closing' was used loosely, if somewhat more realistically, to mean halving. At face value such ambitious goals are precisely what the wealthy Australian state – here referring to the Commonwealth and state and territory constellation of political institutions and bureaucratic fields – should be doing to address historically entrenched Indigenous marginality.

Since February 2008 considerable effort has been made by COAG to complete a very complex National Indigenous Reform Agreement (NIRA) that was signed off by all governments in July 2009. At the heart of NIRA is an expanding series of National Partnership Agreements that have seen unprecedented financial commitments of billions of dollars and a shared inter-governmental view on how Indigenous disadvantage should be addressed (COAG 2009). Much of the focus of NIRA is to ensure transparency and accountability in what is being spent on Indigenous citizens. But even as NIRA was being endorsed in July 2009 (COAG 2009), the Productivity Commission, the Australian Government's independent research and advisory body on a range of issues affecting the welfare of Australians, was sounding some warnings. In its biennial *Overcoming Indigenous Disadvantage: Key Indicators 2009* report, the commission highlighted the possibility that gaps may still be growing and that in a number of areas statistical instruments are not available to measure movements in the gaps so meticulously plotted in NIRA (Productivity Commission 2009). These findings replicate independent academic research by Altman et al. (2008), which tracks changes in Indigenous socioeconomic outcomes, in absolute and relative terms, between 1971 and 2006 censuses. This research shows that at the national level things are improving slowly in absolute terms, but that in relative terms gaps are persisting across most indicators; it also makes some very pessimistic forecasts on the likelihood of gap closure based on historical trends.

A critique of Closing the Gap

All Australian governments in the modern policy era have looked to close the gap, even though comprehensive statistics from the national census to measure progress have been available only since 1971. The Closing the Gap framework can be heavily critiqued from an anthropology of development perspective, or a broader social sciences perspective. Indeed this has already been done in another context.[1] Here, we focus our critique on just three aspects of the new framework.

First, its targets have not been based on any consultations with the subjects of the project of improvement. This was noted by the Productivity Commission (2009) as NIRA was launched: what works includes cooperative approaches between the state and community that are bottom up and participatory rather than top down in design.

Second, deeply entrenched development problems have been rendered statistical to such an extent that the Closing the Gap goals have almost become abstractions divorced from the lived reality of Indigenous subjects. This is what Ferguson (1994) has termed rendering development problems technical so as to seek technical, managerialist solutions. It is also a means to depoliticise the problem, the state project of improvement instrumentally operating as an 'anti-politics machine' that fails to address politico-economic relationships that are the structural and historical sources of inequality (Li 2007). This narrows the frame of the public discourse, closing the space for pluralism and diversity. Importantly, the voice from the local, or of the subject, is effectively marginalised and silenced.

Third, the nature of the principles articulated to achieve Closing the Gap outcomes makes no concession either to diversity of Indigenous circumstances or to Indigenous subjects adhering to beliefs, values, social relations and practices that can remain distinct from mainstream norms. In Australia there is a recognition in social sciences scholarship that probably everywhere Indigenous social norms retain a degree of contestation between customary and western norms. These norms are manifest in diverse combinations that are termed intercultural or bicultural.

At one level this new state goal to normalise Indigenous subjects by closing the gaps and assuming shared social norms is not new at all. In 1961, it was stated:

> The policy of assimilation means in the view of all Australian governments that all aborigines and part aborigines are expected eventually to attain the same living as other Australians... enjoying the same rights and privileges, accepting the same responsibilities, observing the same customs and influenced by the same beliefs, hopes and loyalties as other Australians. (Altman and Nieuwenhuysen 1979, 24)

In 2009, the NIRA principles suggested that investments should aim to improve participation in education or training and in the market economy and to reduce welfare dependence, but also to alter behaviour by promoting personal responsibility and behaviours consistent with positive social norms (COAG 2009, E-79). Exactly whose social norms are deemed positive is unaddressed. Probably for the first time ever the Australian state has explicitly articulated a goal to bring Indigenous human action into the domain of the market. The similarities between 1961 and 2009 indicate adherence to a highly problematic form of evolutionary thinking linked to the modernisation paradigm.

At another level, the neoliberal state is different from the Keynesian welfare state, although both were transnational political projects in advanced societies. In particular, neoliberalism seeks economic deregulation and the wholesale adoption of market or market-like mechanisms; redefinition of subjects, not as citizens with rights, but as clients to be managed; and a cultural trope of individual responsibility and an expansion of intrusive state institutions (Wacquant 2009).[2] Indeed, theorists like Wacquant would identify this as a classic example of the capitalist revolution from above in the era of triumphant neoliberalism. Scott (2009) might see this, unsurprisingly, as part of the state project to homogenise communities and view the ideal civilised subject as the 'no gaps' subject. There is no doubt that the neoliberal state's framing can be viewed as a means to creatively destroy distinct Indigenous institutions in the name of individualism, private property and the market, as suggested in global contexts by Harvey (2005). Bourdieu (1998) asks rhetorically whether neoliberalism is just a program for destroying collective structures that impede pure market logic.

Remote Indigenous Australia: People, land and economy

What is clear from available statistics is that while inequalities between Indigenous and other Australians are evident everywhere, they are greatest in remote or sparsely settled regions (termed in the Accessibility/Remoteness

Index of Australia as remote and very remote). Geographically, these regions cover 86 per cent of the Australian continent. In population terms, 26 per cent of Australia's estimated Indigenous population of 517,000 live remotely, compared with only two per cent of the non-Indigenous population (of just under 22 million). A combination of factors, including demographic proportion and a narrative of 'recent' failure, has seen much of the focus in NIRA on these communities.

We shift our focus now from abstract statistical notions of gap closing to empirical remote Australia today. We highlight this region for several reasons, including the paradox that, while a disproportionate policy focus is on remote Australia, prospects for closing the gap here are poorest, owing to linked structural, historical and cultural reasons. We are not saying that such policy focus is not warranted, only that in terms of statistical targets, outcomes in remote Australia are likely to be most difficult to achieve, according to the normative social indicators that are used to define these targets.

In Figure 9.1, the distribution of discrete Indigenous communities in remote Australia is provided. There are an estimated 100,000 Indigenous people living in 1200 discrete communities in this region, nearly 1000 called 'homelands' or 'outstations', with a population of less than 100. This in itself presents a major challenge for the state in universal provision of services. Hence the new national principle to focus infrastructure support and service provision on larger and more economically sustainable communities, despite no evidence that socioeconomic status improves for those moving up the settlement hierarchy (Biddle 2009). One must ask for whose benefit is such centralisation being advocated if not yet implemented?

Equally paradoxically, over 99 per cent of Indigenous-owned land is in remote Australia, with over 20 per cent forming a part of the Indigenous estate estimated at some 1.5 million square kilometres. The restitution of ancestral lands to traditional owners has occurred slowly over the past 30 years via an array of land rights and native title laws, some passed for social justice reasons, others as a result of judicial decisions. In most cases Indigenous land owners have needed to demonstrate legal continuity of customs and traditions and of connections to qualify under Australian law as traditional owners of their ancestral lands. The relatively late encroachment of colonisation on remote Australia meant that much land here was either belatedly reserved by the colonial state for Aboriginal people, or unalienated and available for land claim. Land rights have empowered remote communities to pursue different livelihoods, as well as a degree of

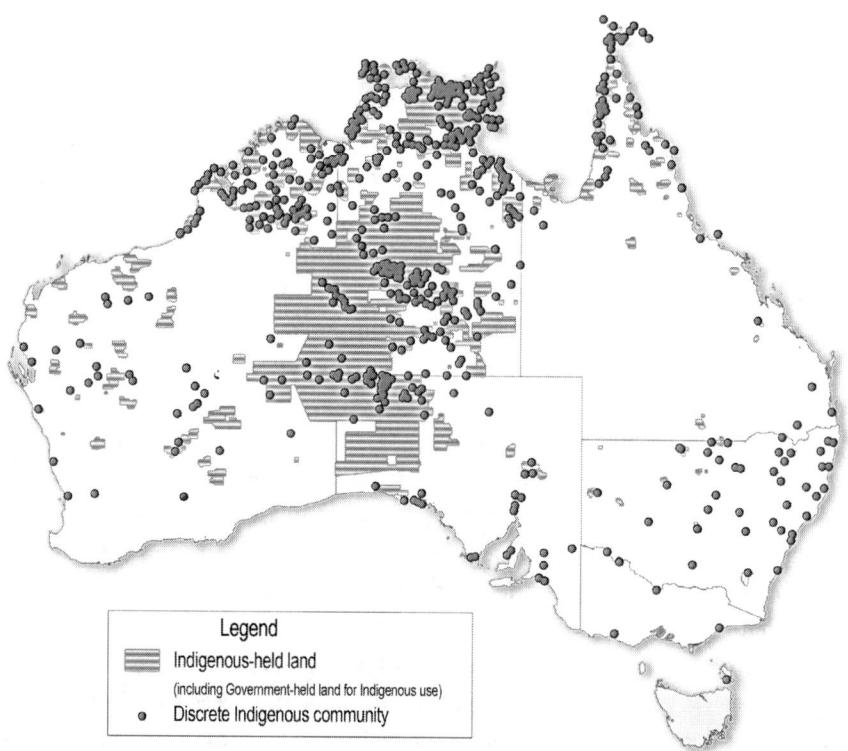

Figure 9.1: Discrete Indigenous communities and Indigenous-owned land
Source: Adapted from Altman et al. 2007.

leverage, to negotiate with commercial interests. In the remotest places Indigenous people are almost beyond the reach of the state and may have learnt 'the art of not being governed' (Scott 2009). On Aboriginal land, groups have been able to maintain beliefs, values, kin-based social relations, languages and practices that are non-mainstream and distinctly Indigenous, although, as noted earlier, these ways of being are modern and intercultural rather than pre-colonial.[3]

Nadasdy (2003), in his study of bureaucrats and hunters, notes, with reference to Weber's work on the nature of bureaucracy, that the development of a money economy is a presupposition of the bureaucracy, as is the current Australian state supposition that development (and closing the gap) will require a full embrace of the market economy. But the relatively late colonisation of remote Australia resulted in a less destructive transformation of the pre-colonial hunter-gatherer economy and today important elements of the customary (or non-market) economy remain intact. This provides a means to maintain land-based ways of life in many situations and has resulted in the emergence of a complex form of hybrid economy that includes state, market and customary sectors (Altman 2009b). This economic reality in remote areas is actualised through an array of sectoral overlaps that influence everyday livelihood strategies. An example that we will return to below is when rangers are employed by the state to provide environmental services using Indigenous knowledge, while at the same time being at liberty to harvest wildlife for domestic use. The hybrid economy model illustrated in Figure 9.2 properly illustrates the complex nature of Indigenous economies in remote Australia beyond the usual private and public duality.

The hybrid economy is different everywhere, in form and in the nature of sectoral overlaps (areas 4, 5, 6 and 7 in Figure 9.2), where most productive activity is undertaken. This is partly explained by structural, cultural and environmental factors. In some places market opportunities in mining or tourism employment might exist. In all situations the precise nature of interculturality, the trade-offs individuals and groups make between engagements in kin-based domestic moral economies or market-based opportunity vary, as does the availability of game or access to fisheries. The existence and resilience of a customary sector is anathema to neoliberalism and its goal of bringing all human action within the realm of the market (Harvey 2005). For many Indigenous groups, however, it provides a means to reduce dependency and associated risk of excessive state intrusion, and to preserve customary ways and to live by them.

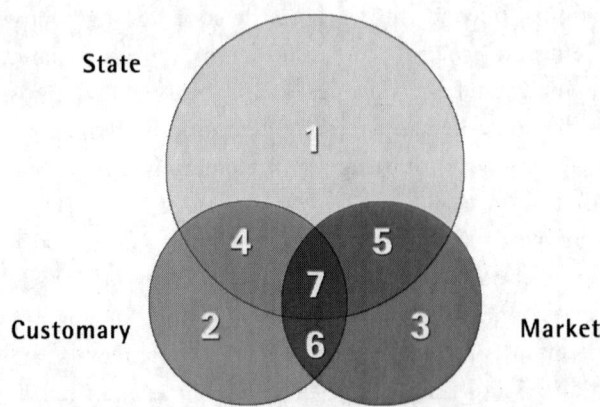

Figure 9.2: The hybrid economy model

Source: Altman 2009b.

Development futures in the hybrid economy

Land and native title rights have facilitated the maintenance of hybrid economies and the emergence of what Comaroff and Comaroff (2009) have termed 'Ethnicity, Inc', the dialectical relationship between the often legal corporatisation of identity and the commodification of culture, sometimes requiring protection using 'lawfare'. Like Comaroff and Comaroff, we do not seek to present this emergence as unproblematic – indeed in Australia the 'repressive authenticity' (Wolfe 1999) and contested identity politics required to claim back land invariably result in conflict in the Indigenous domain and the emergence of winners and losers, although the extent of such competition for land is influenced greatly by region and variable colonial histories. Similarly, the commodification of culture – in tourism, the arts or, most recently, in the provision of environmental services utilising Indigenous knowledge – can be highly problematic.

The growth and diversification of the Indigenous visual arts sector in remote Australia has been a well-documented exemplar of intercultural production in the hybrid economy. Artistic production draws its inspiration from connections to land, the sentient landscape and the sacred places in that landscape that are owned by groups of land owners and that are sometimes enacted in ceremonial contexts. Aboriginal art embodies cultural values that have a high degree of commensurability with western aesthetics and economic values. The value of this sector has probably grown tenfold in the past 20 years as new place- and identity-based movements continue to spring up. The production and marketing of art sits squarely in the intersection of customary, state and market sectors: inspiration and skills acquisition is customary, while cross-cultural mediation with the market requires state patronage.

Perhaps of even greater potential is the emergence over the past decade or so of an Indigenous community-based, grassroots, 'caring for country' movement that is seeing the use of Indigenous and local knowledge in the paid provision of a range of environmental services. It has been estimated that in 2006 just on 400 Aboriginal people were employed as rangers in the northernmost part of the Northern Territory (Northern Land Council 2006, 11) compared with 176 Aboriginal people employed in the mining industry throughout the Northern Territory (in the 2006 Census).

The Indigenous estate that covers 20 per cent of the continent includes some of the most biodiverse lands in Australia. Official natural resource atlas maps indicate that many of the most intact and nationally important wetlands, riparian zones, forests, rivers and waterways are located on the

Indigenous estate. Mapping also shows that these lands are at risk of species contraction and face major threats from feral animals, exotic weeds, changed fire regimes, pollution and over-grazing (Altman et al. 2007). On top of these threats, the latest available climate science suggests that substantial biodiversity impacts on this crucial part of the continental landmass are inevitable.

In the face of this, there has been a slowly growing support from state environmental agencies for Indigenous community-based efforts to ameliorate threats and minimise adverse biodiversity outcomes. Since 1997, 33 Indigenous Protected Areas (IPAs) have been declared over 230,000 square kilometres of Aboriginal-owned land that features natural and cultural heritage values and that will be managed using forms of management that satisfy International Union for the Conservation of Nature (IUCN) guidelines. IPAs make up 23 per cent of Australia's National Reserve System and there are plans to increase national coverage by 40 per cent in the next five years. In 2007 a Working on Country program was established to pay Indigenous rangers wages that had previously been garnered from a range of sources, including the Community Development Employment Program and the Natural Heritage Trust. Figure 9.3 shows the location of the 33 declared IPAs; there is a high correlation between IPAs and people living on their land at small outstation communities.

In late 2007 a research project titled 'People on country, healthy landscapes and Indigenous economic futures' was established (CAEPR 2009) to work with seven community-based Caring for Country projects in the Northern Territory (and one in Western Australia), four of which are now declared IPAs. The projects cover about 70,000 square kilometres and employ just over 100 rangers.

The two most recent IPA declarations in September 2009 (numbers 32 and 33) are Warddeken and Djelk in western Arnhem Land and are two of our research partners; they are people with whom we have collaborated for many years. We provide two vignettes about these new IPAs as exemplars of what activities IPA rangers actually undertake.

Case 1 – Warddeken Land Management Ltd: The Warddeken IPA is declared over 14,000 square kilometres of Arnhem Land escarpment as an IUCN, Category VI protected area, with sustainable use of natural resources. Twelve employed Manworrk Rangers work with traditional owners from over 30 clans to undertake feral species management, record Indigenous knowledge, manage critical aquatic habitats, record native biodiversity health, undertake

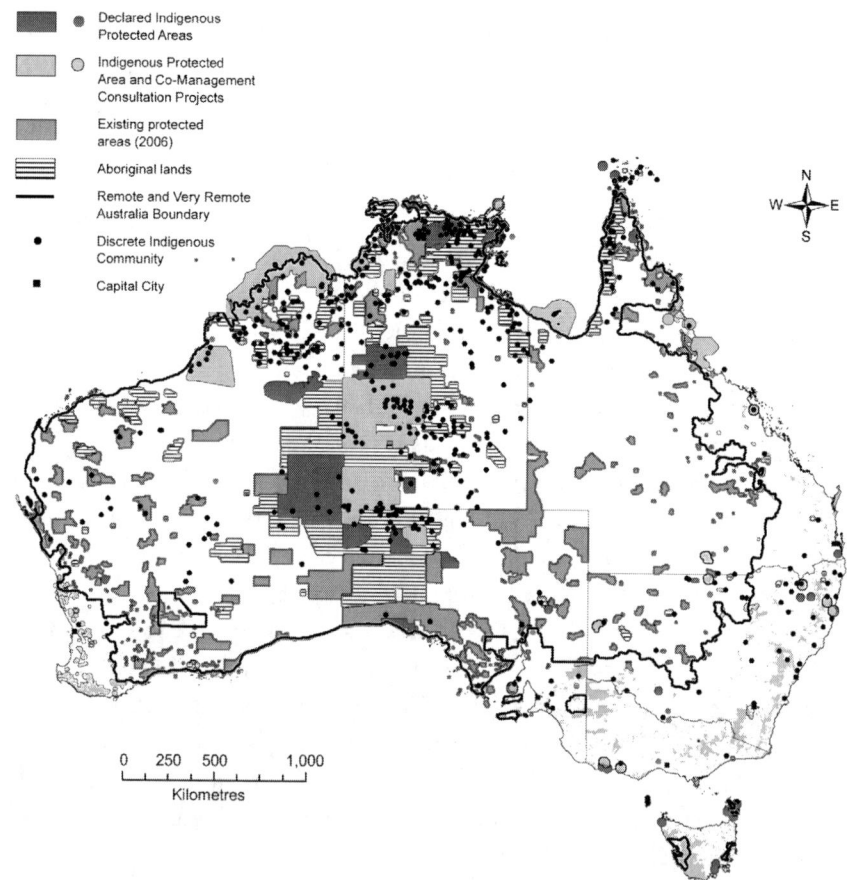

Figure 9.3: Indigenous protected areas and discrete Indigenous communities

Source: Based on http://www.environment.gov.au/indigenous/ipa/map.html.

species autopsy for Australian Quarantine, and participate as core partners in the West Arnhem Land Fire Abatement (WALFA) project. Funds to manage of the Warddeken IPA are sourced primarily from government (75 per cent) but also from private and philanthropic sources (25 per cent). The WALFA project is Australia's only carbon abatement project that has a contract with a multinational corporation to abate a verified 100,000 tonnes of carbon-equivalent greenhouse gases per annum. The Manworrk Rangers have a heavy focus on partnerships with neighbouring ranger groups (like Djelk) as well as scientific, environmental, academic and cultural interest groups. The Warddeken IPA aims to create a reserve of international significance (Warddeken Land Management Ltd 2009).

Case 2 – Bawinanga Aboriginal Corporation Djelk Rangers: The Djelk IPA is declared over 6700 square kilometres of Arnhem Land as an IUCN Category VI protected area, with sustainable use of natural resources. The Djelk Rangers have operated as a community-based Caring for Country project since 1991; currently 30 are employed in land and sea management. In collaboration with traditional owners from 102 clans, rangers undertake prescribed burning to reduce fuel load as part of the WALFA project and use cybertracking technology to accurately monitor burning work. They also undertake feral animal control and exotic weed management and provide cultural and economic site protection. The Sea Rangers undertake marine management and marine debris control over 2000 square kilometres of sea country that will be declared as a protected area in 2010. Women rangers mainly engage in commercial utilisation of wildlife and in bush food enterprises. In 2008–09, the Djelk Rangers undertook 20,800 kilometres of coastal patrols, 8800 kilometres of aerial prescribed burn and 14,000 kilometres of ground burning covering 11,500 square kilometres. Income is earned from WALFA as well as commercial sale of wildlife (mainly estuarine crocodiles and turtles) and the provision of surveillance services under contract to Australian Customs and Australian Quarantine. The Djelk Rangers collaborate in a junior rangers program with the local Maningrida Community Education Centre to provide students with access to country and knowledge transfer from rangers' work (Bawinanga Aboriginal Corporation 2009; Schwab 2006).

Education for diverse futures

Finally, we get to education. We have used working on country as an example of a particular form of intercultural enterprise, largely underwritten by the state, where participants recognise the need to combine two toolkits – Indigenous local knowledge and western science and technology. It is noteworthy that, in the two cases we refer to, rangers are using sophisticated cybertracking, global positioning and satellite surveillance technology and state-of-the-art approaches to manage wild fires, feral animals, exotic weeds and marine pollution – while also drawing on deep Indigenous knowledge on seasonality, the environment and species behaviour. Traditional owner governance of common property is also fundamental to these environmental services enterprises. In remote education there is an emerging dialectical relationship between rangers, providing opportunity for Indigenous and scientific knowledge transfer to school students, which simultaneously provides a conduit to improved school attendance, pathways to skills development, literacy and numeracy acquisition and employment on country.

However, education in remote areas has become a key agent of the neoliberal state's renewed project of modernisation and market-driven notions of success (Wheelahan 2010). Mirroring much of the discourse surrounding employment in the 'real economy' and 'development' as a highly individualised pursuit, the frame through which education is currently being viewed has become increasingly narrow; the aim has become to close the gap. There is no doubting that education for Indigenous students has long been an incredibly complex and challenging policy arena. Difficulties in delivery, logistics, staff retention and quality, purpose and connections to employment have long vexed the sector. Indeed, we do not offer any definitive solutions to such complexity here. Rather, we challenge the current hegemony in thinking about this issue.

While formal educational outcomes in remote Indigenous education in Australia are consistently poor, the discourse in public debate has increasingly ignored the critiques of standardised benchmarking and the complexities of remote educational delivery. For example, 2008 and 2009 National Assessment in Literacy and Numeracy (NAPLAN) results[4] have been instrumental in showing that Indigenous students in remote areas are performing markedly worse against these benchmarks than their non-Indigenous peers in the rest of Australia.[5] Yet, without wishing to 'problem deflate', there is some question as to what such benchmarks are actually testing. Since Thorndike invented formal achievement tests in the early twentieth century, they have been heavily critiqued, particularly in their application to minority populations. As McKenna (1977, 8) noted over 30 years ago, 'such tests use vocabularies and illustrations unfamiliar to those who are not of white middle class cultures or for whom English is a second language: that is, the tests are culturally and linguistically biased'.

Similarly, for over four decades statistics show the poor attendance at school by Indigenous students in Australia, particularly in remote areas. Recent research in the Northern Territory has shown that in some areas, on any given day, as few as a quarter of the potential school-aged cohort are actually going to school (Taylor and Stanley 2005). However, it is also clear that low levels of attainment and attendance are linked to poverty, poor health, inadequate housing, inequitable access to government services (including schools) and low socioeconomic status (MCEETYA 1999, 21). The links between such barriers and attendance are well documented in the international education literature, regardless of ethnicity or location.

While none of this is new, it is surprising that the dominant narrative of policy debate has instead cast the disengagement of Indigenous students as a function of the economic 'failure' or unsustainability of remote Indigenous communities, welfare dependence and/or irresponsible parenting (Pearson 2009; Hughes 2007). Such discursive positions are replete with 'the politics of crisis' and demand prescriptive pedagogic integration, punitive measures against parents and the physical relocation of the educative process away from remote areas. This is especially the case in relation to small outstation schools. COAG (2009, 79) notes that while there is recognition of Indigenous peoples' cultural connections to homelands, policy will now avoid 'expectations of major investment in service provision where there are few economic or educational opportunities'. No research has been undertaken to assess the comparative performance of such schools.

While literacy and numeracy outcomes have increasingly come to represent the whole of education, instead of just one part, the function and form of education in remote areas has stagnated. The national policy remedy seems to be a concerted effort to supply more of the same prescriptive pedagogic solutions. Meanwhile, the need for educational programs geared to the intercultural and multilingual realities of daily life in remote contexts is being ignored by educationalists, policy makers and bureaucrats. There appears to be no capacity to reflexively consider the 'crossed purposes' (Folds 2001) in educational provision, or any capacity to rigorously assess the value or actual performance of past and current experimentation with 'two-way' (Harris 1990) and bilingual education, which is in the process of being dismantled in the Northern Territory (Simpson et al. 2009).

The challenge we wish to highlight is embodied in the following questions: How can a future in remote regions that entails life, employment and activity in a hybrid economic reality be augmented and supported by an appropriate 'hybrid' pedagogic structure? Is education in remote Indigenous Australia providing the skills and knowledge needed by students to maximise their life chances in the extremely restricted labour markets in which most will be engaging and competing in the immediate future?

There is an obvious related question: To what extent is the neoliberal state able to countenance a level of plurality in curriculum design and delivery specifically for remote Indigenous students? Given the imminent advent of a national curriculum in Australia, which has already been released in draft form, the answer may be: Very little. Despite this, there is increasing evidence that strong pedagogic design based in the local can provide for skill sets that are transferable to the global employment market, allowing Indigenous students mobility beyond their home community labour market. Clearly, such an approach would require commitments to research and educational provision far beyond current policy settings or imaginings.

In analysing some of these issues, researchers at the Centre for Aboriginal Economic Policy Research (CAEPR) have been examining the links between education, training and Indigenous futures, including pathways, links and synergies between Indigenous land and sea management and education in remote communities (Fordham and Schwab 2007). They have found that schools and rangers, for example, are engaging in innovative programs in a few remote sites like the Djelk example above, without policy or institutional support, and without any recognition of their role in re-engaging Indigenous students and the community in education processes. As a recent and growing employment pathway, Indigenous land and sea management is not supported by appropriate educational development. This is despite the fact that there are many more employed in ranger work than in mining in jurisdictions like the Northern Territory. We are concerned about the myopic return to abstract human capital theory, as in the NIRA, that links education and training with employment in the mainstream labour market, without considering backgrounds, aspirations, location, opportunities or institutional settings.

We do not question that a focus on literacy should remain a high educational priority, but sufficient resources are also required to provide local Indigenous knowledge and science-related curricula that our research indicates will be beneficial to NAPLAN outcomes. At the same time, there is an urgent need for solid pedagogical foundations that will allow the development of the skills and understandings essential for future employment in land, sea and resource management. Such a learning program would involve customary skills and knowledge, life skills and ranger skills, delivered both within the classroom and on country, utilising the specialist knowledge of teachers, rangers, scientific experts and the community, including senior traditional owners of land who are Indigenous and vernacular knowledge specialists (Evans 2009).

Challenging the dominant policy paradigm

The NIRA, with its apparent shared goals and authoritarian moralism signed off by all Australian governments, might suggest that the neoliberal state is monolithic and monopolistic. However, as Wacquant (2009, 289) reminds us, in his reading of Pierre Bourdieu, the state cannot be construed as monolithic but rather as a splintered space of forces vying over the definition and distribution of public goods in what he terms 'the bureaucratic field'.

Today the bureaucratic field is locked in struggle between what Bourdieu identifies as the Right Hand and Left Hand of the state. At present the Right Hand appears to be in the ascendancy, shaping both discourse and policy, to transform Aboriginal societies from being welfare dependent, communal and gap ridden, to being employed, individualistic and gap free. And yet the Left Hand has championed the development and growth of new programs; clearly there is a degree of values commensurability between the environment department and the desire of Indigenous people living on the land they own to continue doing so, to manage it, and strive to restore environmental values or ensure their maintenance. At the same time, the environment department pays lip service to the Right Hand with its published material noting that 'employment is supported by the Australian Government as part of Closing the Gap under the Working on Country Program' (Department of the Environment, Water, Heritage and the Arts 2009, 2).

Clearly, Aboriginal groups need to learn similar strategic skills to ensure that in the political power/knowledge struggles their diverse perspectives are clearly heard (Bourdieu 1991). This in turn will require diverse education so that an expert Indigenous discourse is readily available for the debates over key emerging issues like global warming, climate change and biodiversity protection. Importantly, this must include contributions that Indigenous knowledge systems and hybrid economies in remote Australia can make to the national interest. At the same time, both the neoliberal state and Indigenous communities need to negotiate for educational approaches that maximise, rather than foreclose, opportunities in whatever sector of the hybrid economy Indigenous people choose to participate, bearing in mind the reality of considerable occupational mobility between sectors. The rich Australian state needs to consider innovative forms of educational provision rather than assuming one approach will suit all. Aboriginal people need to have the option to live in two worlds, but also between them.

Conclusion

In this chapter we have focused on remote Australia in part because so much of current Australian policy is focused there, but also because the neoliberal state's goal of closing the gap will be most difficult to achieve in such situations. We note a fundamental tension between this goal, with its emphasis on sameness and homogenisation, and Indigenous aspirations for self-determination, choice, diversity and difference. There is a clear tension between the goals of statistical equality and ethnic plurality, with the former currently in the ascendancy in policy discourse and practice. The powerful neoliberal state is unwilling to consider investment in small and dispersed Indigenous communities or to provide real choice to land-linked Indigenous groups. As Blaser (2004) notes, state development projects and Indigenous life projects may be very different; in much of the material we have presented they clearly are, but not in all cases.

We are concerned that NIRA might, to paraphrase Edelman (1977), amount to 'an agreement that succeeds but with policies that fail'. Closing the gap is part of a national narrative that the rich Australian state needs to construct to avoid domestic and international embarrassment. But the state also needs to heed the warnings of theorists like Ferguson (1994) and Li (2007) and its own Productivity Commission (2009) that development cannot be imposed in a technical and managerial manner from above: it will require partnership and especially opportunity for communities to shape the diverse forms of development that they aspire to have.

Just as closing the gap requires recognition of cultural and structural difference and diversity, so educational approaches will need to consider particular local needs and aspirations, including for bilingual education and vocationally oriented practical skills acquisition. At present the entire focus of education policy is on imagined approaches to meet national benchmarks that, even if met, are only calibrated to ensure success in the mainstream. There is need to consider other forms of education that might better serve those looking for robust engagement in hybrid economies in remote Australia.

Endnotes

1 Elsewhere Altman has critiqued the framework from a number of perspectives: development by numbers; project of improvement defined by the Australian state, rendered technical; while appearing to be statistically based, statistics in fact are abstractions that have little to do with local solutions and cultures; fundamentally reflects a discourse of power; reflects western not Indigenous notions of outcomes; and that social norms of dominant society, reflected in statistical measures, ignore different lifeworlds etc (see Altman 2009a).

2 The Australian Institute of Criminology (2009) reports Indigenous imprisonment rates increased from 1653 per 100,000 in 2000 to 2223 per 100,000 in 2008. The gap between Indigenous and non-Indigenous imprisonment rates increased from 13.5 times to 17.2 times.

3 This is very clearly evident across a range of language and culture and social networks and support variables reported in the *National Aboriginal and Torres Strait Islander Social Survey 2008* (Australian Bureau of Statistics 2009). For example, 73 per cent of Indigenous people aged 15 years and over in remote Australia spoke, or spoke some words of, an Aboriginal or Torres Strait Islander language.

4   NAPLAN results are reported using five national achievement scales, one for each of the NAPLAN assessment domains of Reading, Writing, Spelling, Grammar and Punctuation, and Numeracy. Each scale consists of 10 bands, which represent the increasing complexity of the skills and understandings assessed by NAPLAN from Years 3 to 9 (MCEECDYA 2009).

5   For example, 90 per cent of students nationally are performing at or above the national minimum standard in each of the key areas assessed, as opposed to the results in the Northern Territory where 14 per cent of very remote Indigenous students met the national reading standard for Year 3, eight per cent for Year 5, 14 per cent for Year 7, and 13 per cent for Year 9 (Gillard 2008).

References

Altman, J C. 2009a. 'Beyond closing the gap: Valuing diversity in Indigenous Australia'. CAEPR Working Paper No. 54. Canberra: Centre for Aboriginal Economic Policy Research, Australian National University. Accessed 21 October 2009. Available from: http://www.anu.edu.au/caepr/working.php.

Altman, J C. 2009b. 'The hybrid economy and anthropological engagements with policy discourse: A brief reflection', *Australian Journal of Anthropology* 20 (3): 318–329.

Altman, J C; Biddle, N; Hunter, B H. 2008. 'How realistic are the prospects for "closing the gaps" in socioeconomic outcomes for Indigenous Australians'. CAEPR Discussion Paper No. 287/2008. Canberra: Centre for Aboriginal Economic Policy Research, Australian National University.

Altman, J C; Buchannan, G; Larsen, L. 2007. 'The environmental significance of the Indigenous estate: Natural resource management as economic development in remote Australia'. CAEPR Discussion Paper No. 286/2007. Canberra: Centre for Aboriginal Economic Policy Research, Australian National University.

Altman, J C; Nieuwenhuysen, J P. 1979. *The Economic Status of Australian Aborigines*. Cambridge: Cambridge University Press.

Australian Bureau of Statistics. 2009. *National Aboriginal and Torres Strait Islander Survey, 2008, Summary*. Cat. No. 4714.0 (released 30 October 2009). Canberra: Australian Bureau of Statistics.

Australian Institute of Criminology. 2009. 'Indigenous imprisonment rates'. Crime Facts Info No. 195, 17 July 2009. Canberra: Australian Institute of Criminology.

Bawinanga Aboriginal Corporation. 2009. *Djelk Rangers 2009 Annual Report 2008–2009*. Maningrida, Northern Territory: Bawinanga Aboriginal Corporation.

Biddle, N. 2009. 'The geography and demography of Indigenous migration: Insights for policy and planning'. CAEPR Working Paper No. 58. Canberra: Centre for Aboriginal Economic Policy Research, Australian National University.

Blaser, M. 2004. 'Life projects: Indigenous people's agency and development'. In *In the Way of Development: Indigenous Peoples, Life Projects and Globalization*, edited by Blaser, M; Feit, H; McRae, G. London and New York: Zed Books: 26–44.

Bourdieu, P. 1991. *Language and Symbolic Power*. Cambridge: Polity Press.

Bourdieu, P. 1998. 'The essence of neo-liberalism'. *Le Monde Diplomatique*. Accessed 20 October 2009. Available from: http://mondediplo.com/1998/12/08bourdieu.

CAEPR (Centre for Aboriginal Economic Policy Research). 2009. 'People on country, healthy landscapes and Indigenous economic futures'. Canberra: CAEPR, Australian National University. Accessed 20 October 2009. Available from: http://www.anu.edu.au/caepr-old/country/index.php.

COAG (Council of Australian Governments). 2009. National Indigenous Reform Agreement (Closing the Gap). Accessed 21 October 2009. Available from: http://www.coag.gov.au/coag_meeting_outcomes/2009-07/02/docs/NIRA_closing_the_gap.pdf.

Comaroff, J; Comaroff, J. 2009. *Ethnicity, Inc.* Chicago: Chicago University Press.

Department of the Environment, Water, Heritage and the Arts (DEWHA). 2009. *Djelk Arnhem Coast, Northern Territory.* Canberra: DEWHA.

Edelman, M. 1977. *Political Language: Words that Succeed and Policies that Fail.* New York: Academic Press.

Evans, N. 2009. *Dying Words: Endangered Languages and What They Have to Tell Us.* Malden, Massachusetts: Wiley Blackwell.

Ferguson, J. 1994. *The Anti-Politics Machine: 'Development', Depoliticization and Bureaucratic Power in Lesotho.* Minneapolis: University of Minnesota Press.

Folds, R. 2001. *Crossed Purposes: The Pintupi and Australia's Indigenous Policy.* Sydney: UNSW Press.

Fordham, A; Schwab, R G. 2007. 'Education, training and Indigenous futures'. Canberra: Centre for Aboriginal Economic Policy Research, Australian National University. Accessed 21 October 2009. Available from: www.anu.edu.au/caepr/education.php.

Gillard, J. 2008. The Hon Julia Gillard MP. 'NAPLAN national report released'. Media release 19 December 2008.

Harris, S. 1990. *Two-way Aboriginal Schooling: Education and Cultural Survival.* Canberra: Aboriginal Studies Press.

Harvey, D. 2005. *A Brief History of Neoliberalism.* Oxford: Oxford University Press.

Hughes, H. 2007. *Lands of Shame: Aboriginal and Torres Strait Islander 'Homelands' in Transition.* St Leonards, Sydney: Centre for Independent Studies.

Li, T. 2007. *The Will to Improve: Governmentality, Development, and the Practice of Politics.* Durham, North Carolina: Duke University Press.

MCEEDYA (Ministerial Council for Education, Early Childhood Development and Youth Affairs). 2009. 'National Assessment Program Literacy and Numeracy Summary (NAPLAN) Report'. Canberra: Australian Government Publishing Service. Accessed 21 October 2009. Available from: www.naplan.edu.au.

MCEETYA (Ministerial Council on Education, Employment, Training and Youth Affairs). 1999. Task Force on Indigenous Education. 'Exploring Multiple Pathways for Indigenous Students: A Discussion Paper'. Canberra: Australian Government Publishing Service. Accessed 21 October 2009. Available from: http://www.curriculum.edu.au/verve/_resources/exploringmultiplepathways_file.pdf

McKenna, B. 1977. 'What's wrong with standardized testing?' *National Education Association Reference and Resource Series.* Washington, DC: National Education Association.

Nadasdy, P. 2003. *Hunters and Bureaucrats: Power, Knowledge, and Aboriginal-State Relations in the Southwest Yukon.* Vancouver: UBC Press.

Northern Land Council. 2006. *Celebrating Ten Years of Caring for Country: A Northern Land Council Initiative.* Darwin: Northern Land Council.

Pearson, N. 2009. *Up From the Mission: Selected Writings.* Melbourne: Black Inc.

Productivity Commission. 2009. *Overcoming Indigenous Disadvantage: Key Indicators 2009.* Melbourne: Productivity Commission.

Rudd, K. 2008. 'Apology to Australia's Indigenous Peoples'. House of Representatives, Parliament House, Canberra. Speech as Prime Minister of Australia, 13 February. Accessed 20 October 2009. Available from: http://www.pm.gov.au/media/speech/2008/speech_0073.cfm.

Schwab, R G. 2006. 'Kids, skidoos and caribou: The Junior Canadian Ranger program as a model for re-engaging Indigenous Australian youth in remote areas'. CAEPR Discussion Paper No. 281/2006. Canberra: Centre for Aboriginal Economic Policy Research, Australian National University.

Scott, J C. 2009. *The Art of Not Being Governed: An Anarchist History of Upland Southeast Asia*. New Haven: Yale University Press.

Simpson, J; Caffery, J; McConvell, P. 2009. 'Gaps in Australia's Indigenous language policy: Dismantling bilingual education in the Northern Territory'. AIATSIS Discussion Paper 24. Canberra: Australian Institute of Aboriginal and Torres Strait Islander Studies.

Taylor, J; Stanley, O. 2005. 'The opportunity costs of the status quo in the Thamarrurr region'. CAEPR Working Paper 28/2005. Canberra: Centre for Aboriginal Economic Policy Research, Australian National University.

Wacquant, L. 2009. *Punishing the Poor: The Neoliberal Government of Social Insecurity*. Durham, North Carolina: Duke University Press.

Warddeken Land Management Limited. 2009. *Warddeken Indigenous Protected Area: Bringing our People Home to Look after the Rock Country*. Darwin: Warddeken Land Management Limited.

Wheelahan, L. 2010. 'Tertiary education as insurance against risk – What are the outcomes? For whom?' In *Risk, Responsibility and the Welfare State*, edited by Marston, G; Moss, J; Quiggin, J. Melbourne: Melbourne University Press: 165–184.

Wolfe, P. 1999. *Settler Colonialism and the Transformation of Anthropology: The Politics and Poetics of an Ethnographic Event*. London: Cassell.

Closing the Gap in Education by Addressing the Education Debt in New Zealand

Russell Bishop
University of Waikato

Introduction

New Zealand is one of many first world countries in which there are striking disparities between the sectors that enjoy a relatively high standard of living and prosperity and those that endure conditions of hardship and significant poverty. Although some progress has been seen in recent times, Maori people, the Indigenous people of New Zealand, continue to have higher levels of unemployment, are more likely to be employed in low-paying work, have much higher levels of incarceration, illness and poverty, and are generally under-represented in the positive social and economic indicators of society. This chapter addresses the question of whether and how the substantial financial and other resources of the more affluent segment of society within New Zealand is able to bring better standards and opportunities to those in the poorer sections, especially the members of the Indigenous population. The chapter draws on the substantial body of evidence that demonstrates how education can make a significant contribution. Through the implementation of *education reform* that is successful, sustainable and scalable, it is possible to institute measures to repay the significant *educational debt* that is owed to those students who have been mistreated by our education system. To achieve this goal, *education reform* that seeks to raise achievement and reduce disparities needs to be part of a broad, system-wide attempt to address systemic minoritisation. This chapter suggests a model of education reform that promotes successful interventions that are sustainable and scalable.

GPILSEO at the system level

I would suggest that there are seven interdependent elements for successful, sustainable and scalable education reform. These elements are gathered together in the reform model labelled GPILSEO, an acronym for Goals, Pedagogy, Institutions, Leadership, Spread, Evidence and Ownership. The model is based on that developed by Coburn (2003) and extended in Bishop and O'Sullivan (2005). The model's central understanding is that a reform initiative must have these seven elements present from the very outset, at a variety of levels: in classrooms and schools and within the wider system. While it is essential that the GPILSEO model be implemented at all levels in education – the classroom, school and system – the focus here is on the system level to develop, implement, sustain and extend theory-based education reforms.

Specifically, at the system level, there needs to be:

1. *goals:* national policy goals to realise the potential of those least well served by the system by raising their overall achievement, thereby reducing historical disparities
2. *pedagogy:* a means whereby inservice professional learning opportunities and professional development for teachers is on site, ongoing and dialogic, addresses the dominance of deficit discourse among teachers and where preservice teacher education is aligned with inservice professional development so that each supports the other in implementing culturally responsive pedagogies of relations
3. *institutions*: the development of supportive policies and infrastructure that provide incentives for teachers and support for schools that is ongoing, interactive and consistent
4. *leadership:* national-level support and professional development for leaders to promote distributed instructional/pedagogical leadership models and policies where accountabilty is supported by the provision of capacity-building activities
5. *spread:* collaboration between policy funders, researchers and practitioners that is responsive to community needs and aspirations, in an iterative process of interaction, feedback and adaptation

6. *evidence:* national-level support for the production of appropriate evidence that will enable collaborative, formative problem solving and decision making that is ongoing and interactive, and from which grow supportive policies regarding standards, assessments and the mix of accountability and capacity building
7. *ownership:* national ownership of the problem and the provision of sufficient funding and resources to see solutions within a defined period of time, and in an ongoing, embedded manner.

1. Goal setting: The education debt

Reducing disparities and raising achievement have long been conflated with addressing the achievement 'gap' in many western nations. Further, fundamental to these policy frameworks is the notion that increasing student achievement can be accomplished primarily in the nation's classrooms.[1] Although it is clear that classrooms are the most effective sites in which to commence educational reform (Alton-Lee 2003; Hattie 2003), it is vital to remember that classrooms are situated in, and inextricably linked to, the school and the wider education system. This suggests the need for reform to include the systemic level because, as Coburn (2003) suggests, teachers are better able to implement and sustain change when there are 'mechanisms in place at multiple levels of the system to support their efforts' (6). Teachers are further strengthened in their ability to sustain change if they are supported by a broader systemic focus on reform at school, and when this is reflected at the national level. Therefore, rather than focusing on realising potential or closing the achievement gap, long-term, system-level policy attention needs to be focused on what Ladson-Billings (2006) identifies as the *accumulation* of achievement disparities, which she terms the 'education debt'.

Using the notion of the national debt as a metaphor, Ladson-Billings (2006) suggests that it is the *annual accumulation* of achievement gaps – as seen in New Zealand since educational disparities were first identified in the Hunn report in 1960 – that need to be addressed, rather than any one gap. As the accumulation of annual fiscal deficits produces an economic debt, so the accumulation of achievement gaps over time has produced an education debt, a debt the education system owes to Maori children who have been short-changed by the system for generations. The long-term intergenerational legacy of an education system oriented to the interests of the dominant group has created this education debt and moving policy foci to 'realising potential' will severely exacerbate this pattern. Ladson-Billings quotes Robert Haverman, an eminent economist, who suggests that the education debt is:

> the forgone schooling resources that we could have (should have) been investing in (primarily) low income kids, which deficit leads to a variety of social problems (eg crime, low productivity, low wages, low labor force participation) that require on-going public investment. This required investment sucks away resources that could go to reducing the achievement gap. (5)

However, it is not just a matter of more funding. Ladson-Billings (2006) argues that the 'historical, economic, socio-political, and moral decisions and policies that characterize our society have created the education debt' (5). Christine Sleeter (2005) agrees:

> Like the US, New Zealand has spent over a century building an educational system, infrastructure, and set of beliefs around the education of students of European descent. The severe underachievement of Maori students reflects this history. Although it is not clear that conventional teaching processes that emphasize transmitting knowledge didactically promote the most optimal learning among students of European descent, it is clear that this system has been abysmal for Maori students. Conventional classroom processes and their supporting beliefs have a very strong weight of tradition and on-going institutional support, which makes them extraordinarily difficult to change. (4)

Sleeter (2005) continues by suggesting a way forward:

> Ultimately, the only way to reconfigure the schooling process so that it works for *both* Maori and Pakeha students is to reconfigure schooling around Maori ways of knowing, using a focus on Maori student achievement as the touchstone for evaluating changes to the processes and systems of education. What will emerge from a sustained focus on reconstructing classroom processes for Maori student achievement will be schooling that works better for both Maori and Pakeha students. (6)

Ranginui Walker (1990) has long maintained that Maori educational failure is a product of an unjust social order that has arisen out of the colonial experience. Through the process of colonisation, Maori history, knowledge and ways of being have been devalued and replaced with those of the coloniser, with educators often ignoring or denying Maori a voice or a place within the education system, education itself serving to reproduce the cultural practices and values of the dominant group (Tuuta et al. 2004). Such a situation means that schools allow for the transmission and reproduction of validated and socially approved knowledge and cultural practices, typically of the dominant social group, while excluding or negating knowledge and cultural practices of minority, indigenous or diverse groups (Bishop and Glynn 1999; Bertanees and Thornley 2004). Current government policy does little to acknowledge that classrooms are situated in and inextricably linked to the broader school and its systems, reflecting the wider society, and how the patterns of discrimination and inequality that exist in the wider society may well be reflected in the arrangements of the education system, schools and classrooms.

2. Systemic support for pedagogic reform: The provision of effective learning opportunities for teachers

At a policy level, providing effective professional learning opportunities for teachers to better understand the basis of their core business is probably the most effective school-based change initiative that any policy maker and funding agency can undertake. Building the capability of those currently working within the education system will increase the capacity of the whole system to bring about effective educational reform (Elmore 2004). However, realising this aspiration is not simple, especially as we have identified the discursive positioning of their teachers as the major influence on the educational outcomes of Maori students (Bishop and Glynn 1999; Bishop et al. 2003; Shields et al. 2005).

Recently in New Zealand the policy focus has shifted to one of 'realising Maori potential' (Ministry of Education 2008), predicated on the notion that including an ethnic orientation in policy frameworks will improve Maori student achievement. However, this shift is problematic, as it deflects the focus from educators needing to address the disparities in outcomes that exist between Maori and non-Maori students, and the part they themselves might play in perpetuating these disparities, to a situation where those who have traditionally held the power in defining what constitutes Maori potential, the non-Maori majority, retain this power. Further, as the vast majority of teachers are non-Maori (91 per cent), they are the ones who will continue to define what constitutes Maori potential on a day-to-day basis. This approach remains problematic because currently the majority of teachers are defining Maori potential in deficit terms (Bishop et al. 2003; Shields et al. 2005).

In a study of Maori students' schooling experiences (Bishop and Berryman 2006), where teachers were positioned within discourses in which they blamed Maori students' learning difficulties on the students, their homes or the school and/or schooling system (the dominant discourse), Maori students felt alienated, marginalised and failed to engage effectively with learning tasks. Where the teachers drew from a discourse that emphasised the power of caring and learning relationships, the students were able to thrive. These understandings need to be reflected at a national policy level by promoting educational reforms that address deficit theorising and associated pathologising practices among educators, and that support educators to develop understandings of how they may discursively reposition themselves in a sustainable, scalable manner.

In addition, currently professional developers are mainly external to schools, and tend to provide professional development opportunities outside the school or on a limited basis in-school. In a detailed investigation of the provision of professional learning opportunities for teachers, Timperley et al. (2007) argue:

> [I]t is generally accepted that listening to inspiring speakers or attending one-off workshops rarely changes teacher practice sufficiently to impact on student outcomes. Yet, at least in the United States, this type of activity is the predominant model of professional development. The popularity of conferences and one-day workshops in New Zealand indicates that it is not too different in this country. (xxv)

A number of researchers have found that the most effective professional development is on-site, ongoing and collaboratively reflective (Hall and Ramsay 1994; Bishop et al. 2001a; Bishop et al. 2001b). The teachers in these studies suggested that effective professional development requires a model of dynamic interactions that result in the establishment of power-sharing relationships between the professional developers and the program participants. This dynamic model suggests a spiralling approach that initially involves collaborative reflection on the experiences, and then the ongoing development of relationships among participants.

Timperley et al. (2007) support this approach to professional development. Their investigation of 97 core studies of teacher professional learning and development programs with substantive student outcomes found that there are seven elements in the professional learning context that have positive impacts on student outcomes:

- providing sufficient time for extended opportunities to learn, and using the time effectively (ie the quality of the use of time is as important as the amount of time)
- engaging external expertise, which requires funding
- focusing on engaging teachers in the learning process, which is more important than being concerned about whether they volunteered or not
- challenging problematic discourses, which involves iterative cycles of teachers considering alternatives and the impact on student outcomes of a range of discursive positions
- providing opportunities to interact, in a community of professionals, that focus on analysing the impact of teaching on student learning in an iterative, ongoing manner
- ensuring content is consistent with wider policy trends
- in school-based initiatives, having leaders actively leading the professional learning opportunities. (xxvi)

This has been supported by the development of a number of initiatives that are evidence based and focus on enhancing student achievement. These include the National Education Monitoring Project (NEMP), examining what achievement looks like across the curriculum and across the schooling sector since 1995 (NEMP 2009).[2] Along with NEMP, national education exemplars have been developed, providing examples of authentic pieces of student achievement at each level across the curriculum for teachers to match their students' progress and inform the next learning steps. These exemplars have been developed for both English- and Maori-medium schooling. Finally, TTle (Assessment Tools for Teaching and Learning) is a large, flexible, electronic bank of test items that teachers can draw on for formative and summative use in English and Maori, again developed and trialled by teachers in conjunction with researchers.

The development of these national 'smart' tools helps teachers implement achievement-focused and evidence-based teaching policy. The tools are implemented with professional development support at a national level by programs such as AtoL (Assess to Learn), a program that supports schools to gather and analyse student data, introducing more effective learning programs based on the analysis of student performance. The professional development programs both update and implement the findings of the Best Evidence Synthesis program in an iterative way. The shifts in policy have assisted development of smart tools and professional development programs that inform, support and implement the policies that seek to make education for Maori and other marginalised students more effective.[3]

Alignment between preservice and inservice teacher education

In a recent international study, Cochran-Smith and Zeichner (2005) identified the lack of links between preservice teacher education, inservice practice and the perceived hierarchies within the education sector as major impediments to comprehensive educational reform. In New Zealand there is need for policy-driven systemic amendments of this misalignment between preservice teacher education and inservice professional development, so that each can support the other in implementing the benefits of large-scale, theory-based educational reforms. Such alignment would create ongoing systems, supporting teachers as lifelong learners: as Smylie (1995) notes, '[w]e will fail… to improve schooling for children until we acknowledge the importance of schools not only as places for teachers to work but also as places for teachers to learn' (92).

One example of this misalignment was evident in the Te Kotahitanga project (Bishop et al. 2007), which found that of the 422 teachers surveyed, 60 per cent had been to teacher education institutions in the previous five years. They expressed their desire to implement a wide and effective range of classroom interaction types, aspiring to actively engage their students in lessons, utilising students' prior knowledge, using group learning processes, providing academic feedback, involving students in planning lessons, demonstrating their high expectations, stimulating critical questioning and including the culture of students in their lessons. However, detailed measured observations of their classrooms showed that 86 per cent of their interactions were of a traditional nature, where they engaged in the transmission of predetermined knowledge, monitoring to see if this knowledge had been passed on, and providing behavioural feedback in order to control the class. Only 14 per cent of their classroom interactions allowed opportunities to create the sorts of learning relationships to which they aspired. In short, despite the teachers' aspirations, the dominant classroom interactions remained active teacher and passive students, the very learning environment that Maori students identified as limiting their opportunities to engage with learning (Bishop and Berryman 2006).

Elmore and Burney (1996) and Bishop (2007) suggest that preservice teacher education programs need to emulate the practices outlined above for the implementation of theory-based educational reforms in schools. Preservice teachers should be organised into professional learning communities. This would enable familiarity with modes of assessment that allow collaborative analysis of the multitude of data that are routinely collected about children to inform and modify teaching practice. These findings signal the need for preservice educators to integrate the theory and practice of teaching and learning in a systematic manner, using evidence of student-teachers' instructional practice and student achievement for formative purposes. They also signal that schools need to provide similar classroom support to inservice teachers, giving them ongoing objective analysis and feedback on classroom interactions, which they critically reflect on in a collaborative problem-solving setting.

Preservice programs conducted at universities are well placed to support ongoing teacher learning by developing a program and culture of teacher research, because such research 'is a way of organising professional development in such a way that it remains closely related to what teachers acknowledge as their domain of professional autonomy' (Tillema and Imants 1995, 142). Introducing such practices at both preservice and inservice levels would allow the reform and associated paradigm shifts to become self-monitoring on a day-to-day basis. The research may also enhance the status of the reform because it would be 'closely related to meaningful school development in which there is a close connection among development, reflection, professionalization, and school renewal' (Tillema and Imants 1995, 146).

3. Institutionalisation

Systemic-level support is necessary for those structural and organisational changes that schools need to undertake to support the sustainability of educational reform. Policy makers need to examine how reform projects and schools are funded so that changes in personnel, resourcing for in-school professional developers and the overall structure of the school can be made by the school's governance and management without jeopardising the reforms. Fullan (2007) points to the example of the Ontario Literacy and Numeracy Strategy, which sought to substantially improve literacy and numeracy within one election period for all 72 school districts and all 4000 or so elementary schools in the province (246). One of the eight interlocking strategies developed to implement the policy was that the budget for education for the province of Ontario be increased by 22 per cent in the first three years of the initiative: 'Much of the new money is devoted to capacity building, with all those in challenging circumstances receiving additional earmarked resources. All this as the government is working to reduce an overall budget deficit' (255).

This example shows the level of commitment needed at the funding level to support large-scale educational reform. It is insufficient to promulgate policies that are responsive to identified needs, and yet not provide sufficient funding to make the reform a reality. The danger of embarking on a reform and its foundering due to lack of funding is too great. Many teachers are wary of what Fullan (2007) calls 'initiative-itis', where more and more programs are promulgated, many without sufficient long-term funding support. Similarly, schools are loath to reprioritise their own funding until they have firm evidence that the professional learning program is going to be productive in terms of enhanced student outcomes. Hence the government needs to provide substantial upfront *and* long-term monies to get the whole process going in such a way that the reform will be able to be successfully embedded. The government needs to see this initial and long-term funding as an investment rather than a cost – an investment that will be financially beneficial for society in the long run in terms of the reduction in costs for downstream services such as welfare, health, crime prevention and incarceration needed by those students currently not well served by education.

Supporting schools to reform their organisational structures

The recent evaluation of the role of in-school facilitators in implementing professional development found that these knowledgeable individuals are essential to support the implementation and sustainability of educational reform programs (Hindle et al. 2007). Drawing on two case-study projects, Te Kauhua and Te Kotahitanga, Hindle et al. (2007) found that at the school level it is essential that a permanent position of professional development facilitator is confirmed within project schools to sustain gains made. Hindle et al. (2007) suggest that policy makers should identify effective reform initiatives through robust qualitative and quantitative means and continue to support these initiatives on an ongoing basis so they become normal, embedded in the system and culture of the schools (cf Fullan 2005; Hall and Hord 2006; Hargreaves 2006). Just as schools are funded for maths teachers and guidance counsellors, so too there needs to be an allocated fund for professional development facilitators so that teacher capacity building continues.

Hall and Hord (2006) and McLaughlin and Mitra (2001) go further, suggesting that removal of funding from those responsible for educational reform within the schools (eg in-school professional development facilitators) will mean the end of the project and a waste of all money expended. McLaughlin and Mitra (2001) suggest that '[m]aking provision for the resources necessary to sustain a reform effort is a "bottom line" reformers need to negotiate at the outset with the implementing site or with funders' (305).

These findings indicate that development of a cadre of professional developers within schools rather than externally based providers will become a necessary feature of schools' staffing entitlement in the near future. Just as classroom teachers have been joined by guidance counsellors, social workers, RTLBs (Resource Teacher: Learning and Behaviour) and teacher aides, professional staff developers will be among the next group of support staff to be added to the staffing entitlements of schools. As Elmore (2004) and Guskey (2005) explain, change in teaching practice is incremental and teachers need ongoing support to work through the steps to implement reform practices in line with reform principles.

The message for national policy makers is that once a reform project is proven successful in addressing its identified goals, it is essential to see it as an integral part of schooling and no longer as an adjunct. In effect, system-level support is needed for the development, at both national and school levels, of what St John (2002) terms the 'improvement infrastructure'. The *project* then becomes a *program*, a normal part of what schools are funded to provide for their communities. The message is clear: unless this essential step takes place, unless the project becomes funded as part of schools' ongoing core business, then the project and its goals will always remain peripheral to schools' business, and national goals of addressing educational disparities will always remain goals and never be realised.

4. Leadership: Accountability and capacity building

According to Fullan (2007), governments can support the development of systemic leadership by promoting *accountability*, providing *incentives* and fostering *capacity building*. Getting the right balance between these three approaches to policy development is crucial to supporting large-scale reform. Fullan (2007), along with Elmore (2004) and Guskey (2005), argue that systems promoting accountability and/or providing incentives at the expense of capacity building do not produce successful educational reforms.

In the US, No Child Left Behind, an accountability-heavy policy, was legislated in 2002. It required all states to establish a series of annual standardised reading and mathematics tests for Grades 3 to 8, and reading and mathematics tests in Grades 10, 11 and 12. Tests are administered to at least 95 per cent of all students enrolled in each grade level. The legislation requires that each school demonstrate annually adequate progress according to a set of targets predetermined by the policy. If a school fails to meet these targets, there is a sequence of consequences, culminating in being placed in a 'restructuring' category after year five, when they may be closed down or merged with a more successful school.

There are a number of problems with such approaches to national testing. Fullan (2007) reports that so much time is taken at the school and classroom level complying with assessments for students to measure their proficiency that there is 'little time left for doing the actual work of improvement' (241). More problematic is the situation where an external accountability scheme does not allow for building the capacity of staff to undertake the 'work of improvement'. As Elmore (2004) argues, no external accountability scheme can succeed in the absence of internal school-level accountability, defined as 'the capacity (knowledge, skills, resources) of the entity for individual and collective responsibility to engage in daily improvement practices' (241). An overemphasis on accountability systems seriously underestimates the importance of school-based capacity building. Indeed, capacity building needs to precede accountability, or at least be part of a dialogue, with a realistic time frame so that both can be present.

Elmore (2004) and Fullan (2007) are both highly critical of policies promoting accountability-focused systems, with Fullan (2007) reporting that in the US 'the gap between high and low performance has widened since 2000, precisely the opposite of what [No Child Left Behind] so forcefully intended' (242). What is essential in New Zealand is that we learn from these experiences and do not introduce policies of national testing for students without support from appropriate capacity-building programs. Fullan (2007) also warns of the tendency of past governments to implement centralised high-stakes accountability systems without providing for appropriate supportive capacity building linked to results. Capacity building as a means of guiding and directing people's work must be 'carried out in a highly interactive professional learning setting. All else is clutter. Policies need to be aligned to minimize distractions and mobilize resources for continuous improvement' (263).

5. Spread

From their detailed examination of a number of large-scale reform projects in North America, Glennan et al. (2004) distil some general lessons about producing widespread, deep and lasting educational reform: 'No matter the target of reforms or the design construct, the scale-up process is necessarily iterative and complex and requires the support of multiple actors. This is likely to remain so for the foreseeable future' (647). From an examination of the core tasks for scaling up the respective reforms in their study, they also note that '[i]f the scale-up is to succeed, the actors involved – including developers, district officials, school leaders, and teachers – must jointly address a set of known, interconnected tasks, especially aligning policies and infrastructure in coherent ways to sustain practice' (648). In other words, collaboration between policy funders, researchers and practitioners in an iterative process of interaction, feedback and adaptation is part of the wider picture that supports the sustainability of theory-based educational reforms (Datnow and Stringfield 2000).

Communities of practice

Wenger (1998) describes a 'community of practice' as a community of practitioners that shares practice and understanding in order to be effective in certain specified domains. Surrounding community practices are boundaries across which 'brokers' may transfer understanding and procedures. In this light, the education system may itself be conceptualised as comprising a 'constellation' of communities bound together by the overall institutional enterprise, achieving transfer between various groups to foster a collective response to Maori and national aspirations for effective educational reform for Maori students at all levels of the system. In other words, at a system level, unless all are involved in a reciprocal, iterative manner, ownership of the reform is unlikely.

Just as schools as institutions can do much to create a context in which communities of practice can thrive, so too can system-wide communities of practice gather round a common agenda, share understanding and practices that go towards the effective application of the reform in question and go beyond the specific project to co-construct new policies and practices in other areas. The actions of such communities lead to achievement of Coburn's (2003) normative coherence, ie spreading the reform norms, beliefs and principles within schools and beyond.

6. Evidence to enable collaborative formative problem solving and decision making

Different forms of assessment of learning and behaviour in schools produce evidence that can reinforce or undermine the motivation of students to strive for future achievement. Student achievement may be constrained by the forms of assessment used, as assessment practices can affect students' belief in their own potential (Murphy 2002). Assessments should therefore acknowledge the importance of students developing positive learning identities. There is strong argument for assessment, the prime purpose of which is formative, designed to offer constructive support towards achieving competence. There is also a need to acknowledge that learning takes place in multiple localities (Street 1993; Gee 2000); meaning processes that seek to assess the learning and behaviour of students need to take into account students' real-life experiences. This emphasis implies a broader conceptualisation of what needs to be assessed beyond simply the characteristics of the individual learner and what has been achieved over a particular period of time. If evidence is to effectively inform educational reform, assessments need to be responsive to the different knowledges, experiences and cultural understandings within diverse communities in which students live and are educated.

We need to question whether some government-supported assessment policies and practices such as standardised tests serve to keep students in a marginalised position. The assumptions associated with identification of individual difficulties in learning through, for example, norm-referenced testing, intrinsically contradict notions of inclusion. Statistical, norm-referenced tests often lead to deterministic views of ability and restrict expectations of achievement for some student groups. This identification of a few *problem* students results in reproduction of underprivileged groups in society. Furthermore, poor scores on normative tests are often associated with *blaming* student attributes rather than opening up discussion about amending pedagogy to support learning and behaviour. Access to available resources and the need to determine eligibility for additional services (special educational provision) are typically argued as justification for norm-referenced assessments. Such assessments compare individual students' achievement against those of their peers (Cline 1992). Standardised tests such as these reflect a view of intelligence as an innate capacity, assumed to be randomly distributed throughout populations. Norm-referenced tests of ability and attainment can therefore 'determine selectively the way in which issues are discussed and solutions proposed' (Broadfoot 1996, x). The underlying assumption of such approaches is inconsistent with the view of students as having the potential to achieve highly, given the right learning opportunities. The influence of psychometric approaches to measuring human achievement therefore lends support to deterministic views of ability and achievement.

A similar problem is that of measuring Maori students against progress made by non-Maori students, especially those in the same class. Durie (1995) warns that such comparisons are perpetuating non-Maori being seen as the norm – the standard against which all others are measured – ignoring the advantage non-Maori students have had. He suggests Maori students' progress should be measured against their peer group.

In Bourdieu and Passeron's (1973) terms, schools use these practices to reproduce patterns of control and subordination within society that are linked to economic context. The rhetoric of education to promote equality is not supported by the reality: that the system of education functions to maintain the children of underprivileged groups in powerless positions in society. From this perspective, 'success' and 'failure' are social categories, in which the labels serve the vested interests of dominant, powerful groups in society. They are not simply givens; rather, some students' lack of achievement in the education system may be understood as a function of the societal, economic and political status quo that requires some children to fail.

Learning is 'a fundamentally social phenomenon, reflecting our own deeply social nature as human beings capable of knowing' (Wenger 1998, 3). However, the competitive climate encouraged currently by some governments, intent on target setting and narrowly conceived achievement, contradicts policies that seek to create an inclusive classroom environment where all students have the potential to achieve. Ironically, such conflicting aspirations are visible in the same policy documents. Assessment can be a powerful contributor to the promotion of effective learning if used in the right way. However, there is little evidence that increasing the amount of testing will enhance learning. Rather, the focus needs to be on helping teachers to use assessment and promote teaching and learning in ways that will raise the achievement of students. To be successful, learners need to be able to take ownership of their learning, understanding the goals they are aiming for and developing the motivation and skills to achieve success. Ongoing formative assessment can provide teachers with formal and informal opportunities to notice what is happening during learning activities, recognising where the learning of individuals and groups of students is going and how they can help take learning further.

7. Ownership

There are two major implications for government policy from the above analysis. The first is that to address the current educational crisis afflicting Maori and also New Zealand's potential to realise aspirations of becoming a 'knowledge' society, there needs to be national ownership of the problem. This requires that policy makers intentionally and explicitly maintain the primary focus of educational policy on Maori student achievement in ways that make sense to Maori. Policies that promote the whole range covered by the GPILSEO model – goals, pedagogies, institutions, leadership, spread and evidence – need to demonstrate national-level ownership. Evaluation and support of the potential benefit of any proposed action should be undertaken with reference to its impact on Maori students.

The second implication is that policies regarding funding need to be specific. To address the economic marginalisation of Maori associated with the education debt, current government policies such as that outlined in *Ka Hikitia* (Ministry of Education 2008) to 'realise Maori potential', need to be amended to set specific government funding targets for outcomes for Maori. The government has been able to set specific dates and has allocated specific resources, albeit limited, to see an end to the process of addressing historical grievances under the Treaty of Waitangi. In a similar vein, the government needs to set specific dates and allocate specific resources in association with its education policy documents to see an end to educational disparities within a set period of time.

Current approaches to professional development by the New Zealand Ministry of Education generally run to a short-term funding timetable, where initial funding is provided for a limited period of time, reduced, then withdrawn. The expectation is that the schools will reprioritise funding to support the long-term implementation and maintenance of the reform from their own resources. The reality is that this rarely happens. Sarason (1990) identifies this as one of the main causes of 'the predictable failure of school reform': the failure to provide schools with sufficient ongoing funding to support effective reforms in the face of competing claims for limited funding.

A number of common outcomes result from this type of policy. The first is that schools shift from reform to reform – not one of which is ever embedded in the school – as the funding becomes available from the central government agency. The second is that insufficient money is invested in schools to develop the necessary infrastructure that will allow the reforms to flourish. The third is the lack of opportunities to provide responsive support for schools in a climate that promotes curriculum content reforms such as those that focus on literacy and numeracy. Current government policies seeking to reduce educational disparities through raising the educational achievement of those students who are not currently well served by the education system are necessary, but also insufficient to create appropriate conditions for addressing the long-term education debt, evident in the statistics of educational disparities in this country. What is needed is a long-term policy that is not subject to the electoral cycle, one that in Fullan's (2001) terms provides an expansive rather than a contracting resource base for individual schools, and seeks to reallocate to Maori people their fair share of the benefits that our society has to offer.

Such a vision needs to be taken on by the nation as a whole, in an approach that goes beyond party politics and the three-year electoral cycle, to acknowledge that New Zealand society and economy cannot survive with an increasing demographic of non-participating young people. In many ways, Maori people's future is New Zealand's future. The questions that stand out for our political leaders are: Who has the courage to take on this challenge? Who has the courage to address the education debt that is owed to Maori and the nation as a whole? As a nation, we had the courage to address women's suffrage, the need for a welfare state and nuclear ship visits – among other world firsts. Now we need to summon the courage to address the long-term education debt that will otherwise cripple us as a people and a country unless we attend to it with haste and determination.

Acknowledgment

Thanks to my colleagues Mere Berryman, Dominic O'Sullivan and others in the Te Kotahitanga project for their support over the years.

Endnotes

1   The New Zealand Ministry of Education for example is clear in its 2004 document that the first means of addressing educational disparities is quality teaching: 'The research is unambiguous – effective teaching is the single biggest influence over a student's learning and success. Good teaching is powerful and can offset many factors that can exert a negative influence in a student's life' (Ministry of Education 2004, 5). The second is to support families and communities to play a greater part in the education of their children: 'Supportive families and communities are also powerful influences on learning outcomes. The better the formal learning environment respects and affirms the learner's home environment and community, and incorporates this into the learning process, the higher the level of likely achievement' (5). The third means of improving learning outcomes is to support quality providers that are first

and foremost focused on student achievement: 'We need to help create a culture of professional debate and provide professional support that helps make a real difference for students' (5).

2   The researchers and developers of this project use teacher experiences at all levels, including the development of test items, marking and evaluation. Teachers also undertake the testing, providing them with valuable professional learning opportunities to take back to their classrooms and schools.

3   However, currently there are no structured ways of introducing the best evidence synthesis documents themselves into schools, other than simply posting them out and providing lectures on their content. Part of the irony of this approach is that it is these documents that have synthesised what we know about the approaches that best support teacher learning. There is a need to use this knowledge to effectively introduce these publications to schools in ways that best reflect the learning.

References

Alton-Lee, A. 2003. 'Quality Teaching for Diverse Students in Schooling: Best Evidence Synthesis'. Wellington: Ministry of Education.

Bertanees, C; Thornley, C. 2004. 'Negotiating colonial structures: Challenging the views of Pakeha student teachers'. *Asia-Pacific Journal of Teacher Education* 32 (2): 81–93.

Bishop, R. 2007. 'Lessons from Te Kotahitanga for teacher education'. In *International Research on the Impact of Accountability Systems*, edited by Detrechin, L F; Craig, C J. Lanham, Maryland: Rowman & Littlefield Education: 225–239.

Bishop, R; Berryman, M. 2006. *Culture Speaks: Cultural Relationships and Classroom Learning*. Wellington: Huia Publishers.

Bishop, R; Berryman, M; Cavanagh, T; Teddy, L. 2007. 'Te Kotahitanga Phase 3 whanaungatanga: Establishing a culturally responsive pedagogy of relations in mainstream secondary school classrooms'. Wellington: Ministry of Education.

Bishop, R; Berryman, M; Richardson, C. 2001a. 'Te Toi Huarewa: Effective teaching and learning strategies, and effective teaching materials for improving the reading and writing in te reo Maori of students aged five to nine in Maori medium education'. Wellington: Ministry of Education.

Bishop, R; Berryman, M; Richardson, C; Glynn, T. 2001b. 'Teachers' perceptions and use of Aro Matawai Urunga-a-kura (AKA). Final report'. Wellington: Ministry of Education.

Bishop, R; Berryman, M; Tiakiwai, S; Richardson, C. 2003. 'Te Kotahitanga: The experiences of year 9 and 10 Maori students in mainstream classrooms'. Wellington: Ministry of Education.

Bishop, R; Glynn, T. 1999. *Culture Counts: Changing Power Relations in Education*. Palmerston North: Dunmore Press.

Bishop, R; O'Sullivan, D. 2005. 'Taking a reform project to scale: Considering the conditions that promote sustainability and spread of reform'. A monograph prepared with the support of Nga Pae o te Maramatanga, The National Institute for Research Excellence in Maori Development and Advancement. Unpublished manuscript.

Bourdieu, P; Passeron, J C. 1973. *Reproduction in Education, Society and Culture*. London: Sage.

Broadfoot, P. 1996. *Education, Assessment and Society*. Buckingham, Pennsylvania: Open University Press.

Cline, T, ed. 1992. *The Assessment of Special Educational Needs*. London: Routledge.

Coburn, C. 2003. 'Rethinking scale: Moving beyond numbers to deep and lasting change'. *Educational Researcher* 32 (6): 3–12.

Cochran-Smith, M; Zeichner, K. 2005. *Studying Teacher Education: The Report of the AERA Panel on Research and Teacher Education*. Hillsdale, New Jersey: Lawrence Erlbaum Associates.

Datnow, A; Stringfield, S. 2000. 'Working together for reliable school reform'. *Journal of Education for Students Placed at Risk* 5 (1): 183–204.

Durie, M. 1995. 'Principles for the development of Maori policy'. Paper presented at the Maori Policy Development AIC Conference, Wellington.

Elmore, R. 2004. *School Reform from the Inside Out: Policy, Practice and Performance*. Cambridge, Massachusetts: Harvard Education Press.

Elmore, R F; Burney, D. 1996. *Staff Development and Instructional Improvement: Community District 2*, New York City. Philadelphia: Consortium for Policy Research in Education.

Fullan, M. 2001. *The New Meaning of Educational Change*. 3rd edn. New York: Teachers College Press.

Fullan, M. 2005. *Leadership and Sustainability: Systems Thinkers in Action*. Thousand Oaks, California: Corwin Press.

Fullan, M. 2007. *The New Meaning of Educational Change*. 4th edn. New York: Teachers College Press.

Gee, J. 2000. 'New people in new worlds: Networks, the new capitalism and schools'. In *Multiliteracies: Literacy Learning and the Design of Social Futures*, edited by Cope, B; Kalantis, M. London: Routledge: 43–68.

Glennan, T K; Bodilly, S J; Galegher, J R; Kerr, K A. 2004. *Expanding the Reach of Education Reforms: Perspectives from Leaders in Scale-up of Educational Interventions*. Santa Monica, California: RAND Research.

Guskey, T. 2005. 'Taking a second look at accountability'. *National Staff Development Council* 26: 10–18.

Hall, A; Ramsey, P. 1994. 'Effective schools and effective teachers'. In *The Professional Practice of Teaching*, edited by McGee, C; Fraser, D. 1st edn. Palmerston North: Dunmore Press: 196–227.

Hall, C; Hord, S. 2006. *Implementing Change: Patterns, Principles, and Potholes*. Boston: Pearson Education.

Hargreaves, A. 2006. 'From recovery to sustainability'. *Journal of Reading Recovery* 5 (2): 39–44.

Hattie, J. 2003. 'New Zealand educational snapshot: With specific reference to the years 1–13'. Paper presented at the Knowledge Wave 2003 leadership forum, Auckland, New Zealand.

Hindle, R; Marshall, M; Higgins, J; Tait-McCutcheon, S. 2007. 'A study of in-school facilitation in two teacher professional development programmes'. Wellington: Ministry of Education.

Ladson-Billings, G. 2006. 'From the achievement gap to the education debt: Understanding achievement in US Schools'. *Educational Researcher* 35 (7): 3–12.

McLaughlin, M; Mitra, D. 2001. 'Theory-based change and change-based theory: Going deeper, going broader'. *Journal of Educational Change* 1 (2): 24.

Ministry of Education. 2008. 'Ka Hikitia: Managing for success: Maori Education Strategy 2008–2012'. Wellington: Ministry of Education.

Murphy, S. 2002. 'Literacy assessment and the politics of identities'. In *Contextualising Difficulties in Literacy Development: Exploring Politics, Culture, Ethnicity and Ethics*, edited by Soler, J; Wearmouth, J; Reid, G. London: Routledge Falmer: 87–101.

NEMP (National Education Monitoring Project). 2009. Dunedin: Ministry of Education. Accessed 21 December 2009. Available from: http://nemp.otago.ac.nz.

Sarason, S. 1990. *The Predictable Failure of Educational Reform: Can We Change Course Before It Is Too Late?* San Francisco: Jossey-Bass.

Shields, C M; Bishop, R; Mazawi, A E. 2005. *Pathologizing Practices: The Impact of Deficit Thinking on Education.* New York: Peter Lang.

Sleeter, C. 2005. *Un-standardizing Curriculum: Multicultural Teaching in the Standards-based Classroom.* New York: Teachers College Press.

Smylie, M. 1995. 'Teacher learning in the workplace: Implications for school reform'. In *Professional Development in Education: New Paradigms and Practices*, edited by Guskey, T; Huberman, M. New York: Teachers College Press: 92–113.

St John, M. 2002. 'The improvement infrastructure: The missing link or why are we always worried about "sustainability"'. Paper presented at the second annual conference on Sustainability of Systemic Reform, Cambridge, Massachusetts: Centre for School Reform at TERC.

Street, B, ed. 1993. *Cross-cultural Approaches to Literacy.* New York: Cambridge University Press.

Tillema, H H; Imants, J G M. 1995. 'Training for the professional development of teachers'. In *Professional Development in Education: New Paradigms and Practices*, edited by Guskey, T; Huberman, M. New York: Teachers College, Columbia University: 135–150.

Timperley, H; Wilson, A; Barrar, H; Fung, I. 2007. 'Teacher Professional Learning and Development: Best Evidence Synthesis Iteration (BES)'. Wellington: Ministry of Education.

Tuuta, M; Bradnum, L; Hynds, A; Higgins, J; Broughton, R. 2004. 'Evaluation of the Te Kauhua Maori mainstream pilot project'. Wellington: Ministry of Education.

Walker, R. 1990. *Ka Whawhai Tonu Matou: Struggle Without End.* Auckland: Penguin Books.

Wenger, E. 1998. *Communities of Practice: Learning, Meaning and Identity.* Cambridge: Cambridge University Press.

If This Is Your Land, How Do You Teach Your Stories?

The Politics of 'Anthologising' Indigenous Writing in Australia

Adam Shoemaker
Monash University

This chapter is about 'closing the gap' between student and teacher, reader and text, Indigeneity and non-Aboriginal knowledge. It concerns Aboriginal people in Australia but – more particularly – the migration of their stories from (and to) different forms. Above all, it has to do with questions of access, choice and influence in what can only be described as the fraught world of Australian publishing.

The case study I examine here is the landmark publication, *Macquarie PEN Anthology of Australian Literature*, a major and challenging work in scope, size and intent. The anthology was released in various locations around the world in July/August 2009, after over six years of preparation and editorial work. The editorial team, led by Professor Nicholas Jose and a talented group of (mostly) Sydney-based editors, tackled the concept of representing Australian writing by portraying it in the most inclusive possible way (Jose 2009). The end result was impressive and mammoth: a 1464-page hard-cover anthology that weighed over 1.7 kilograms and cost in excess of $1.5 million dollars to produce.

This is a major tome in anyone's language. It is a significant cultural achievement for Australian publishing – and a diplomatic barometer of the times. For example, the Deputy Prime Minister, Julia Gillard (whose portfolio includes the fields of education, employment and workplace relations as well as social inclusion), launched the book at the Australian Consulate in New York City on 7 October 2009. More of that later;

the significant point here is that the book became – on that night and subsequently – a diplomatic incident.

Even more: the anthology was co-published in the United States not by Macquarie or Allen & Unwin, but by the venerable American university literary text publisher, W.W. Norton. Norton anthologies are iconic in North America: the New York-based publishing house specialises in producing mammoth first-year set texts in literary genres, which find their way into compulsory reading lists in thousands of university syllabi in hundreds of colleges and universities the length and breadth of North America.

In one sense, then, the publication of this anthology is the literary equivalent of an Australian violinist debuting with the New York Philharmonic on her first tour overseas, or of an expatriate Australian actor landing a leading role in a James Cameron blockbuster straight after graduation from the Victorian College of the Arts or NIDA. Read one way, this is really 'making it'. And, judged by the criteria that literary agents would employ, this was undoubtedly a first for Australian publishing.

So the questions then arise: What does all of this have to do with a comparative Southern Worlds Conference at Monash South Africa on the crucial theme of closing the gap in education, specifically Indigenous education? What is the role of such an anthology in the world of teaching and what is my role in analysing it?

Surprisingly, there is a single answer to these questions. Put simply, it is that the *Macquarie PEN Anthology of Australian Literature* has the highest proportion of material written by Indigenous people of any such representative national collection ever published. Even more: this material is interpolated throughout the entire volume rather than being gathered – as is so often the case – as a kind of preface before the 'collection proper' begins. The contributions embrace work by Aboriginal and Torres Strait Islander people from every region of Australia and range across all genres: from the diary to the petition; from oral poetry to drama; from children's verse to the novel; and from journalism to polemic. Beginning with Bennelong's letter of 1796, the Indigenous contributions are intentionally recuperative and restitutional. As the two editors of the 'Aboriginal literature' strand of the *Macquarie PEN Anthology* – Anita Heiss and Peter Minter – observe:

> But just as the Crown's acquisition of 1770 had made sovereign Aboriginal land *terra nullius*, it also made Aboriginal people *vox nullius*… For Aboriginal people, the use of English became a necessity within the broader struggle to survive colonisation. (Heiss and Minter 2009, 8)

Despite the overt W.W. Norton survey-style format, this is no typical anthology. It embraces a particular agenda, that of centralising Indigenous creativity at the core of Australian literary achievement. The question is, 'Does it succeed?'

In a scathingly statistical mood, the launcher of the book at the British High Commission in late September, the redoubtable Clive James, observed that the anthology contained exactly 12.6 per cent of so-called 'Indigenous content'. And he continued, shocking many of those in the audience (not least the Australian High Commissioner to the United Kingdom), by *denouncing* that fact. James was reported to have said that there were 'far too many aboriginal [sic] writers included… when this ethnic minority is not noted for its literary tradition' (ALR Blog 2009). According to the *Evening Standard*, all hell broke loose when James continued his critique with the words, 'This tokenism was at the expense of good writers competing on a world stage who should have been included.' And James ended with the words, 'Don't tell Kevin Rudd, the current Labour [sic] PM who has apologized to the aboriginals. He won't like it' (ALR Blog 2009).

So literature can be – and is – highly political, especially where Indigenous writers are concerned. This is despite the fact that 87.4 per cent of the *Macquarie PEN Anthology* is faithfully devoted to non-Aboriginal poetry and prose and is entirely in English (with the exception of the rare translated word). Clearly, it is not a matter of inclusiveness, or representativeness, or even (dare I say it) Australianness that is being considered, but a particularly narrow invocation of literary culture. This is disturbing because, in so many other areas, Indigenous Australians are proportionally underrepresented in national life – from the percentage of Indigenous young people who graduate from university to the number of Aboriginal doctors in hospital wards or the ratio of Indigenous magistrates who preside over Australian courtrooms. Yet, for some, this 12 per cent contribution to the *Macquarie PEN Anthology* is simply beyond the pale. I argue that this should be a matter for celebration, just as we laud the fact that, in 2009, 82 players – or about 12 per cent of those competing at the highest levels of the Australian Football League – were from Indigenous backgrounds, with that number having risen astronomically over the past 15 years (AFL 2010). Or to quote an even more apposite example: 'between 25 and 50 per cent of all working Australian visual artists' (Ryan et al. 2008, 284) are Indigenous Australians and their work has created a signature export industry that is estimated to be worth as much as $500 million per year (Papunya Tula Artists Pty Ltd 2006), up strongly from a figure of $100 million to $300 million per annum in 2002 (Altman et al. 2003).

Of course, this anthology – and the teaching that accompanies it – can also be described as an export industry, as much as I dislike the commodification of literary works. The pertinent question here is: Without volumes such as this one, how will those in other nations – Canada, New Zealand, South Africa and many others – be able to teach with Indigenous people, about Indigenous cultures, in a way that advances first nations people socially, economically and educationally? What is our role? What is *my* role as an educator in this field? How do non-Aboriginal scholars 'profess' in this area in a way that is both ethical and liberating?

I submit that the *Macquarie PEN Anthology* shows us some of the ways to proceed and some of those to avoid. For the reality is that all of us who teach and research require tools with which to open minds. This anthology is one such tool. The manner of its creation, the critiques of its size (one critic said, 'This massive tome... edited by Nicholas Jose and with a foreword by Thomas Keneally, is even fatter than William Shawcross's Queen Mum' (ALR Blog 2009)) all make it a fascinating and revealing test case for intercultural and cross-border education.

Even more: the trenchant criticisms of its Indigenous dimensions are suggestive of deep-seated controversy and debate at the core of the Australian literary community; for instance, the Melbourne critic Peter Craven (2009) wrote in his *Australian Book Review* assessment of the book:

> This leaves the final glaring failure of the PEN anthology. It overflows with Aboriginal writing, much of which has no literary value whatever... the sheer quantity of Aboriginal writing included in this volume – much of it devoid of literary quality or even literary ambition – is an egregious mistake.

This review tells us as much about the predilections of Peter Craven as it denotes the inherent value (or otherwise) of the project. Expressed in another way, this book does not reflect the literary content – or image – of what Craven sees as a suitable national anthology.

In a similarly personal vein (but with an almost diametrically opposed line of reasoning), Robert Dessaix took the debate further at the Adelaide Festival Writers' Week of March 2010. In a special session that focused on the anthology, he addressed the role of such literary collections in a globalised world of national erasure and abnegation. Put simply, his critique of the anthology was that it was attempting to define a fruitlessly unitary sense of Australianness in an era in which that was impossible. In Dessaix's words:

> Anthologies... like retrospectives... search for lost or unformulated unities. We had a country there for a while, post-war... The editors of the PEN anthology have left their run a little late to create an artificial unity... they wanted to give Australian literature the place it has been losing in a globalised world [but] in 2010 anthologies will have little discernible effect on Australian identity except in the classroom... [The editors] have done a marvellous job – I just doubt that it is a job that needs doing. (Dessaix 2010)

So for Dessaix it is not Indigeneity per se that is the problem, but the basic thrust and goal of the project *as an anthology* at the end of the first decade of the twenty-first century. And this is – above all – an educational issue, for even Dessaix admits that the role of such works 'in the classroom' is of a particular type and significance.

My point is that we should not shy away from such controversies in our teaching and research; indeed, they often provide the springboard for deeper understandings of race relations and Indigeneity, of the migration of cultures locally, domestically and internationally. They also give us a more nuanced appreciation of generational change in the academy and in the world outside the campus.

I have to confess that there is a personal dimension too. As an editor myself (one who co-edited the first national anthology of Indigenous Australian writing in 1990 and edited the literary and photography anthology, *A Sea Change*, published in association with the Sydney Olympic Games in 1998), I think that Peter Craven is reaching towards a partly valid conclusion but gets bogged on the road towards it in his racialised analysis of the *Macquarie PEN Anthology*.

Briefly, my own critique relates to editorial policy. The general editor of the work, Nick Jose, together with Peter Minter and Anita Heiss, has chosen to opt for a thoroughly genre-exploding, chronological treatment of the panoply of Australian literature. As a concept, 'inclusiveness' has been elevated to the status of a literary arcadia, with over 300 authors represented in the collection. This is 'so far so good' – as far as it goes. In the general editor's words:

> The first and foremost aim of this book is to make available to readers and students a sampling of the range of Australian writing, putting striking works from recent times together with works from the past that have become less familiar. By ordering the material chronologically... and by encompassing a jostling variety of genres and styles, including letters, journals, speeches and songs, we intend

that the anthology show the phases of change and development in Australian literature. (Jose 2009, 2)

This embrace of differing genres sounds marvelous, but is actually undercut by the manner and presentation of the excerpted works. For example, as influential critics such as Katharine Brisbane (2009) have pointed out, it is wildly unfair to maintain that a principle of editorial *inclusivity* has been operative when set alongside the fact of *exclusivity* that applies in the case of Australian theatrical literature. As Brisbane points out, 'among the 300 authors represented – and twice as many extracts – 10 plays have been chosen. Some 27 of the 300 wrote for the stage and might have been considered. Scores of equal contenders have been rejected'.

The truth is that Australian writing for the theatre has witnessed huge breakthroughs over the past 50 years. It was the plays of David Williamson that broke into the West End of London in the 1970s and the plays of Jack Davis that did the same a decade later. It was (and continues to be) theatre that has acted as a catalyst for the cross-over influence of Indigenous writing in nearly every capital city of Australia over the past 35 years: from Bobby Merritt's *The Cake Man* in the late 1970s to the work of Leah Purcell (*Box the Pony*) and Josie Ningali Lawford (*Ningali*) in the late 1990s to the continuing directorial breakthroughs of Wesley Enoch in recent years. Indeed, in her wonderfully evocative speech launching the *Macquarie PEN Anthology* at Admiralty House in Sydney, the Australian Governor-General, Her Excellency Ms Quentin Bryce (2009), noted that in July she had seen Sam Watson's biographical play, *Oodgeroo: Bloodline to Country*, and observed: 'In the line it draws between past and present, we felt the electric thrill of a literary culture that is alive and flourishing'.

The cross-fertilisation of genres evidenced by the migration of plays such as Jimmie Chi's *Bran Nue Dae* from the stage in 1990 to the screen in 2009 (directed by Rachel Perkins) is yet another index of the importance of drama by, about and for Indigenous people in this country. Finally, the inherently episodic nature of writing for the stage lends itself particularly to anthologisation. Given the explicit orientation of the *Macquarie PEN Anthology* in the direction of Indigenous literature, it is difficult to understand why more extracts of Australian theatre – both Aboriginal and non-Aboriginal – are not included in this collection.

The editors' approach is similarly flawed because of the attempt to include too much, too briefly. The choice of extracts has been so exacting – just a few pages from classic works like Marcus Clarke's *For the Term of his Natural Life* or Sally Morgan's *My Place*, and the juxtapositions so sudden that the sum-total effect is one of discordant fragmentation. Even more: those Indigenous contributions that are written versions of originally oral storytelling material suffer the most in this mistranslation on the page. The book is so segmented that reading it is like travelling down a suburban road with scores of intellectual potholes and speed bumps obstructing the journey. I believe it is this to which the critics are responding when they target – unfairly – the Indigenous extracts in the collection.

In short, it is not a matter of weak Indigenous writing but one of frequently staccato editorial practice in this anthology. This gives the reader the uncomfortable sensation of skipping across the surface without ever really landing inside the works themselves. Ironically, despite its massive overall length, the contributions to the anthology are – within themselves – almost all too short and abrupt. This renders the collection even more open to criticism, in that it is more akin to a superficial survey than an in-depth tribute. Finally, this feature is equally a liability when the collection migrates to the teaching environment in other countries: in Canada, in Germany, in Korea, in New Zealand.

But what of South Africa? How would this book be received there? Indeed, would it even be *published* in that country, when it is so culturally specific, so massive and so expensive in relative terms (the list price is A$69.95). And how is such anthologised literature perceived in a country in which the black majority now rules a fast-changing democracy? It is fascinating to speculate which tools, which readings and which intellectual sources will be the most appropriate when it comes to teaching about black and Indigenous education internationally and in this nation. It is entirely possible that only the online extracts from this volume will be used in Durban, Dakar or Denpasar.

Ironically, in the end this chapter is not about an anthology per se. It is about a country's desire to *represent itself*; about a book that displays an Australian Government coat-of-arms on its title page, along with those of its major university and corporate sponsors. Thus the anthology looks and feels at times like a gargantuan writers' festival prospectus rather than a publisher-initiated project.

Finally, this is a case study about the means by which the academy enters into an often fraught public space. It is about reading, about politics, about education and about learning across cultures. Surely it is a comment on the insertion of governmentalism into the project: at the launch of the anthology at the Australian Embassy in Washington, Julia Gillard felt she had to defend the book against its critics. As reported by the Melbourne *Age* on 9 October 2009:

> The debate about the quality of the Aboriginal entries has raged in Australian literary journals, blogs and forums, but Ms Gillard was determined to deal with it upfront and move on when she launched the US version of the book in Washington DC on Wednesday. [The minister said,] 'This is an anthology for its time. Like any great historical text it will – and in Australia already has – stirred a fierce debate and feeling concerning its composition'. (Davies 2009)

But, as we know, migration and reception of meaning change everything. As the report continues:

> But there were mutterings about the omission of writers such as Geraldine Brooks, a best-selling Australian writer who won America's highest literature award, the Pulitzer Prize for fiction, in 2006, for her novel *March*. Others remarked on the omission of Ruth Park, popular overseas as well, and Colleen McCulloch, who has been wildly successful in the US. (Davies 2009)

So there it is. Clearly, if there is a gap to be closed in the area of Indigenous Education, works like this one will – in part – help to generate the productive debate that leads in that direction. Conversely, it will also be the *critique* of works like this that emphasise the fact that Aboriginal words, Aboriginal narratives, Aboriginal forms of storytelling cannot and should not be artificially constrained by a strictly predetermined anthology format. It is one step from anthologising words to anthologising (or regimenting and controlling) the lives of Indigenous peoples themselves. We are well aware of the disasters that this attitude has caused in the history of race relations in all southern societies.

References

AFL. 2010. Accessed 14 March 2010. Available from: http://www.afl.com.au/.

Altman, J C. 2003. 'Developing an Indigenous Arts Strategy for the Northern Territory: Issues Paper for Consultations', Working Paper No. 22. Canberra: Centre for Aboriginal Economic Policy Research, ANU.

ALR Blog. 2009. 'Clive James responds'. 'A Pair of Ragged Claws', ALR Blog, *Australian*. Accessed 14 October 2009. Available from: http://blogs.theaustralian.news.com.au/alr/index.php/theaustralian/comments/clive_james_responds/.

Brisbane, K. 2009. 'More drama over the PEN anthology'. *Crikey*, Tuesday 3 November. Accessed 11 November 2009. Available from:
http://www.crikey.com.au/2009/11/03/more-drama-over-the-pen-anthology.

Bryce, Q. 2009. 'Address by Her Excellency Ms Quentin Bryce, AC, Governor-General of the Commonwealth of Australia, on the occasion of Launch of the Macquarie PEN Anthology of Australian Literature, Admiralty House, Sydney, 30 July'. Accessed 14 March 2010. Available from:
http://www.gg.gov.au/governorgeneral/speech.php?id=586.

Craven, P. 2009. 'Obscuring the heritage'. *Australian Book Review*. September: 8.
Davies, A. 2009. 'Gillard defends anthology as one for its time'. *Age* online, 9 October 2009. Accessed 17 May 2010. Available from: http://www.theage.com.au/news/entertainment/books/gillard-defends-anthology-as-one-for-its-time/2009/10/08/1254701101238.html.
Dessaix, R. 2010. 'The Macquarie PEN anthology of Australian literature'. A session with Chloe Hooper, Malcolm Knox and Michelle de Kretser at the Adelaide Festival Writers' Week. Accessed 15 March 2010. Available from: http://www.abc.net.au/tv/fora/stories/2010/03/15/2845779.htm.
Heiss, A; Minter, P. 2009. 'Aboriginal literature'. In *Macquarie PEN Anthology of Australian Literature*, edited by Jose, N. St Leonards: Allen & Unwin.
Jose, N. 2009. 'General introduction'. In *Macquarie PEN Anthology of Australian Literature*, edited by Jose, N. St Leonards: Allen & Unwin.
Papunya Tula Artists Pty Ltd. 2006. Submission to 'Inquiry into Australia's Indigenous visual arts sector'. Canberra: Environment, Communications, Information Technology and the Arts Committee, Australian Senate.
Ryan, M D; Keane, M; Cunningham, S. 2008. 'Australian Indigenous art: Local dreamings, global consumption'. In *Cultures and Globalization: The Cultural Economy*, edited by Anheler, H K; Isar, Y R. London: Sage Publications.

Beyond the 'Digital Divide'

Engaging with New Technologies in Marginalised Educational Settings in Australia

Ilana Snyder
Monash University

The term 'digital divide' refers to the gap between those with and those without access to computers and the Internet and, as a result, their participation in the information age. The term became popular under the Clinton administration after the publication by the US National Communications and Information Administration (NTIA 2000) of the report 'Falling through the net: Defining the digital divide' (Warschauer 2003; Haythornthwaite 2007). When first used, the term served an important rhetorical purpose. It drew attention to a significant social and cultural phenomenon: dramatic differences of access to computers and the Internet among population groups. However, the notion of a digital divide and what it implies – that educational problems can be dealt with by providing computers and access to the Internet – have become increasingly problematic. Four stories, each with two versions, help illustrate this point.

The hole in the wall

The first story is located in India and is about the 'hole in the wall' experiment. Version one tells of an Indian academic and researcher, Sugata Mitra, who knocked a hole through the wall of his NIIT (National Institute of Information Technology) laboratory in New Delhi so that children in the adjoining slum could play on one of his computers. He wanted to see whether unschooled children would teach themselves how to use the

Internet if left to their own devices. Mitra discovered that the children quickly taught themselves how to surf the net, read the news and download games and music.

From this grew the Hole-in-the-Wall Education Ltd (HiWEL) project, a joint venture between NIIT and the International Finance Corporation (a part of The World Bank Group). It set up 23 outdoor computer kiosks in some of the poorest slums in India, where children had never had access to a computer. The computers were in a booth and the monitors protruded through holes in the walls. Instead of a mouse and keyboard, there were specially designed joysticks and buttons. The computers were connected to the Internet through dial-up access. A volunteer inside the booth kept the connection going and no teachers were provided. Each time the results were similar: within hours and without instruction, the children began browsing the Internet. It was hailed as a ground-breaking project offering a model of how to bring India into the computer age.

At the end of five years, the schools reported that their English, maths and science scores were all going up. Moreover, the experiment had an unexpected impact in Hollywood, as the 'hole-in-the-wall' project provided the inspiration for *Slumdog Millionaire*, the British film that won the Best Picture award at the Oscars in 2008. The movie is based on the novel *Q and A*, by Vikas Swarup, India's Deputy High Commissioner to South Africa. In an interview following the Oscar success, Swarup said:

> My book is about hope, optimism and triumph of the human spirit. I was inspired by the Hole-in-the-Wall project, where a computer with an internet connection was put in a slum in Delhi. When the slum was revisited after a month, the children of that slum had learnt how to use the worldwide web without any supervision. That got me fascinated and I realised that there's an innate ability in everyone to do something extraordinary, provided they are given an opportunity. (Swarup 2009)

The second version of the story provides a more sober account of the 'hole in the wall' experiment. Eminent researcher in the field of literacy and technology studies Mark Warschauer (2003) – University of California, Irvine – reports that overall the project was not very effective. The Internet seldom functioned, no special educational programs were made available and no special content was provided in Hindi, the only language the children knew. Further, parents had ambivalent attitudes to the kiosks. Some welcomed the initiative but were concerned that the lack of organised instruction took away its value. Others complained that it distracted the children from homework. According to Warschauer (2003), children taught themselves basic operations, including how to click and drag objects; select different menus; cut, copy and paste; launch and use programs such as Word and Paint; get on the Internet; and change the wallpaper. The children learned to manipulate joy sticks and buttons, but almost all their time was spent drawing with paint programs or playing computer games.

Warschauer's evaluation resonates with early research findings about the use of computers in schools. There has been much evidence demonstrating that when computers are used, the students in privileged socioeconomic school environments are given intellectually demanding assignments that require creative and complex application of the technologies. By contrast, in poorer schools the emphasis is on pre-packaged drill-and-skill exercises with little evidence that the skills transfer to other learning settings and situations (Snyder 2008). Although not located in formal school contexts, the 'hole in the wall' experiment has similar characteristics. The children in India had access to computers and the Internet, but the activities with which they engaged were low level and educationally unchallenging. The research findings suggest that questions always need to be asked about not simply physical access to technology, which is largely a matter of income and/or interventionist policies, but also about the quality and nature of the access. How the technologies are used is also influenced by the cultural resources children and their families can bring to bear on their relationship with technology (Snyder et al. 2004).

The $100 laptop

The second story is about the $100 laptop program in Brazil. The first version tells of Boston 'Brahmin' Nicholas Negroponte's bold initiative, which aimed to provide hundreds of millions of the world's poor children aged six to 12 with portable, Internet-enabled computers. Negroponte and his team at MIT designed $100 laptops, aiming to sell them to the governments of technologically underdeveloped countries. The plan was to distribute the computers en masse to the participating countries' children.

By November 2005, the One Laptop per Child (OLPC) not-for-profit organisation was in operation and a prototype was unveiled. Negroponte's vision of the $100 laptop – special design, free and open-source software, special display, no movable parts and low energy use – became a reality: 'the children's machine' was launched by Nicholas Negroponte and Koffi Anan in 2005 at the World Summit on the Information Society in Geneva (ITU

2009). From the beginning the project acknowledged that there is more to do than just distribute the hardware. It is not based on a one-size-fits-all model and, in the strong educational tradition of the Media Lab at MIT, promotes a constructionist approach to learning. Negroponte pointed out that considerable work would be devoted to teachers – not so much to learn what and how to teach, but more in terms of their own self-confidence and comfort with the machines.

In Brazil it became the President's project and was called *um computador por aluno* (one laptop per student) rather than 'one laptop per child'. The change in name signifies that in Brazil the project is located firmly in education and involves both the government at the highest level (the presidency) and the Ministry of Education. It has three objectives: to change the educational paradigm by initiating pedagogical innovation in education; to promote digital inclusion, with the students taking the laptops home so that members of the family can use them; and to contribute to the IT industry in Brazil, with the laptops being built locally (Valente 2008). The program also involves a committee of professors who work with the technologies (GTUCA) to advise the government – both the presidency and the ministry. The committee's role is to advise about the pedagogical implementation of the project in schools, develop teacher training strategies and produce evaluation criteria. Research has been initiated in five schools across Brazil and the preliminary findings published by the advisory committee of academics are very positive (Valente 2008).

The alternative version of the $100 laptop story is that the project in Brazil has met with difficulty after difficulty. Brazil has been a particular frustration to Negroponte, even though President Lula da Silva initially expressed support. Negroponte's not-for-profit foundation, which promised to produce the laptops, decided not to compete when the Brazilian Government opened up the tendering process to other bidders and imposed specifications. In the end, Brazil awarded a contract for 150,000 laptops to an Indian-based company. When interviewed about the Brazilian laptop project, Larry Cuban, professor emeritus at Stanford and a leading scholar on the history of the use of technology in education, said: 'If there's a lack of electricity, basic health care, [acceptable] facilities, and especially teachers, it's not such a good idea to begin with laptops'. Dismissing the contention that laptops can replace teachers, he added: 'Effective teaching is based on a relationship between an adult and children, and machines don't create those kinds of relationships' (Hatch 2009). One-hundred-dollar laptops have also reached Australia, where they have been donated to students in some remote Indigenous schools by the not-for-profit One Laptop Australia. Shepherdson College on Elcho Island is one recipient community. Two others are the Rawa Community School in Western Australia and Newcastle Waters School in the Northern Territory (Guest 2009). Research investigating the effects of their implementation has yet to emerge.

eGranary

The third story is about a proposal for a research project to use eGranary (WiderNet Project 2009), an off-line digital archive developed by the University of Iowa Foundation, in Uganda. The first version tells of a group of academics from North America who are working with colleagues in Uganda on a project to bring the children of that developing nation into the age of the Internet (Mutonyi and Norton 2007). The research team has chosen eGranary as the technological resource that will underpin the project. The eGranary digital library provides millions of digital educational resources to institutions lacking adequate Internet access. Through a process of garnering permissions, copying websites, and delivering them to intranet web servers within the partner institutions in developing countries, eGranary delivers millions of multimedia documents that can be instantly accessed by patrons over their local area networks at no cost. The researchers would prefer to provide Ugandan children with direct access to the Internet but, as this goal is unachievable, the team has chosen eGranary archival software as a viable alternative.

The second version of this story is not yet available, as the project is still under consideration for major funding, but the very idea raises a number of important questions that confront all such initiatives. To raise just a few: Is providing inferior digital resources to a developing country better than no resources? What criteria were used in the selection of the educational resource to include in the archive? What was excluded? Are the resources in the archive so culturally specific that they won't be as useful as imagined?

An education revolution

The fourth story is located in Australia. The first version tells of prime ministerial aspirant Kevin Rudd promising a revolution in education if Labor were elected. As soon as his government came into office in November 2007, Rudd moved to initiate the revolution. Integral to the policy is the 'digital education revolution' (DER). Its aim 'is to contribute sustainable and meaningful change to teaching and learning in Australian schools that will prepare students for further education, training and to live and work in a digital world' (DEEWR 2009).

Through the DER, the government has allocated $2.2 billion over six years to provide computers for all secondary schools with students in Years 9 to12; support high-speed broadband connections to Australian schools; collaborate with states and territories and deans of education to ensure that new and continuing teachers have access to training in the use of information and communication technologies (ICT) 'that enables them to enrich student learning' (DEEWR 2008); provide online curriculum tools and resources that support the national curriculum and specialist subjects such as languages; enable parents to participate in their children's education through online learning; access support mechanisms to provide vital assistance for schools in the deployment of ICT. The execution of the DER will be guided by the Digital Education Revolution Implementation Roadmap (AICTEC 2009). A revolution indeed, if successfully implemented.

Although not explicitly part of the DER, in July 2009 the Council of Australian Governments announced that the federal government would spend $7 million on providing public Internet access facilities in remote Indigenous communities over the next four years, as part of its Closing the Gap initiatives, and will also deliver training in basic computer and Internet use in up to 60 remote communities a year (Dearne 2009). Clearly, schools are likely to benefit from this investment in IT infrastructure.

By contrast, the second version of the story begins from a position of some scepticism in response to the very notion of engineering a 'revolution' in education. The digital education 'revolution' has been dismissed in the media, by critics from both the left and the right, as pure hyperbole – a lot of high-minded promises, not well thought through, and without sufficient funds to resource them (eg Donnelly 2008; McShane 2009). The roll-out of computers to secondary-school students has also been the subject of persistent criticism. Concern has been expressed about the emphasis on providing the hardware with not sufficient allowance for technical support systems and provision for teachers' professional learning. There have even been instances of principals refusing to accept the computers because they do not have the funds to resource these essentials (Milne 2008).

Further, the rationale offered by the state government leaders as to why there is a need to ensure access to technology is questionable. According to the Joint Ministerial Statement on ICT in Australian education and training, 2009–2011: 'Australia will have technology enriched learning environments that enable students to achieve high quality learning outcomes and productively contribute to our society and economy' (DEEWR 2008). But does access to technology 'enable' students to achieve 'high quality learning outcomes', which is code for improved scores on the NAPLAN (National Assessment Program – Literacy and Numeracy)?

There has been much research investigating this question since computers first entered schools in large numbers in the late 1970s. In my own field of literacy studies, the initial question was: Does the use of computers improve the quality of students' writing? A more recent version of this question asks: What is the impact of computers on students' literacy outcomes? The findings have been consistently equivocal: about half the studies claim an impact, about half claim no impact, while some even claim that the use of new technologies actually makes things worse (Andrews 2004; Snyder 2008). Such a mix of findings does not provide a strong evidence base to inform policy decisions.

In 2009 The Le@rning Federation, a joint initiative of the state, territory and federal governments of Australia and New Zealand, published a report on a series of research projects investigating the effectiveness of using digital curriculum resources with Indigenous students in remote, regional and urban settings (Le@rning Federation 2009). The study found that the resources supported motivation and engagement – not to be scoffed at – but not higher scores as measured in the NAPLAN. There is simply no persuasive evidence that demonstrates the existence of a causal relationship between the use of computers and improved outcomes as measured in test scores.

A far more compelling argument for providing students with ICT access is that new technologies are playing such a critical role in society, culture and economics that unequal access can have devastating consequences for individuals and communities. Manuel Castells' (1996) vision of the network society, elaborated in the mid-1990s, still holds: when access is inequitable, the more privileged become the 'interacting', with the skills, knowledge and resources to select or create their multimedia circuits of communication, while the less privileged become the 'interacted', limited to passive access to pre-packaged choices. In other words, the interacting are those with the skills and capital to shape the multimedia context of the future and the interacted are those who are recipients of multimedia content created by others (Warschauer 2009).

To return to the Australian Government's DER policy documents, there is no reference to supporting Indigenous students, particularly those located in remote communities. The rhetoric of the revolution is to provide resources for *all* Australian students. Clearly, there is much value in focusing on the diverse digital needs of *all* Australian children and young people, but it sounds a little like the one-size-fits-all approach to education that innovative educational reformers such as Negroponte have tried hard to avoid, and which researchers know don't work if sustained change is the goal.

In a speech to launch a book at the Institute of Public Affairs in Melbourne in September 2009, conservative historian Geoffrey Blainey made a plea for the 'quiet burial' of the phrase education revolution, branding it more a slogan than a model for educational change (Wilson 2009). Blainey pointed out that the last time there was a revolution in education in Australia was in the late nineteenth century, when the state of Victoria led the charge for compulsory education. This was a step that placed Australia, a vast land where many could not read and write, ahead of most other nations in terms of educational opportunities. But, Blainey added, even this 'real' education revolution failed to reach most Aboriginal settlements. 'Since then, primary education has retreated in many Aboriginal regions. In that sense, the real education revolution of the 1870s is still uncompleted.' Blainey urged the government, at whatever cost, to revitalise primary schools for Aboriginal children and encourage them to attend regularly.

Drawing the threads together

The four projects in India, Brazil, Uganda and Australia were motivated by a genuine attempt to improve children's educational opportunities through access to new technologies. In India, Brazil and Uganda, the focus has been on marginalised children; in Australia, on 'all' children. However, in each case there have been unexpected difficulties that have limited the sought-after educational outcomes. With the emphasis too often on providing hardware and software, not enough attention has been given to the social systems that must also change for technology to make a difference. Access to new technologies with the potential to produce significant consequences for users involves more than the provision of computers and connection to the Internet. What is required is a more complex explanation of access that involves not only physical and digital resources but also human resources and social relationships, as the new technologies are embedded in existing social relations, which influence their social distribution and impact.

As Warschauer (2003) emphasises, content and language, literacy and education, and community and institutional structures must all be taken into account if meaningful access to new technologies is to be provided. But even when efforts are made to complicate the notion of the digital divide in such ways, its original sense is so strongly associated with the availability of computers and connectivity rather than with issues of content, language, education, literacy or social resources, that it is difficult to replace it with an alternative sense in people's minds.

Another problem with the notion of the digital divide is the implication that society is split into two: the haves and the have-nots. In reality, these two monolithic groups do not exist, yet they continue to be invoked. What does exist is perhaps better captured by the notion of a 'spectrum of access' (Haythornthwaite 2007). Compare, for example, a professor at Monash Australia with a high-speed connection in her office, a student in Cape Town who occasionally uses an Internet café, and a teacher in a remote part of Brazil, who has no computer or phone line but whose colleagues in the Ministry of Education print out digital materials for her to use in her school setting. These are just three examples of the spectrum of possible access.

The notion of a binary divide between the haves and the have-nots is too simplistic to capture the complexity of social barriers to Internet use (Willis and Tranter 2006). It is also probably patronising because it fails to acknowledge the resources that people manage to exploit in unexpected and creative ways. In Australia, Indigenous Australians are often portrayed as being on the wrong side of the digital divide, when in fact access varies by, at the very least, income group and location. Just as it is inaccurate to present a monolithic vision of Aboriginal people in Australia that fails to acknowledge the multiplicity inherent in Indigenous cultures – manifest in the many language groups, diverse histories and different experiences of Indigenous people – so too is it inaccurate to present Indigenous Australians, particularly those in remote communities, as the technology have-nots who lack access to computers and the Internet (cf McConaghy and Snyder 2000).

Descriptions of Indigenous Australians as located on the wrong side of the digital divide contain traces of 'Aboriginalism' (Hodge 1990; Attwood 1989; 1992), the discursive regime that has been particularly effective in producing a dominant representation of Indigenous Australians. Drawing on Said's (1978) notion of orientalism, 'Aboriginalism' refers to the production of texts about Indigenous Australians that emerge as integral to the imposition of authority and power over them. The Aboriginalist project is described by Bain Attwood (1992) as taking three interdependent forms: researching and speaking about Indigenous people; constructing 'them' as oppositional to 'us';

and maintaining institutions for the disciplining, administering and ruling over Indigenous Australians.

A related way of thinking about the discourses of Aboriginalism is through the lens of 'culturalism' (McConaghy 2000). Integral to this framework is the assumption of two immutable and oppositional cultures: 'Indigenous' and 'western'. McConaghy argues that culturalism has for many decades sustained a politics of racialisation in a wide range of Australian social institutions and academic disciplines, including education. The framework demands that before issues of policy, curriculum and pedagogy can be debated, issues of culture must be considered. Reflections of the two contrasting cultural formations are everywhere – in the research literature, in policy documents, in the media and in popular discourses.

Take, for example, the continuing debate in Australia over teaching bilingualism in remote communities, which heated up recently, again. In July 2009 the Northern Territory Government dismantled bilingual and bicultural education because it claimed that it was responsible for lower literacy levels. The new policy requires teachers to provide Indigenous children with intensive English classes for four hours each day, which does not leave much time for the children to learn in their own languages. The plan has generated impassioned debate among educators, academics and Indigenous community members, with critics arguing that the proposal will severely limit the opportunities for Indigenous involvement in education – that it devalues Indigenous languages and language learning. This action by the Northern Territory Government has had a full range of responses in the media – praise, condemnation and resistance – and all were evident in the September ABC *Four Corners* program that focused on the change in policy (Whitmont 2009). Evident in the journalist's questions and narration, and in the views of those interviewed, were traces of culturalism.

Culturalism favours 'culture' as an explanatory tool for understanding matters of social difference and uses the notion indiscriminately to explain diverse issues in contrasting contexts. It views 'cultures' as essentially knowable, bounded and separate. The word 'culture' is used to include every action and every belief in a total system, as a way of life, and members of different cultures are thought to share world views (McConaghy 2000). Like Aboriginalism, culturalism is reductive and unhelpful, as too often it is used as an excuse to stymie the tough policy decisions needed to move things forward in Indigenous education (Pearson 2009).

Describing Indigenous Australians in remote communities as located on the wrong side of the digital divide feeds off popular narratives about

Indigenous education that are informed by Aboriginalist and Culturalist representations. Integral to these narratives is the notion of 'the essential Aborigine', a construction that has long been associated with 'Indigenous incapacity' (Hodge and Mishra 1991). As a direct consequence, pedagogical efforts are directed towards dealing with a 'lack' of some sort among Indigenous Australians. In the context of this chapter, Indigenous children 'lack' digital literacy, that is, the literacy skills associated with the use of computers and the Internet. The children are in 'deficit' as they lack 'functional' digital literacy, a label that expresses a narrow understanding of literacy. Brian Street (1984) calls this an 'autonomous model' of literacy – that literacy, defined independently of cultural context and meaning, will have effects, creating inequality for those who 'lack' it and advantages for those who gain it (Street 2009). Thus providing access to computers and the Internet becomes a project aimed at redressing the 'lack' of digital literacy skills among Indigenous children.

Despite vigorous debates within Indigenous education in Australia, the polarisation of black and white Australians works to sustain beliefs in Indigenous incapacity, poverty of expression and general primitiveness. Martin Nakata's (1991) analysis of the positioning of 'the Torres Strait Islander' in this literate/illiterate binary is useful here. He explains how constructions of literacy and illiteracy were used as a technology for colonial subjugation – for the degeneration and dehumanisation of Torres Strait Islanders. In a similar way, Bain Attwood's (1996) work has promoted more awareness of how Aboriginalism sustains repressive dichotomies or dualisms between black and white. Constructions of digital literacy skills and the lack of them perpetuate the regime of bifurcating white and black Australia.

The limitations of representing complex social and educational issues as simple dichotomies are manifold. But there is an alternative – a more productive way forward. Today the ability to access, adapt and create knowledge using new technologies is critical to full social participation. A focus on social participation shifts the discussion of the digital divide from something to be bridged by providing material resources to social challenges to be met by integrating technology into communities, institutions and societies. Most important is not so much the physical availability of computers and the Internet – although that of course is important – but the ability of children and young people in peripheral communities to use the technologies to engage in meaningful social practices in the social, cultural and economic dimensions of their lives.

Social participation rather than a digital divide

Despite the significant differences in access to computers and the Internet between Indigenous and non-Indigenous communities, and between remote and non-remote communities, the notion of the digital divide is unhelpful (see Hunter 2005 for statistical evidence of the differences). It tends to suggest digital solutions – computers and telecommunications – to the exclusion of other equally if not more important factors. Computers and connectivity do not exist as material resources to be inserted from the outside to produce desired educational outcomes. Technologies are always deeply enmeshed in social systems, processes and practices (Lankshear and Snyder 2000).

The goal of using computers and the Internet with marginalised groups is not to overcome a digital divide but to advance processes of genuine social participation. To accomplish this goal, both the material resources and the social changes required need to be considered. The digital divide was a useful concept historically – it helped to draw attention to inequity – but today finding language that supports social participation and more accurately portrays the complex issues involved is likely to be more productive.

Social participation refers to the extent to which individuals, families and communities are able to take part in society and control their own destinies, taking into account a variety of factors related to 'economic resources, employment, health, education, housing, recreation, culture, and civic engagement' (Warschauer 2003, 8). Social participation is not only about sharing resources, but also about contributing to the determination of individual and collective life chances. It overlaps with socioeconomic equality but is not equivalent. There are many ways that Indigenous Australians in remote communities can enjoy fuller participation, even though they lack an equal share of resources. The concept of social participation does not ignore the role of race and location but recognises that a broad array of other variables helps shape how different forces interact.

A focus on 'digital equality' draws attention to the variables involved: the hardware and software, the users' skills and capabilities, and the level of support and purpose for which the technologies are used. Of particular importance here is the notion of 'capabilities' (see Tikly this volume). It draws on the work of Sen (2002) and Nussbaum (2000) and embodies what children and young people in remote Indigenous communities are actually able to do and be in the context of the use of new technologies. Capabilities comprise at least two aspects: 'primary goods' – the knowledge and skills to act – and 'agency' – the freedom to make choices. Digital literacy capabilities thus imply more than simply digital literacy skills in a narrow sense. They also imply the opportunity for children and young people in remote communities to convert their resources into achievements and outcomes of different kinds. The notion of capabilities offers an alternative to the predominant global focus on economic wealth as a measure of development; it has the potential to bridge and extend human capital, and human rights and entitlements, approaches to education (see Snyder 2008).

When these factors are taken into account, the focus shifts to the relationship between access and the use of technology for social and economic equality. Success at school is vitally important, but not if the sole emphasis is on raising children's test scores, which is a highly politicised and contested terrain in Australia (Snyder 2008), as it is in New Zealand and South Africa. Rather, the concern for education in remote communities becomes how to provide classroom opportunities for technology-mediated practices that are related to achieving social, economic and educational power. These essential practices include finding, critiquing and deploying sophisticated multimedia texts.

Beyond 'closing gaps' and 'bridging divides'

'Divides to bridge' and 'gaps to close' are powerful metaphors in terms of their rhetorical impact. They demand people's attention, appear to pinpoint the key issues and provoke conversation and action. As the title of an important conference, 'Closing the gap' did the trick. It was sufficiently appealing to attract the participation of leaders in education from around the world. It highlighted the fact that there are pressing issues of inequality that urgently require solutions. It was the catalyst for important conversations across national borders and suggestions for moving forward. However, these metaphors are also profoundly problematic. They are reductive, crude and polarising. They reflect a tradition in Australia of dividing people into two monolithic groups.

Said's notion of 'making the voyage in' offers a more constructive metaphor, as it embodies hope for Indigenous education in remote communities by suggesting that progress is possible. In *Culture and Imperialism*, Said (1993) argues that the imperial politics of identity has worked to endorse separatism on racialised grounds. He advocates an alternative project of 'worldliness' to reintegrate those people once reduced to marginal or peripheral status with the rest of the human race, to assist them to make 'the voyage in', to have a voice that counts. A key challenge facing Australian education is to enable

Indigenous children and young people in remote communities to acquire the critical digital literacy capabilities necessary for active and meaningful social participation. This is their right and entitlement but, like all universal rights, it needs to be socially and culturally situated to be both meaningful and potentially democratic. Indigenous education needs to be accessible to universal rights and entitlements while providing for culturally specific and localised self-determination. The achievement of this vital educational goal involves getting the best possible mix of both imperatives. It also involves close scrutiny of the policies that make recommendations for providing access to new technologies for Indigenous children in remote communities: what they say and what they don't say, but also how they say it. These are some of the ongoing issues in regard to marginalised educational settings with which we must continue to engage.

References

AICTEC (Australian Information and Communications Technology in Education Committee). 2009. 'Digital education revolution implementation roadmap'. Canberra: Australian Government. Accessed 21 September 2009. Available from: http://www.digitaleducationrevolution.gov.au/.

Andrews, R, ed. 2004. *The Impact of ICT on Literacy Education*. London: RoutledgeFalmer.

Attwood, B. 1989. *The Making of the Aborigines*. Sydney: Allen & Unwin.

Attwood, B. 1992. 'Introduction'. In 'Power, knowledge and Aborigines', edited by Atwood, B; Arnold, J. Special edition of *Journal of Australian Studies* 35, i–xvi.

Attwood, B. 1996. 'Introduction. The past as future: Aborigines, Australia and the (dis) courses of history'. In *In the Age of Mabo. Histories, Aborigines and Australia*, edited by Attwood, B. Sydney: Allen & Unwin: vii–xxxviii.

Castells, M. 1996. *The Rise of the Network Society, Vol. 1, The Information Age: Economy, Society and Culture*. London: Blackwell Publishers.

Dearne, K. 2009. '$7m internet boost for indigenous communities'. *Australian IT* 2 July.

DEEWR (Department of Education, Employment and Workplace Relations). 2009. 'Digital education revolution'. Accessed 21 September 2009. Available from: http://www.deewr.gov.au/Schooling/DigitalEducationRevolution/Pages/default.aspx.

DEEWR (Department of Education, Employment and Workplace Relations). 2008. 'Success through partnership: Achieving a national vision for ICT in schools'. Strategic plan to guide the implementation of the digital education revolution initiative and related initiatives. Accessed 21 September 2009. Available from: http://www.deewr.gov.au/Schooling/DigitalEducationRevolution/Documents/DERStrategicPlan.pdf.

Donnelly, K. 2008. 'Chairman Rudd's education revolution'. *Quadrant Online* 7 October. Accessed 2 October 2009. Available from: http://www.quadrant.org.au/magazine/issue/2008/12/chairman-rudd-s-education-revolution.

Guest, D. 2009. 'Laptop "magic" lures young back to school'. *Australian IT* 27 April.

Hatch, D. 2009. 'Have laptop will travel'. *National Journal* 4 November. Accessed 21 September 2009. Available from: http://laptop.org/images/pdf/2009_apr_11_OLPC_National_Journal.pdf.

Haythornthwaite, C. 2007. 'Digital divide and e-learning'. In *The Sage Handbook of E-learning Research*, edited by Andrews, R; Haythornthwaite, C. Los Angeles and London: Sage: 97–118.

Hodge, B. 1990. 'Aboriginal truth and white media. Eric Michaels meets the spirit of Aboriginalism'. *Continuum* 3 (2): 201–205.

Hodge, B; Mishra, V. 1991. *Dark Side of the Dream: Australian Literature and the Postcolonial Mind*. Sydney: Allen & Unwin.

Hunter, B H, ed. 2005. *Assessing Recent Evidence on Indigenous Socioeconomic Outcomes*. Canberra: ANU E Press.

ITU (International Telecommunication Union). 2009. 'World summit on the information society'. Accessed 3 October 2009. Available from: http://www.itu.int/wsis/index.html.

Le@rning Federation. 2009. 'Using The Le@rning Federation digital curriculum resources to enhance the education of Indigenous students'. Report prepared by The Le@rning Federation. Melbourne: Curriculum Corporation. Accessed 27 September 2009. Available from: http://www.tlf.edu.au/verve/_resources/Indig_Report_web_version.pdf.

Lankshear, C; Snyder, I; Green, B. 2000. *Teachers and Technoliteracy: Managing Literacy, Technology and Learning in Schools*. Sydney: Allen & Unwin.

McConaghy, C. 2000. *Rethinking Indigenous Education: Culturalism, Colonialism and the Politics of Knowing*. Flaxton, Queensland: Post Pressed.

McConaghy, C; Snyder, I. 2000. 'Working the web in postcolonial Australia'. In *Global Literacies and the World Wide Web*, edited by Hawisher, G E; Selfe, C L. London and New York: Routledge: 74–92.

McShane, I. 2009. 'After the revolution'. *Inside Story / Current Affairs and Culture*. Accessed 2 October 2009. Available from: http://inside.org.au/after-the-revolution/.

Milne, G. 2008. 'Criticism for Rudd school plan'. *Daily Telegraph* 6 April.

Mutonyi, H; Norton, B. 2007. 'ICT on the margins: Lessons for Ugandan education'. *Language and Education* 21 (3): 264–270.

Nakata, M. 1991. 'Constituting the Torres Strait Islander: A Foucauldian discourse analysis of the national Aboriginal and Torres Strait Islander education policy'. Bachelor of Education (Hons) thesis, Queensland: James Cook University.

NTIA (National Telecommunications and Information Administration). 2000. 'Falling through the net: Toward digital inclusion'. Washington, DC: US Department of Commerce. Accessed 3 October 2009. Available from: http://www.ntia.doc.gov/ntiahome/digitaldivide/.

Nussbaum, M. 2000. *Women and Human Development*. Cambridge: Cambridge University Press.

Pearson, N. 2009. 'Radical hope : Education and equality in Australia'. *Quarterly Essay 35*. Melbourne: Black Inc.

Said, E. 1978. *Orientalism: Western Conceptions of the Orient*. London: Penguin.

Said, E. 1993. *Culture and Imperialism*. London: Chatto and Windus.

Sen, A. 2002. *Rationality and Freedom*. London: Harvard University Press.

Snyder, I. 2008. *The Literacy Wars: Why Teaching Children to Read and Write is a Battleground in Australia*. Sydney: Allen & Unwin.

Snyder, I; Angus, L; Sutherland-Smith, W. 2004. '"They're the future and they're going to take over everywhere": ICTs, literacy and disadvantage'. In *Doing Literacy Online: Teaching, Learning and Playing in an Electronic World*, edited by Snyder, I; Beavis, C. New Jersey: Hampton Press: 225–244.

Street, B V. 1984. *Literacy in Theory and Practice*. Cambridge: Cambridge University Press.

Street, B V. 2009. 'Literacy inequalities in theory and practice: The power to name and define'. Keynote presentation at Literacy Inequalities: An International Conference,

September 1–3. Norwich, UK: University of East Anglia.
Swarup, V. 2009. 'Oscar favorite…'. PR-inside.com. Accessed 21 September 2009. Available from: http://www.pr-inside.com/oscar-favorite-slumdog-millionaire-inspired-r1064438.htm.
The Le@rning Federation. 2009. 'Using the Le@rning Federation digital curriculum resources to enhance the education of Indigenous students'. Report prepared by The Le@rning Federation. Melbourne: Curriculum Corporation. Accessed 27 September 2009. Available from: http://www.tlf.edu.au/verve/_resources/Indig_Report_web_version.pdf.
Valente, J A. 2008. 'Brazilian project: One laptop per pupil'. Presentation at the Knowledge Lab, Institute of Education, University of London.
Warschauer, M. 2003. *Technology and Social Inclusion: Rethinking the Digital Divide.* Cambridge, Massachusetts: MIT Press.
Warschauer, M. 2009. 'Digital literacy studies: Progress and prospects'. In *The Future of Literacy Studies,* edited by Baynham, M; Prinsloo, M. London: Palgrave Macmillan: 123–140.
Whitmont, D. 2009. 'Going back to Lajamanu'. *Four Corners,* Australian Broadcasting Commission, 14 September. Accessed 2 October 2009. Available from: http://www.abc.net.au/4corners/content/2009/s2683288.htm.
WiderNet Project. 2009. 'eGranary: The eGranary digital library'. University of Iowa Foundation. Accessed 29 January 2010. Available from: http://www.widernet.org/digitallibrary/.
Willis, S; Tranter, B. 2006. 'Beyond the "digital divide": Internet diffusion and inequality in Australia'. *Journal of Sociology* 42 (1): 43–59.
Wilson, L. 2009. 'Bury revolution: Geoffrey Blainey'. *Australian,* 16 September.

Closing the Quality Gap in South African Education

An Analysis and Critique of the Education Roadmap

Leon Tikly
University of Bristol

Introduction

This chapter provides an analysis and critique of contemporary debates concerning the quality of education in South Africa from a social justice perspective. In particular, it focuses on the Education Roadmap, which has gained support from a range of stakeholders in South Africa, including key members of the government. It considers the Education Roadmap in relation to dominant approaches integral to understanding education quality, namely the human capital and human rights based approaches. The chapter argues that the Roadmap shares characteristics of both approaches, although it is especially influenced by the former.

An alternative approach based on social justice principles is set out. This approach, while developing and extending aspects of the dominant ones, is pertinent because it articulates historical struggles around education in South Africa. The chapter suggests that, although the Roadmap demonstrates limited characteristics of a social justice approach, it falls short in other key aspects and it is these aspects that must form the basis for ongoing struggles for a more equitable education system.

Background

A full account of the background to the Education Roadmap is provided by Bloch in this volume (see chapter 3). As Bloch points out, concerns about the parlous state of the South African education system were forcefully expressed at the ANC conference in Polokwane in 2007. The conference had itself sought to outline a more grassroots approach to policy linked to popular mobilisation. The impetus for the Roadmap, however, came from the Board of the Development Bank of South Africa (DBSA). Prompted by the recognition of a severe skills shortage in South Africa, the Chair of the Board, Jay Naidoo, a respected political figure, brought together three key people to instigate the Roadmap process. They were the education minister at the time, Naledi Pandor; the Head of the ANC education sub-committee, Zweli Mkhize; and Jay Naidoo himself. Between them they instigated a process of stakeholder consultation that, while not fully representative, included 'ANC and non-ANC aligned institutions, unions, government officials, academics, NGOs and other commentators' (Bloch 2009a, 150). Of particular importance was the presence around the same table of both the government and the main teachers union, the South African Democratic Teachers Union (SADTU).

The role of the DBSA was significant to the Roadmap process from at least three respects. At an economic level, the DBSA could present a convincing overarching rationale for focusing on education quality, namely the critical shortage of skilled manpower. At a political level, the bank appeared neutral and could position itself as an 'honest broker' in the face of sometimes conflicting interests. At a discursive level, the key role of the DBSA finds expression in the predominance of human capital concerns that relate to its function as a development bank.

The Roadmap is presented 'as only a beginning', that is, the first stage in a longer term project of consultation around education quality (Bloch 2009a). Bloch, who was involved in instigating the Roadmap as an education specialist employed by the DBSA, suggests that the process goals of the Roadmap – in the sense of bringing together a broad and representative range of stakeholders to arrive at consensus over what can be done – were at least as important as the recommendations that arose as a result of the process.

It is also important to understand the Education Roadmap as *contested*. Although it purposefully disavows any single ideological position, preferring instead the language of neutral pragmatism, it can in fact be seen as the outcome of different ideological/discursive orientations, both within and between the organisations involved in the process of formulating it. For instance, although the DBSA is understood here primarily as a financial institution and government para-statal – operating within a global, neoliberal climate, explicitly embracing human capital approaches[1] – both Bloch and Naidoo, as veterans of the anti-apartheid struggle, have in the past been staunch advocates of human rights and social justice concerns in education, as have members of SADTU and indeed the ruling ANC. Nonetheless, this chapter argues that the content as well as the tone and language of the document reflect the predominance of the powerful political and economic interests in shaping it.

In a recent book, Chisholm (2004) and the contributors to the volume have identified the formation of a new middle class that includes not only the historically advantaged groups but also the new black middle class. They make the case that education policy is currently skewed in favour of this group. With its advocacy of neoliberal 'solutions' to the education crisis, the Roadmap is likely to further entrench the interests of the middle classes, including the new black middle class, and thus it plays a legitimising role in relation to these interests. Although this chapter is critical of key aspects of the Roadmap, the intention is to contribute towards a more radical reworking of the Roadmap idea, but in the interests of historically marginalised groups.

Turning to the Roadmap itself, six areas that are perceived to hold back education are highlighted. These include the impact of intergenerational social disadvantage; the role of teachers' poor subject knowledge, teaching practices, lack of adequate numbers and of performance evaluation; dysfunctional, badly managed and poorly supported schools; a continuing lack of basic resources, including libraries and computers; poverty effects, including malnutrition and HIV/AIDS, gangs and drugs; and a lack of support for schools at provincial and district levels. The Roadmap draws on a framework developed by a leading economist of education, Martin Carnoy, which identifies three levels for action: in-school, support for school, and societal. A 10-point program was fashioned around these levels.

At the in-school level, the Roadmap prioritises getting teachers to be in class on time, teach and use textbooks; focus on the quality of early childhood development; conduct external tests of Year 3 learners annually and provide results to parents; ensure effective evaluation of teachers; enhance the recruitment of quality teachers and strengthen teacher development; offer bursaries to attract quality students into teacher training and enhance preservice and inservice teacher training; ensure that teacher unions have a formal and funded role in teacher development. At the level of support for the school, the plan prioritises the strengthening of management capacity, including bringing it in from the private sector, increasing the use of ICT in education and improving national–provincial alignment and efficiency. At the societal level, the Roadmap calls for a social compact for quality education that includes processes of community mobilisation and the implementation of poverty reduction measures involving a nutrition program (with health), basic infrastructure for schools and social support for children.

The Education Roadmap in relation to dominant approaches to understanding quality

In this section, the Roadmap is considered in relation to a critical discussion of the two dominant global discourses concerned with understanding education quality: the human capital and the human rights approaches. These have been described at length elsewhere (see Tikly and Barrett forthcoming). In reality, it is possible to trace the overlap between them.[2] However, it is useful to distinguish between them, as each involves a different underlying view of development and of how education quality is perceived and measured in relation to development. Although the Roadmap does not set out its evidential base, Bloch's (2009a) book, *The Toxic Mix*, together with a report to a parliamentary committee (Bloch 2009b) and some other technical background materials (DBSA 2008; Taylor et al. 2008), help to illuminate the overall thinking behind the document and the evidence drawn upon during the consultation process. The analysis of the Roadmap has been undertaken against a reading of these accompanying texts.

The human capital approach

Several authors have provided a summary of the shifting nature of human capital discourses globally since the 1970s (see Ilon 1994; Tikly 2004; Robertson et al. 2007; Unterhalter 2007). The central rationale for investing in education (including more recently education quality) lies in the contribution that education can make to economic growth. Here GDP is understood as the most significant indicator of development. The role of education in relation to economic growth, however, has shifted over the years. An initial focus on manpower planning gave way in the 1970s to understanding better investment choices at different levels of education through rates of return analysis. In the context of the shift from the Washington to the Post-Washington consensus (see Robertson et al. 2007), human capital theory has begun to complement a continued interest in rates of return with an interest in education's role in alleviating poverty and promoting social welfare, including women's welfare, as a basis for improving growth and human security. This has prompted a shift in political commitment from cost sharing to free primary education (Jones 2007). Nonetheless, exponents of human capital theory continue to advocate market-led, neoliberal policies as a basis for reform. While primary education has traditionally been identified by exponents of human capital theory as a priority in terms of investment, the current emphasis is widening to include secondary and post-basic levels of education and training to equip populations with the skills required to participate in the 'global knowledge economy'. It is in this context that economists working within a human capital framework have begun to show a keen interest in the quality of education (eg Wils et al. 2007; Hanushek and Wößmann 2008; Vegas and Petrow 2008).

Human capital theory had an ambiguous relationship with education policy during the transition from apartheid to democracy. Although some themes – including manpower planning and rates of return – have entered into the policy debate, they have generally been subordinate in policy terms to Afrikaner nationalist ideologies during the apartheid era and a commitment to rights-based approaches in the immediate post-apartheid phase (Chisholm and Fine 1994). However, the uptake of human capital themes in the Roadmap, particularly those concerned with decentralisation and the introduction of user fees, have become increasingly influential, as a recent collection of essays has highlighted (see Chisholm 2004). Contributors to the collection argue that the Roadmap represents a further shift in South African education policy towards the take-up of human capital themes, including the recent trend of linking the quality of education with economic growth.

In this regard, Hanushek and Wößmann (2008) argue that there is a statistically and economically positive effect of the quality of education on economic growth that is far larger than the association between quantity of education and growth. They suggest that quality, as measured by student achievement on standardised tests, correlates more strongly with economic growth than simply years spent in school. Others have argued from a human capital perspective that countries that have the highest levels of inequality in the education sector (of any kind) also have the slowest national growth rates (Wils et al. 2007). Although these findings are based largely on empirical work in high-income countries, it is claimed that there are lessons for countries such as South Africa, given the deep-seated and pervasive nature of educational inequalities. Indeed, South Africa is one of the most unequal societies in the world, with the distribution of wealth currently more unequal than it was a decade ago,[3] and these inequalities are mirrored in the education system. Human capital theory does not provide a framework for understanding education quality. Influential texts on education quality published by the World Bank have therefore often adopted school effectiveness approaches (Lockheed and Verspoor 1991; Heneveld and Craig 1996). The preferred school effectiveness frameworks are based around what can be described as a 'process model'. Inputs (in the form of financial and material resources), teacher and student characteristics are acted on by educational processes producing outcomes. The Roadmap is based around a process model developed by Carnoy (cited in Bloch 2009a) and this is discussed below.

In terms of strategies to raise the quality of education, human capital theorists typically propose market-led solutions. These are often premised on a version of rational choice theory in which individuals are presumed to act in their own economic best interests. Hanushek and Wößmann (2008), writing from a human capital approach, emphasise three key areas that reform initiatives will have to address to raise quality: creating greater choice and competition between schools, which will encourage schools to improve outcomes; greater school autonomy, including local decision making, fiscal decentralisation and parental involvement; and greater accountability through the publication of school performance data, the use of external examinations and benchmarking, including participation of countries in international tests.

From this brief overview of the human capital approach, it is clear that it has been influential in shaping the Roadmap. Although the document does not make explicit its view of development or of the relationship between education quality and development, as Bloch (2009a, 2009b) has suggested, a key rationale behind its instigation was the skills crisis and its likely impact on the economy, which is consistent with the DBSA's overall uptake of human capital themes (see also DBSA 2008). Neither does the Roadmap offer a definition of education quality. In keeping with human capital approaches, however, it clearly associates quality with the results of standardised test scores.

There are several criticisms that can be levelled at the human capital approach to education quality that apply in turn to the Roadmap. For example, it is problematic to assume a linear relationship between inputs, processes and outputs of education that is often implied by a process model. Rather, the inter-relationships between student background, resource inputs, educational processes and outputs are complex and vary according to context. The danger with a model such as that presented in the Roadmap is that it presents a one-size-fits-all approach to quality that is insensitive to the learning needs of different groups of learners and diverse learning environments. Further, the over-reliance on standardised assessments of cognitive learning as a measure of quality can also be problematic (Barrett 2009). Readily measurable cognitive outcomes shift from being privileged indicators of quality to *defining* quality. When this happens, qualitative indicators and a concern with the processes of teaching and learning in classrooms can be easily overlooked (Alexander 2008).

Further, the empirical evidence linking education quality with growth needs to be treated with caution. As Hanushek and Wößmann (2008) point out, for education quality to lead to increased wages, a strong macroeconomic and labour-market environment is necessary. This is significant for South Africa, where the macroeconomic environment has become increasingly vulnerable in the context of the global financial crisis and where large sections of the historically disadvantaged population are unemployed (eg Bhorat 2004). The danger is that education is perceived as a panacea for problems that have their root causes elsewhere in the wider economy and society.

There is also a contradiction between the concern with educational inequality in human capital theory and some of the market-led 'solutions' that are proposed. As a recent UNESCO report has highlighted, policies based on greater 'choice', competition, decentralisation and local accountability often exacerbate rather than reduce inequality (see UNESCO 2009 for a discussion of these). This has been the case in South Africa (Chisholm 2004). As various commentators have argued (Chisholm 2004; Fleisch 2007), devolving power and permitting historically advantaged schools to determine the level of fees has contributed to a growing gulf in quality between these schools and historically disadvantaged schools. This has offset other government efforts to redress historic inequalities in funding.[4] There is also limited evidence to suggest that greater local accountability and choice results in improved outcomes, particularly for disadvantaged groups (UNESCO 2009). A priority in the Roadmap document is to provide parents with more information about how schools are performing in standardised tests, so that they can hold schools to account and presumably have a basis on which to choose between schools. However, such a policy assumes that parents are able to access and interpret whatever information may be provided by schools and are in a position to influence school policy. This is a problematic assumption, given that many parents have low levels of education and lack opportunities for genuine participation in school governance, particularly the parents of disadvantaged learners (Grant Lewis and Naidoo 2004). Further, the majority of parents, particularly in the rural areas, have very limited choice of schools (Tikly and Mabogoane 1997). Thus, while these policies may provide greater choice and opportunities to urban elites, they are less likely to benefit disadvantaged learners.

As we have seen, the Roadmap identifies a raft of issues relating to teachers as a major cause of the education crisis. The background documents provide evidence about poor subject knowledge and teaching practices and a lack of qualified teachers (DBSA 2008; Taylor et al. 2008). The Roadmap correctly identifies improvements in preservice and inservice training as important for raising quality, including better coordination between different aspects of professional learning (Lewin and Stuart 2003; Sayed 2004). However, there is less evidence for some of the other, more market-led 'solutions' to the teacher crisis. For example, there is limited evidence to support the recommendation in the Roadmap to implement performance-related pay linked to performance evaluation as a means to raise quality. What international evidence that does exist suggests that it is often a mixture of factors related to professional status, overall levels of pay, job satisfaction, conditions of service, including housing and intrinsic rewards from teaching, that motivate teachers and raise achievement of learners and that the mix depends very much on the context (Bennell 2004; Muralidharan and Sundararaman 2009). There is also limited evidence that creating competition by rewarding schools that are successful at raising achievement will benefit disadvantaged learners. Indeed, such policies have often had a negative impact on equity because they have favoured schools that are already successful (UNESCO 2009). More evidence is also needed about the impact of providing incentives to graduates to address the teacher shortage. There is no guarantee that graduates drawn into the scheme will end up teaching in historically disadvantaged schools.

A final point in relation to the influence of human capital approaches is the emphasis on the 'efficiency' of the education system, which is a priority in the Roadmap. On the one hand this is a legitimate concern for South Africa, which spends a relatively high proportion of its GDP on education but has poor returns in terms of measurable outcomes. In *The Toxic Mix*, Bloch (2009a) identifies a range of issues relating to administrative capacity and lack of skills to sheer incompetence and corruption, which contribute to inefficiency. Importantly, the effects of inefficiency impact most heavily on disadvantaged learners (UNESCO 2009). What is less clear is whether these problems can be tackled through the means identified in the Roadmap.

There is no guarantee that bringing in capacity from other areas of the bureaucracy that are also likely to suffer from capacity issues will help in any way. The private sector is often seen as a panacea for the ills of the public sector, but the evidence relating to the effectiveness of public–private partnerships from other parts of the world is not clear cut. The involvement of the private sector may appear to offer short-term solutions, but it is symptomatic of the underlying issue, which is state failure. An alternative short-term solution would be to provide more and better training for bureaucrats and school principals. Other problems, such as corruption, need to be tackled through transparent processes and a mix of legal, educational and administrative means.[5] Improving efficiency and tackling corruption require a firm will and the moral commitment of leaders. These dimensions are barely addressed in the Roadmap. It is to a discussion of these issues that the chapter now turns.

Human rights approaches

In contrast to the human capital approach, the human rights approach is interested in rights to education, rights in education and rights through education (Subrahmanian 2002; Unterhalter 2007). Whereas in human capital approaches economic growth is the object of development, in rights-based approaches it is the realisation of fundamental human rights. These include the enactment of negative rights such as protection from abuse, as well as positive rights such as celebration and nurturing of learner creativity, use of local languages in schools, student participation in democratic structures and debate. While classroom processes have typically been treated as something of a 'black box' within human capital frameworks, teaching approaches that are broadly identified as learner centred and school structures that are democratic are promoted within the human rights approach. The human rights discourse has become increasingly influential globally (Tikly and Barrett forthcoming); for example, two rights-based quality frameworks have been promoted by UN agencies.

A rights-based approach to education quality has profound significance for South Africa. In this respect, campaigns for basic rights to, in and through education were central to the struggle against apartheid (Christie 1991; Kallaway 2002). In particular, learners campaigned against a profoundly unequal and racially segregated education system, against having to learn in Afrikaans, against racist and authoritarian curricula and against corporal punishment and the sexual harassment of female learners and teachers. Students' organisations argued for learner-centred approaches and for democratic participation in decision making. Since the end of apartheid, there have been some important achievements in terms of realising these rights, including the creation of a unified education system, an attempt at greater equalisation of government expenditure between historically advantaged and disadvantaged schools, and the abolition of corporal punishment. Since 1994 the South African Government has also been proactive in pioneering learner-centred curricula and pedagogy in the form of Outcomes Based Education (OBE), although this has come in for increasing criticism, including in the Roadmap.

In *The Toxic Mix*, Bloch (2009a) articulates a rationale for a focus on education quality informed by rights-based concerns. Drawing on the UNESCO 2005 framework (UNESCO 2004), Bloch argues the case for a quality education as a right in itself and as instrumental in the development of other rights, including those associated with democratic citizenship. Bloch has also articulated rights-based concerns when presenting the Roadmap to parliament (Bloch 2009b). However, these concerns are almost completely non-existent in the Roadmap document itself. Through not making explicit its values basis and seeking to couch the document in the language of 'neutrality', the result has been to reinforce implicit values and interests, including those associated with a market-led approach. There is no statement of right or entitlement to a quality education. Nor is there mention of the need to preserve negative freedoms, such as the right not to be subject to corporal punishment or sexual harassment or to be discriminated against on the basis of race, culture, religion, HIV/AIDS status or sexual orientation, despite the fact that abuses of all of these rights are a regular occurrence in South African schools (Vally 2002). The document is also silent on positive rights, such as the right to have one's culture reflected in the curriculum and to learn in one's mother tongue. Indeed, for the most part, the document can safely be described as a 'value-free zone'. Reading between the lines, however, it is possible to identify two broad areas in which the Roadmap does connect with rights-based concerns.

The first of these is in relation to the curriculum and pedagogy. In contrast to trends elsewhere, the Roadmap takes a step back from learner-centred approaches to instruction, at least as they have been articulated in OBE, which is identified in the background materials concerned with underachievement (DBSA 2008). Rather, the Roadmap embraces a 'return to basics' in the form of the government's Foundations for Learning Campaign, which built on a smaller scale initiative in the Western Cape. In this respect the document reflects broader debates in South Africa around curriculum and pedagogy, in which OBE has often been the scapegoat for wider ills in the system. A concern about the current debate, however, is that it is in important respects rhetorical rather than based on firm evidence. For example, the Chisholm Report (DoE 2000), which undertook a review of the OBE curriculum, criticised its complexity and the implementation process but was supportive of the underlying principles of OBE. The curriculum was subsequently revised and streamlined. Contrary to some of the fears expressed in the media, it is too early to assess any long-term trends concerning the impact of OBE on matriculation rates, as the first cohort to have experienced OBE for the entirety of their schooling graduated only in 2008. It is also important not to conflate learner-centred approaches in general with the specific form that they have taken in South African schools, or to assume that learner-centred approaches are difficult to implement per se.[6] Bloch presents some powerful evidence to support a greater focus on the foundations of literacy and numeracy in the early years.[7] There is considerable international evidence to support this finding (Barrett et al. 2007). The Foundations for Learning Campaign has the virtue of having been piloted, although it is too early to assess the impact of the program. The debate in South Africa is in danger of becoming polarised between advocates of OBE, on the one hand, and of a 'back to basics' approach, on the other, when the international evidence suggests that the most effective approaches to raising the achievement of disadvantaged learners in resource-poor environments often involve a mix of child-centred and more structured forms of pedagogy, depending on the context (UNESCO 2004; Barrett 2007; Barrett et al. 2007).

The second area where the document connects with a rights-based agenda is in relation to the development of a 'social compact for quality education'. The Roadmap proposes the establishment of a National Consultative Forum dedicated to clarifying 'the "nonnegotiables" and performance targets for key stakeholders, and the monitoring thereof' (Bloch 2009a, 157). Although the language of performance targets and monitoring speaks principally of human capital concerns, there is, arguably, an implicit view of the right of stakeholders to participate in a national debate. However, while the idea of a forum does provide a limited basis for grassroots engagement, the process as outlined in the Roadmap is state led. The top-down nature of the document is reflected in the disciplinary tone of the text and background materials. Thus, although 'blame' for the crisis is perceived to lie to some extent with educational bureaucrats, most of the focus is on teacher unions, teachers themselves, managers and 'dysfunctional schools'.[8] Notably absolved from blame are senior politicians, despite the fact that it is they who have consistently failed to deliver on their election promises. The discussion draws attention to a general limitation of a rights-based approach to education quality (Tikly and Barrett forthcoming) –

at least as it has been enacted by governments and development agencies – in that it has often had as its focus the state and its institutions as the locus of change. While legal and policy frameworks are important for guaranteeing basic rights, as suggested below, civil society also has a critical role to play in advocacy and in mobilising for change.

The social justice approach

The aim of this concluding section is to set out a social justice[9] approach to understanding education quality and to use this to assess the extent to which the Roadmap advances social justice principles and concerns. The approach has been described in depth elsewhere (Tikly and Barrett forthcoming) and is summarised here. The underlying view of social justice is based on Nancy Fraser's work. Fraser (2008) defines justice as 'parity of participation' (16). She explains that 'overcoming injustice means dismantling institutionalized obstacles that prevent some people from participating on a par with others as full partners in social interaction' (Fraser 2008, 16). The framework is also informed by ongoing work in the area of capabilities and education (Brighouse 2000; Robeyns 2003; 2006; Unterhalter 2007; Walker 2006; Walker and Unterhalter 2007). The concept of capabilities is taken from the seminal work of Sen (eg 1999; 2009) and Nussbaum (2000; 2006). Capabilities and associated concepts of wellbeing have become increasingly influential in mainstream development thinking. Capabilities have been posited by Sen as an alternative to a focus on economic wealth as a measure of development and described by Nussbaum as 'a species of a human rights approach' (Nussbaum 2006, 78) and thus have the potential to bridge and extend the human capital and rights-based approaches to education quality discussed above. Put simply, capabilities are the opportunities that individuals have to realise different 'functionings'[10] that they may have reason to value and that contribute to wellbeing (Sen 1999; 2009).

Capabilities thus imply more than simply skills in a narrow sense. They also imply the opportunity for individuals to convert whatever resources they may have at their disposal into achievements or outcomes of different kinds. Besides basic literacy and numeracy, other capabilities linked to education might include access to knowledge, critical thinking, problem solving, emotional literacy and autonomy, which – besides their utility in relation to developing useful functionings – have an intrinsic value of their own (Walker 2006). In this sense, 'education quality' may be defined in terms of the opportunities to develop the greater capability set that are afforded to different individuals and groups through the processes of teaching and learning. However, for Sen what counts as a capability is context dependent and needs to be arrived at through processes of public debate and advocacy at different levels. A key focus for debate is elucidating the moral case for a quality education that provides a basis for whatever becomes enshrined in policy and law.

The social justice approach can be summarised in relation to three interrelated principles that provide a benchmark against which social justice within an education system can be evaluated. The first of these, that education should be inclusive, is concerned with ensuring that all learners achieve specified learning outcomes. The focus here is not only on access to the necessary resources to learn, but on overcoming economic, social and cultural barriers that prevent individuals and groups from converting these resources into desired outcomes. A social justice approach does not require all learners to have access to the same kind of quality inputs. Past injustices along with differing educational needs mean that learners require different kinds and levels of resources to develop their capabilities. The second principle is that a quality education must be relevant; that is, that learning outcomes are meaningful for all learners, valued by their communities and consistent with national development priorities in a changing global context. The third principle is that education should be democratic, in the sense that learning outcomes are determined through public debate and ensured through processes of accountability. In the remainder of the chapter each of these principles is applied to the Roadmap.

Turning first to the principle of inclusion, the Roadmap recognises disadvantage in access to a quality education, although there are limitations. For example, the document identifies school feeding as a priority. Evidence from an analysis of the SACMEQ II data set[11] suggests that malnutrition is arguably the most significant barrier to achievement in mathematics and literacy for the poorest 25 per cent of the population in South Africa (Smith 2010; see also Fleisch 2007). Further, the Roadmap prioritises providing more social support for disadvantaged learners, although it is unclear what is entailed by this in practical terms. There is also evidence to support the recommendation in the Roadmap concerning the use of ICTs and audiovisual equipment, although interventions need to focus on *how* technologies are deployed and their fit to desired learning outcomes if they are to be successful in raising achievement (UNESCO 2004). However, research has identified other possible interventions that are not mentioned in the Roadmap. The provision of basic materials such as exercise books, pens and rulers, and having access to a school library, all impact positively on achievement, particularly for the most disadvantaged learners, and such materials are still not uniformly available in South Africa (Smith 2010).

Further, as is the case with human capital discourses more generally, key aspects of socioeconomic inequality are glossed over in the Roadmap. The document does not make any suggestions about how to close the enormous gap in quality between historically advantaged and disadvantaged schools. There is also evidence that where children from socioeconomically disadvantaged backgrounds attend historically advantaged schools there remains a significant achievement gap between them and more advantaged learners (Smith 2010). From a social justice perspective, this implies the need to explore more effective ways to target government funding. A recent UNESCO (2009) report has identified a range of means by which governments effectively target funding to disadvantaged groups. Possible examples here include greater use of school grants to address specific forms of disadvantage; the use of funding formulae to reflect the proportion of disadvantaged learners in schools; packages of measures to attract better qualified and more experienced teachers to historically disadvantaged schools; and the use of incentives to reward schools that raise the achievement of the most disadvantaged learners (in contrast to the neoliberal emphasis on rewarding schools that are already successful in raising achievement). As with any intervention, they would need to be trialled and evaluated to assess their impact. They would also require a more robust informational basis, including a way to assess individual learners' needs, and more robust mechanisms to monitor and track their progress than those currently in place.

The focus on socioeconomic disadvantage in the Roadmap is consistent with the emphasis within human capital discourses. Further, in keeping with these discourses there is a lack of recognition of the justice claims of other marginalised groups. There is compelling evidence suggesting that a major source of underachievement that impacts most heavily on the most socioeconomically disadvantaged learners is the use of a language of instruction in the school that is not spoken widely by the child outside of school (Fleisch 2007; Smith 2010). The Roadmap is completely silent on this issue. Similarly, gender is notable by its absence from the Roadmap, despite the fact that girls in rural areas are less likely to do as well as their urban peers (Smith 2010). Sexualised forms of violence also remain a serious issue in many schools. Besides violating the rights of girls and women, schools that report sexualised violence also have lower scores in maths and literacy (Smith 2010).

Turning to the principle of 'relevance', consideration is given in the last section to the balance between different forms of curriculum content and pedagogy and different outcomes of education. It has been suggested that the Roadmap offers a narrow, instrumentalist view of education quality, focusing almost exclusively on literacy and numeracy. For authors such as Nussbaum and Sen, literacy and numeracy are key capabilities, although they form a part of a potentially much wider capability set. Although very much in its infancy, a capability approach provides a fresh perspective from which to begin to evaluate existing curriculum arrangements, including both OBE and Foundations for Learning, although space does not allow for a full discussion of the implications of this approach here (Walker 2006; Unterhalter 2007; Tikly and Barrett forthcoming). It would entail opening up to informed public debate the extent to which existing curriculum arrangements produce outcomes that learners, parents, communities and society at large have reason to value. This would involve engaging directly with the politics and practicalities of curriculum reform in a context where different stakeholders have access to different degrees of social voice (Chisholm 2003). It would also involve developing an appropriate informational basis on which a range of capabilities can be identified and measured. What is implied is an approach to curriculum change that is considerably more thoroughgoing than that proposed by the Roadmap.

This takes us to the third principle, namely that decisions about what constitutes a quality education should be democratic. This includes debates about national frameworks, but also at the provincial and school levels about how national frameworks can be implemented. What distinguishes a social justice approach is the importance that is attached to the role of grassroots civil society and community-based organisations and NGOs in advocating issues concerned with quality.[12] In the Roadmap civil society is perceived to have a role, but the role is largely confined to one of holding schools and teachers to account for poor examination grades and providing financial and other support for schools and for forms of philanthropy. It does not encompass holding politicians and elites to account for the systemic failures of the system as a whole. As Grant Lewis and Naidoo (2004) have argued, if communities are to have a genuine voice in local decision making, this involves deepening and extending the role of school governing bodies beyond a narrow concern with efficiency.

The struggle against apartheid education is a testament to the importance of advocacy on the part of civil society. A concern with the normative and ethical basis of education, crystallised into the notion of 'people's education' during the 1980s, was a characteristic of the anti-apartheid struggle and of the discourses of the post-1994 government. However, such a clear articulation of principle has been lacking in more recent debates, including in the Roadmap, as civil society has become hollowed out and radical voices incorporated into the new elites or co-opted by government. Speaking from his perspective as a veteran political activist, chapter two of Bloch's (2009a) book is taken up with an account of the apartheid past and of the struggle. What is not clear is how the social justice values and principles that were so clearly articulated during that era, and the moral imperative that drove the struggle forward, resonate with the market-led priorities set out in the Roadmap.

Endnotes

1   This is evident, for example, on the DBSA web page http://www.dbsa.org/Pages/default.aspx.
2   Indeed some of the better known quality frameworks, including that contained in the 2005 Global Monitoring Report (UNESCO 2004), bring together aspects of both.
3   The gini coefficient, which is a measure of economic inequality, has increased over the past decade from 0.64 to 0.66 in South Africa. Most developed countries have scores of between 0.20 and 0.40 (SA Institute of Race Relations (SAIRR) cited in the *Times*, 26 November 2009).
4   These have included attempts to equalise personnel costs in the period after the transition by offering voluntary severance to more experienced teachers in historically advantaged schools, and efforts to skew the infrastructure budget in favour of historically disadvantaged schools through implementing an index of need.
5   See UNESCO (2008) for a summary of evidence relating to ways to overcome corruption in education.
6   In India, for example, a longstanding tradition of learner-centred multi-grade teaching in a minority of schools (Little 2006; Blum 2009) has blossomed into the implementation of activity-based learning in state schools in Chennai and in rural areas (Sriprakash 2008).
7   He points out the appalling statistic that 62.5 per cent of Grade 3 students in former white schools in the Western Cape could read and count at appropriate levels, but that the corresponding figure in African townships was 1 per cent (Bloch 2009b, 2).
8   Bloch uses the term 'dysfunctional schools' to refer to historically disadvantaged schools with significant proportions of underachieving learners. It is suggested that this term is unhelpful because it homogenises schools that undoubtedly face a range of problems and has the effect of pathologising not only the schools themselves, but the teachers, learners and communities around the schools.
9   In applying the principles of social justice, it is important to take account of the western origins of the term and to argue the relevance of the concept for the African continent. We have attempted to do this elsewhere (Tikly and Dachi 2009).
10 Walker (2006) gives some useful examples that assist in distinguishing capabilities from functionings. Thus she distinguishes mobility (a capability) from actually being able to move around (a functioning). Similarly, she separates the capability of literacy from the function of actually reading and the capability of being well educated from acting and being a well-educated person.
11 Southern and East African Consortium for Monitoring Education Quality (SACMEQ). The analysis was carried out by the Research Programme Consortium on Implementing Education Quality (EdQual) and is reported in Smith (2010).
12 An example from elsewhere in the world is Prathan in India. This community-based organisation conducts its own assessments of quality independently of government and is involved in ongoing advocacy work around interventions to raise quality.

References

Alexander, R. 2008. 'Education for all, the quality imperative and the problem of pedagogy'. CREATE Research Monograph No. 20. Sussex: CREATE.

Barrett, A M. 2007. 'Beyond the polarisation of pedagogy: Models of classroom practice in Tanzanian primary schools'. *Comparative Education* 43 (2): 273–294.

Barrett, A M. 2009. 'The education millennium development goal beyond 2015: Prospects for quality and learners'. EdQual Working Paper Quality No. 6. Bristol: EdQual.

Barrett, A M; Ali, S; Clegg, J; Hinostroza, H E; Lowe, J; Nikel, J; Novelli, M; Oduro, G; Pillay, M, Tikly, L; Yu, G. 2007. 'Initiatives to improve the quality of teaching and learning: A review of recent literature'. EdQual Working Paper Quality No. 3. Bristol: EdQual.

Bennell, P. 2004. *Teacher Motivation and Incentives in Sub-Saharan Africa and Asia*. London: Department for International Development.

Bhorat, H. 2004. 'The development challenge in post-apartheid South African education'. In *Changing Class: Education and Social Change in Post-Apartheid South Africa*, edited by Chisholm, L. Pretoria: Human Sciences Research Council.

Bloch, G. 2009a. *The Toxic Mix: What's Wrong with South Africa's Schools and How to Fix It*. Cape Town: Tafelberg.

Bloch, G. 2009b. 'The education roadmap: Taking education forward'. Report to Parliament. Portfolio Committee on Higher Education and Training, 19 August. Accessed 26 March 2010. Available from: http://www.pmg.org.za/files/docs/090819roadmap.doc.

Blum, N. 2009. 'Small NGO schools in India: implications for access and innovation'. *Compare* 39(2): 235–248.

Brighouse, H. 2000. *School Choice and Social Justice*. Oxford: Oxford University Press.

Chisholm, L. 2003. 'The politics of curriculum review and revision in South Africa'. Paper presented at the Oxford International Conference on Education and Development, 9–11 September, at the session 'Culture, context and the quality of education'.

Chisholm, L., ed. 2004. *Changing Class: Education and Social Change in Post-Apartheid South Africa*. Pretoria: Human Sciences Research Council.

Chisholm, L; Fine, B. 1994. 'Context and contest in South African education policy: Comment on Curtin'. *African Affairs* 93: 233–248.

Christie, P. 1991. *The Right to Learn*. Johannesburg: Raven.

DBSA (Development Bank of Southern Africa). 2008. 'Education roadmap: Focus on schooling system'. Background document to the Education Roadmap Process. Accessed 26 March 2010. Available from: http://www.dbsa.org/Research/Roadmaps1/Education%20Roadmap.pdf.

DoE (Department of Education). 2000. 'South African curriculum for the twenty-first century'. Report of the Review Committee on Curriculum 2005. Chisholm Report. Pretoria: DoE.

Fleisch, B. 2007. *Primary Education in Crisis: Why South African School Children Underachieve in Literacy and Mathematics*. Cape Town: Juta.

Fraser, N. 2008. *Scales of Justice: Reimagining Political Space in a Globalizing World*. Cambridge: Polity Press.

Grant Lewis, G S; Naidoo, J. 2004. 'Whose theory of participation? School governance, policy and practice in South Africa'. *Current Issues in Comparative Education*. 10 May: 100–112.

Hanushek, E; Wößmann, L. 2008. *Education Quality and Economic Growth*. Washington, DC: World Bank.

Heneveld, W; Craig, W. 1996. *Schools Count: World Bank Project Designs and the Quality of Primary Education in Sub-Saharan Africa.* Washington, DC: World Bank.

Ilon, L. 1994. 'Structural adjustment and education: Adapting to a growing global market'. *International Journal of Educational Development* 14 (2): 95–108.

Jones, P W. 2007. *World Bank Financing of Education: Lending, Learning and Development.* 2nd edn. London: Routledge.

Kallaway, P. 2002. *The History of Education Under Apartheid: 1948–1994: The Doors of Learning and of Culture Shall Be Opened.* Cape Town: Creda.

Lewin, K M; Stuart, J S. 2003. 'Researching teacher education: New perspectives on practice, performance and policy'. Multi-Site Teacher Education Research Project (MUSTER) Synthesis Report. London: Department for International Development.

Little, A. 2006. *Education for All and Multigrade Teaching.* Springer: London.

Lockheed, M E; Verspoor, A M. 1991. *Improving Primary Education in Developing Countries.* Oxford: Oxford University Press for the World Bank.

Muralidharan, K; Sundararaman, V. 2009. 'Teacher performance pay: Experimental evidence from India'. Accessed 26 March 20010. Available from: http://econ.ucsd.edu/~kamurali/teacher%20performance%20pay.pdf.

Nussabaum, M C. 2000. *Women and Human Development: The Capabilities Approach.* Cambridge, UK: Cambridge University Press.

Nussabaum, M C. 2006. *Frontiers of Justice: Disability, Nationality, Species Membership.* Cambridge, Massachusetts: Belknap Press.

Robertson, S; Novelli, M; Dale, R; Tikly, L; Dachi, H; Alphonce, N. 2007. *Globalisation, Education and Development: Ideas, Actors and Dynamics.* London: Department for International Development.

Robeyns, I. 2003. 'Sen's capability approach and gender inequality: Selecting relevant capabilities'. *Feminist Economics* 9 (2–3): 61–92.

Robeyns, I. 2006. 'Three models of education: Rights, capabilities and human capital'. *Theory and Research in Education* 4: 69–84.

Sayed, Y. 2004. 'The case of teacher education in post-apartheid South Africa: Politics and priorities'. In *Changing Class: Education and Social Change in Post-apartheid South Africa*, edited by Chisholm, L. Pretoria: Human Sciences Research Council: 247–265.

Subrahmanian, R. 2002. 'Engendering education: Prospects for a rights based approach to female education deprivation in India'. In *Gender Justice, Development, and Rights*, edited by Molyneux, M; Razavi, S. Oxford: Oxford University Press.

Sen, A. 1999. *Development as Freedom.* Oxford: Oxford University Press.

Sen, A. 2009. *The Idea of Justice.* London: Penguin.

Smith, M. 2010. 'Socio-economic status and school effects in South Africa'. EdQual Working Paper. Bristol: EdQual.

Sriprakash, A. 2008. 'Negotiating "quality" pedagogy: Child-centred teaching in rural Indian primary schools'. Paper presented at BAICE Annual Conference. University of Glasgow, 4-6 September 2008.

Taylor, N; Fleisch, B; Schindler, J. 2008. 'Changes in education since 1994'. Paper commissioned by the Presidency for the Fifteen Year Review Process. Pretoria: Office of the President.

Tikly, L. 2004. 'Education and the new imperialism'. *Comparative Education* 40 (2): 173–198.

Tikly, L; Dachi, H. 2009. 'Social justice in African education in the age of globalization', in *Handbook of Social Justice in Education*, edited by Ayers, W; Quinn, T; and Stovall, D. Oxford: Routledge: 120-137.

Tikly, L; Barrett, A. Forthcoming. 'Social justice, capabilities and the quality of education in low income countries'. *Journal of International Educational Development.*

Tikly, L; Mabogoane, T. 1997. 'Marketisation as a strategy for desegregation and redress: The case of historically white schools in South Africa'. *International Review of Education* 43 (2–3): 141–161.

UNESCO. 2004. 'EFA global monitoring report 2005: Education for all, the quality imperative'. Paris: UNESCO.

UNESCO. 2009. 'EFA global monitoring report 2009 – overcoming inequality: Why governance matters. Paris: UNESCO.

Unterhalter, E. 2007. *Gender, Schooling and Global Social Justice.* London and New York: Routledge.

Vally, S. 2002. 'Violence in South African schools'. *Current Issues in Comparative Education* 2 (1): 80–90.

Vegas, E; Petrow, J. 2008. *Raising Student Learning in Latin America: The Challenge for the 21st Century.* Washington, DC: World Bank.

Walker, M. 2006. 'Towards a capability-based theory of social justice for education policy-making'. *Journal of Education Policy* 21 (2): 163–185.

Walker, M; Unterhalter, E, eds. 2007. *Amartya Sen's Capability Approach and Social Justice in Education*. Basingstoke: Palgrave Macmillan.

Wils, A; Carrol, B; Barrow, K. 2007. 'Educating the world's children: Patterns of growth and inequality'. Accessed 26 March 2010. Available from: http://www.poledakar.org/IMG/pdf/EPDC-2005-EducatingTheWorldsChildren.pdf.

Section 4:
Enhancing social justice and equity

Stronger Smarter Approaches to Indigenous Leadership in Australia

Chris Sarra
Indigenous Education Leadership Institute, Queensland

When I was the principal at Cherbourg State School in Queensland, I remember on occasions saying to the staff there, 'This work is more than just getting children to read and write. Our work at school here can play a part in transforming the community and, who knows, maybe our work will influence how other teachers have to work with Indigenous children right across the country!' It turns out that in some ways I was right. Under the 'Strong and Smart' philosophy and the efforts of the teachers, parents, children and those solid Indigenous men who worked alongside me as brothers, we set out on that journey. We didn't know it at the time, but in many ways our efforts provoked teachers and school leaders across the country to re-examine their approaches to Indigenous children in their schools and in particular their attitudes and expectations.

Eventually I left Cherbourg State School and, as the founding director of the Indigenous Education Leadership Institute (now The Stronger Smarter Institute) at Queensland University of Technology, I said that I wanted my team to set about changing the tide of low expectations of Indigenous children in schools. To do this we have worked with school and community leaders across Australia in leadership programs to arm them with the belief and the capacity to create high expectations, school cultures that are intent on developing and embracing a positive sense of Indigenous identity, and schools that Indigenous parents can truly connect with and that all Australians can be proud of.

From the outset I have refused to work with those in schools who have to be convinced that delivering better quality education outcomes for our children is a good thing. Instead, we work with those who are ready to be worked with, and who create a critical mass of school leaders who believe that we really can deliver on the promise of a stronger smarter future for Indigenous children.

Those who work with us understand very well the need for our children to be stronger and smarter. It is a fundamental human right of our children to have an education that makes them stronger, in a way that enables them to develop a rich and positive sense of their own cultural identity; and smarter, in a way that enables them to participate in a modern society as any other Australian would. If schools only seek to make Indigenous children smart, without developing any positive sense of cultural identity, then we do little more than assimilate them into the mainstream. In this circumstance we all lose.

I'd like to extend the discussion of the 'strong and smart' philosophy beyond school communities, to a broader application as it relates to Indigenous identity and, specifically, to notions of Indigenous leadership. Obviously, the patterns observed in schools regarding teacher perceptions of Indigenous children can be found in mainstream perceptions of Indigenous people in general. They affect the ways in which government policies and service delivery is shaped for Indigenous people; they also affect Indigenous leadership and potential leadership within Indigenous communities. The strong and smart philosophy applied more generally entails:

- challenging Indigenous Australians' perceptions about themselves and their capacity to sustain themselves
- imagining and articulating a future to which we are all accountable as stakeholders
- asserting and maintaining a culture of high expectations at home, in our communities and in society at large
- aligning our interests in the pursuit of excellence.

It is vital that those of us who are on the main stage, speaking on behalf of and working with Indigenous people, do not find ourselves ascribing to and colluding with self-perceptions that make us powerless to change.

Perceptions of Indigenous Australians

My own research, as well as countless anecdotes readily available in everyday conversations and the news media, suggest that mainstream Australians often have negative perceptions of Aboriginal and Torres Strait Islanders (Sarra 2005). As we all know, perception is interpretation, not reality, so it should be no surprise that a corresponding large number of people hold negative views of people or groups of people they have never met or interacted with.

It is not uncommon to hear the following words or phrases used to describe Indigenous people:

- alcoholics, drunks
- boongs, coons, niggers, black bastards, gins, darkies
- got it good, well kept by government, privileged
- welfare dependent, dole bludgers, handout syndrome
- lazy, won't work
- aggressive, violent, troublemakers, disrespectful.

This is certainly not who we are, which is not to deny that we have these elements in our communities, as all communities do, but it is to affirm that these descriptors are not part of Indigenous cultural identity. These are stereotypes we have acquired, just as movies depict Italians as mobsters. Surely we don't think all Italians are in the Mafia?

What makes these words even more powerful is that there are some Indigenous people who hold such views of their communities; this is particularly true of middle-class Indigenous people who may be embarrassed, disappointed and ashamed of some of the disturbing news reported about our communities. However, ascribing to and maintaining these negative perceptions of Indigenous people is counter-productive in a society committed to social inclusion.

It is our time to assert our place in the nation with honour and dignity. For too long we have been the 'other' in Australian society. Historically, Australia has tried to engineer us as the 'other' – either as little more than slaves or domestics or as hopeless and despicable. They have even rounded up a few of our own to validate this belief and design policy to inflict punishment upon us. Many of us have always known, however, that we are more than this. A different truth has always existed about us and it is time to assert that truth in a way that will not threaten white Australia but, instead, set us all free.

Some Australians think the solutions lie in abandoning the notion of being 'other' in Australian society so that we can all be the same. But this is not an Australian future to which we should aspire. We must be content being the 'other', with no desire to be the 'same' as mainstream Australia. We must choose to be 'other', but only on the grounds that *we* decide what kind of 'other' we will be. We will triumph as Indigenous Australians when we assert ourselves in Australia as the Strong, Smart, Black and Deadly Australians that we are.

In our triumph, it is crucial that other Australians do not feel threatened or divided by this aspiration. Embracing our blackness and celebrating the notion that we are the only Australians who are connected to the oldest human group on the planet, and the true descendants of the very first Australians, has never been about putting white Australians down.

As a people, we have known what it is like to be put down. This is not something that is good to inflict upon other human beings. Of course, we must never forget the sacrifices of our old people in the past, who walked in the long grass to lay a solid platform upon which many of us as Indigenous people could proudly stand. We must also keep in our minds the times when some of us had to fight. The Redfern Riots, the courage of Lex Wotton and the Palm Island riots; while we never want to revisit such times, they serve as reminders to all Indigenous people that our children still have a journey to make into a stronger smarter Australian future. It is a journey they must be armed for. Not with rocks and sticks and petrol bombs, but with intellectual, psychological and spiritual integrity.

For me, a stronger smarter Indigenous identity means that we are proud to be Aboriginal or Torres Strait Islander. We will stand up for ourselves. We may not always agree, but we can commit to working together cooperatively. These are essential ingredients if we are to imagine a better future for ourselves.

Embracing Indigenous leadership

The government, no matter who is in power, is not our solution. We have to be explicit about how to work productively with our communities. We have to be committed to decreasing the health, social and economic gap between Indigenous and non-Indigenous Australians. In the process, we have to understand and figure out what type of Indigenous leadership we want to embrace and align ourselves with, at the community level and at the national level, as these leaders and their ideas can have a direct impact on the lives of Indigenous communities.

So the question is: What kind of leadership do we develop for the twenty-first century to reflect the hopes and aspirations of Indigenous Australians?

I've assessed over time that there seem to be three categories of Indigenous leadership:

- those who focus on being the victim – leaders who make use of the victim culture
- those who focus on booting the victim – leaders who find political leverage in denigrating Indigenous people as part of their 'tough love' strategy
- those who look beyond the victim – leaders who embrace a positive Indigenous cultural identity as complementary (if not essential) to success rather than an impediment to it.

Being the victim

Many Indigenous Australians, and indeed many Indigenous communities around the world, have come to be seen and in turn see themselves as victims of history. It is clear that our colonial histories have left us with the idea that Indigenous people are the victims and that colonisers are the victimisers. In adhering to a victim culture, the two (victim and victimiser) are co-dependent; without each other the culture could not exist.

Over the years, Australian governments for their part have either affirmed or denied their role as victimiser, depending on the politics of the day. In turn, Indigenous communities have affirmed or attempted to shed light on their victimisation, depending on the counter-politics of the day. Some Indigenous leaders have found success in encouraging victimhood, leading a cause that leaves Indigenous people powerless to act on their own behalf and therefore at the mercy of those in power. They are encouraged to see themselves as victims – victims who should be compensated in some way or every way by the victimisers for their historical grievances.

Psychologist Dr Ofer Zur (1994) observes:

> In claiming the status of victim and by assigning all blame to others, a person can achieve moral superiority while simultaneously disowning any responsibility for one's behavior and its outcome. The victims 'merely' seek justice and fairness. If they become violent, it is only as a last resort, in self-defense. The victim stance is a powerful one. The victim is always morally right, neither responsible nor accountable, and forever entitled to sympathy.

Leading through victim status entails pushing for preferential treatment, as will all Indigenous leaders to some extent, but in this model Indigenous communities are likely to be seen as mere receivers of service rather than creators, implementers or consultants. Under this type of leadership things happen 'to' Indigenous communities, not 'with' them, since adhering strictly to victim status means that Indigenous people are not responsible for their own lives and are what Malcolm X called 'zombies', marching to the beat of someone else's orders.

Booting the victim

There are those who have discovered that, while being the victim is compelling at some levels, it is not always politically attractive. Therefore, another group of Indigenous leaders have found political traction by blaming the victim. In this sense, Indigenous communities fare worse than their white counterparts for a variety of reasons, many of them having to do with cultural pathologies and self-destructive values held by Indigenous people. The underlying assumption in blaming the victim is that if Aboriginal and Torres Strait Islanders just got their act together everything would work out fine. This type of leadership dismisses the victim story and promotes assimilation politics as the only way for Indigenous people to better themselves.

For me this is as troubling as focusing on being the victim, because it assumes that mainstream culture, white culture and white values are the standards by which all others should be judged. Indigenous identity is then seen as the thing to be overcome, rather than a society that should be more inclusive.

Some may choose to see booting the victim as a kind of 'tough love', but is it really? Since blame is a psychological construct, there are inherent biases at play when we blame people for outcomes we cannot control, based on expectations we didn't develop. We spend much of our time in this type of leadership blaming Indigenous people for being Indigenous and living in Indigenous communities with other Indigenous people. There is an over-abundance of information to be found and used as proof that Indigenous people are the cause of their own misery. This is possible according to American psychologist Mark Alicke (2000) because the 'evidential standards for blame' are usually lowered, especially when people are specifically 'seeking information to support their blame attribution'. Intentionally or unintentionally, we engage in what he calls 'biased information search' to support our desire to blame the victims for their unfavourable condition.

The need to blame the victim also means that leaders can present themselves, their personal stories and personal achievements, in the mainstream, as replicable by those who commit themselves to the task. What may be exception and particular is presented as general and universal, to be applied to all, even if it will predictably only benefit a chosen few. We have to be honest with ourselves.

There is therefore little discussion about some of the constraints faced by Indigenous communities, be they physical, psychological or situational. There are situational constraints for many Indigenous people in both urban and rural communities that are simply overlooked, such as access to infrastructure including roads, public transit, properly staffed hospitals and schools, culturally appropriate services and school curricula.

In some ways it is easy to see how Indigenous leaders can be seduced into a relationship with white Australians via processes of booting the victim. This is a seductive yet toxic relationship in which Indigenous 'leaders' are embraced readily, for several reasons. Firstly, when Indigenous leaders are intent on booting the victim, they validate the ignorance of those who might share such distaste for Aboriginal people. This in turn enables white Australians to scoff at the need to develop a deeper understanding of the complexities and challenges confronting Indigenous Australians. In their minds they don't need to, as they have an Aboriginal friend who says the same things they do. A convenient relationship indeed, in which white Australians can be content with their ignorance and their hatred is validated, while at the same time Indigenous leaders have the potential to attract tens of millions of dollars for such posturing.

Beyond the victim

While history has no doubt dealt us a bad hand, there is no need to wallow in it so that it cripples us from acting and creating a better present and future for our communities. When people are busy being the victim or booting the victim, very rarely do they stop to ask: What am I doing to contribute to underachievement? What am I doing to contribute to the 'disadvantage' and victimisation of Indigenous communities?

We have to be accountable for our actions; we have to have the hard conversations, focusing less on blaming and more on the plan of action forward. Researchers like Ofer Zur have shown that 'the victim culture' and blaming have not been very helpful and in fact have led to further victimisation. It is clear, then, that it is time we moved away from nurturing victimisation and from blaming Indigenous people for their plight. This is not to say that we should turn away from looking critically at Indigenous communities and behaviours within families and communities that are destructive to self and others. This is also not to shut out the voices of those who are being marginalised by government policies or corporate developments etc.

What I wish to suggest here is how to move beyond the predisposition to see Indigenous people as social inferiors who are either helpless (victims) or culpable (blamed) for their lower economic performance, educational attainment or health indicators.

We have to act under the principles of self-determination, not in the political sense but in the psychological sense, in that we have the power to shape our present and future. In fact, it is *our* responsibility to do so! Neither the mainstream nor the government can *give* us honour and dignity; we must possess it in ourselves. Marcus Garvey, the Pan-Africanist and Black Nationalist leader in the US in the first half of the twentieth century, understood well that to improve conditions leaders need to inspire hope, dignity and a positive destiny.

For me that can only be done if we move beyond victimisation, beyond the appeal to boot the victim for political gain to embrace a kind of Indigenous leadership that is not based on seeing Indigenous identity as a deficit disorder.

Moving beyond the victim status in the stronger smarter philosophy means:

- acknowledging, embracing and developing a positive sense of Indigenous identity
- acknowledging and embracing Indigenous leadership in communities, especially among our youth
- seeking and embracing innovative and dynamic ideas in our complex social and cultural contexts
- seeking and embracing innovative and dynamic people, who are committed to social justice
- committing to high-expectations leadership to ensure high-expectations communities with high-expectations family relationships.

These are five pillars that I think are achievable and necessary to move our communities forward. We've been instilling in school leaders across Australia that embracing a positive Indigenous identity in students is vital to the success of the students and the same is true within the broader society. We cannot expect to get the best out of people when our perceptions and expectations of them are negatively skewed. This is as true for the mainstream as it is for Indigenous leaders who adhere to negative perceptions of their communities. Likewise, Indigenous Australians have to embrace and assert their positive cultural identity, not as victims but as first Australians.

We must accept that there are differences within our communities and embrace them by recognising different types of community leadership. We must also create a space for our young people so that they can contribute to the wellbeing of their communities. If we do not prepare our youth for leadership, dynamic leadership based on a positive sense of Indigenous identity, we can expect that victimisation will continue and it will be our own fault.

We have to recognise that we live in a complex social and cultural space. It's not just about black and white, victim and victimiser: we live in a multicultural space. Our conversations are now about social inclusion and social justice. We have to learn to share the stage without diminishing our message or diluting our aspirations. These are things that can only be done if we are collectively, psychologically self-determined. We cannot tackle, let alone accomplish, this hard task if we see ourselves as helpless victims.

We have to be open to new ideas. This doesn't mean we accept every new idea we hear; it just means we seek out new ways of doing things and allow ourselves time to reflect and consult. We have to commit to doing things differently; to be more participatory in our own lives, in our communities. To have high expectations of ourselves, our children, our families, our communities and our leaders. We have to articulate these expectations and hold ourselves accountable for making them happen.

We have to raise our collective self-esteem and think critically and responsibly about our present, and be hopeful and decisive about our future without forsaking or diminishing our past. Indigenous Australians are not victims of history; we are survivors of circumstances. We are responsible and accountable for our actions. We have a responsibility to each other to work together to create a new way of dealing with each other and with non-Indigenous Australians. The task ahead is not an easy one, but it's a transformation that, like Cherbourg, will be filled with rewards as well as hard work and a solid commitment from all.

References

Alicke, M. D. 2000. 'Culpable control and the psychology of blame'. *Psychological Bulletin* 126 (4): 556–574.

Sarra, C. 2005. 'Strong and smart: Reinforcing Aboriginal perceptions of being Aboriginal at Cherbourg State School'. PhD thesis, Western Australia: Murdoch University.

Zur, O. 1994. 'Rethinking "Don't blame the victim": The psychology of victimhood'. *Journal of Couple Therapy* 4 (3/4): 15–36.

Redressing Marginalisation
A Study of Pedagogies for Teaching Mathematics in a Remote Australian Indigenous Community

Peter Sullivan
Monash University

Robyn Jorgensen
Griffith University

Rebecca Youdale
Community School

Introduction

The discussion in this chapter draws on a series of teaching explorations at an Indigenous community school in a remote region of Western Australia. The school was one of the sites in the Maths in the Kimberleys research project led by Robyn Jorgensen and conducted on the invitation of the Association of Independent Schools of Western Australia. The ongoing project is seeking ways to support the teaching of mathematics in small community-run schools. We see the learning of mathematics as directly connected to modernisation of communities, and that an important focus of support is to enhance the capacity of teachers to engage all students in effective mathematics learning.

The project design recognises the complexity of the educational challenges in such small communities, acknowledges those who have addressed these issues previously, and emphasises collaboration with the respective communities at each stage. This chapter outlines the context of the research, some challenges with teaching and learning mathematics for Indigenous students, the pedagogical model that we are researching, some classroom explorations that exemplify aspects of the pedagogical model, and some reflections on the opportunities and challenges with the model.

The research context

The schools serve communities that are focused on modernisation, they foster commitment to the community and there is active involvement in most schools. Most of the communities served by these schools are alcohol free, there is a mix of traditional activities such as hunting and fishing, and some access to aspects of modern living such as sporting opportunities and health care. School attendance is very good. It appears that the basic conditions for effective schools with high proportions of Indigenous students, as described by Frigo et al. (2003), are being met. In particular, Frigo et al. noted that key features of schools that supported positive outcomes were strong school leadership in partnership with local Indigenous leaders, specific actions to support regular attendance and active engagement, good teaching and Indigenous presence in the school.

The schools conduct a well-supported and highly structured program, Accelerated Literacy, which aims to set high standards for students. It revolves around allocating significant time for literacy and structured, even scripted, actions by teachers. This support for literacy is clearly a prerequisite for educational and community development, although we note that this program, given the allocated resources, has had only mixed success. While both the school leadership and the teachers are active and committed, they are inexperienced, there is a high attrition rate (although substantially less than in similar communities elsewhere) and there is limited induction to the schools, the communities and the challenges the teachers encounter.

Challenges in and approaches to teaching mathematics

Our project is exploring ways to teach the mathematics that is needed for participation in modern societies. We endorse the call by Sarra (2008) that 'Aborigines… be afforded the capacity and freedom to engage in whatever economies in whatever part of the world they choose'. We argue that success at mathematics is a prerequisite to access to opportunities for this engagement.

Yet it seems that performance overall of Indigenous students is not preparing them for these opportunities. Lokan et al. (2001) note that, while some Indigenous students are performing at the highest levels (indeed, the recent Programme for International Student Assessment (PISA) results reported that the proportion of Indigenous students at the highest level was the international average), most are well below the overall means on most aspects of numeracy. Frigo et al. (2003) noted that, while Indigenous students performed well in assessments when commencing school, by the third year of school growth had 'slowed considerably' (xi) and that much of the variation in students' scores was a function of the school. In other words, the challenges of improving access to opportunities include finding ways to improve the overall performance of Indigenous students and arresting the apparent decline in comparison with non-Indigenous students over time.

A number of studies have sought to address this decline. The theme in all of them, as articulated by Perso (2006), is that students improve when teachers recognise differences in background and learning styles, and that failing to do so can lead to teachers adopting a deficit approach, perpetuating marginalisation of these students. Frigo et al. (2003) list key elements of effective numeracy teaching – from across schools serving high proportions of Indigenous students – as teaching skills in real-life contexts, developing sound number skills, reinforcing concepts through structured activities and semi-structured play, offering low-risk opportunities to develop confidence, exploring the language of mathematics, and building on what the students know.

Several studies have attempted to explain why policies and initiatives aimed at improving Aboriginal students' mathematics achievement have often failed (eg Baturo et al. 2004). Howard (1997) argues that the imposition of a 'western' curriculum has meant that 'for many Aboriginal children… the mathematics classroom becomes an alien place characterised by tensions and conflicts about relationships and the value of what they are being taught' (17).

There have been attempts to adapt conventional western pedagogies to Indigenous contexts. For example, the Garma Living Maths program (Perso 2006) describes an approach termed 'two-way learning', indicating acceptance of a mixing of western and Indigenous knowledge, and likens the meeting of these knowledge systems to the meeting of two bodies of water in a lagoon where salt and fresh water come together. A key element in this approach is the notion of not only incorporating community values into teaching approaches, but actively engaging the community in all aspects of the curriculum and pedagogies that are adopted.

An alternative approach, QuickSmart (Pegg et al. 2005), is a four-phase process for addressing the needs of low-achieving students. The approach involves initial teaching, subsequent attempts to address difficulties experienced by some students, collaborative support for teaching by a specialist and, ultimately, withdrawal from class. The approach emphasises automaticity of skills in both reading and computation, and the measures were of the extent to which the improved automaticity enhanced higher-order processing.

Our pedagogical model draws on these various approaches, and also on our understandings of mathematics learning generally. For example, we see mathematics learning as more than the development of low-level skills, and that the strategies that have been successful for learning mathematics elsewhere in the world should also be utilised in our community schools. These include creating opportunities for students to investigate mathematically rich situations, to identify patterns and seek commonalities, and to explain reasoning and justify choices. Our approach seeks to create such opportunities.

Interactive pedagogies

Our approach, termed 'interactive pedagogies', draws on Boaler's (2008) extensive work and has also been informed by Burton's research (2004) on working mathematically and productive pedagogies (Gore et al. 2004).

This approach challenges deficit models of teaching Indigenous students and seeks to promote a rich and deep mathematical learning. The approach is founded on a strong belief that all students can learn mathematics when the pedagogy is appropriate (see Grootenboer 2009; Jorgensen 2009; Sullivan 2009). The key elements of the interactive pedagogies are:

Group work: We see group work as foundational to processes of social learning. By incorporating group work with which students are familiar in out-of-school learning, it becomes possible to draw on the skills and knowledge within a group to solve problems. The roles of the group members create interdependent learning opportunities that are not possible within parallel learning.

Home language: Students are allowed to draw on their home language (in this case, Kriol) to negotiate meanings. When reporting back, they are encouraged to use standard Australian English.

High interactivity: There is a strong focus on quality interactions – within the group work and the reporting-back stage. Good questioning is critical to this approach. Teachers develop good questions to promote learning opportunities for the students as well as students learning to pose good questions to each other.

Multi-representational: Recognising the diversity among learners, we encourage use of tasks that foster, and allow for, various methods of representation that cater for the different skills and dispositions that learners bring to the task. Provided that the result is reasonable, the pathway and mode of representation is valued.

Reporting back: This is a critical part of the lesson, where students report to the class on their approach to solving the task and the responses they have developed. Ideally, students within the classroom pose questions to the reporting group so that there is quality dialogue among peers, which ultimately promotes aspects of working mathematically, such as justifying, clarifying, generalising, conjecturing and so on. The purpose is to encourage dialogue among peers that promotes rich mathematical learning.

Tasks and activities: Our focus in this chapter is on the choice of the task, for which there are three complementary elements:

- The teachers should be clear about what they are intending to teach.
- The lessons should build on what the students know (as distinct from what they do not know).
- Tasks should be mathematically rich and draw on the 'working as a mathematician' approach, in which there should be multiple pathways and entry points for learners and multiple ways of representing thinking and learning that incorporate different learning styles and approaches.

These aspects are elaborated in the following discussion of the explorations in Rebecca's classroom.

The classroom explorations

The project overall involved regular professional learning sessions with teachers on aspects of the interactive pedagogies, supported by occasional school visits by the research team, data collection via the video-recording of lessons by the teachers, and telephone interviews with the principals and teachers. The following discussion focuses on just one aspect of the interactive pedagogies and elaborates considerations about the selection and use of tasks and activities. It draws on observations from a set of 10 lessons, spread over three separate research visits. The lessons were planned collaboratively with Peter and taught by Rebecca.

The purpose of the observations was to examine the implementation of the interactive pedagogies in real time in a classroom. Rebecca was willing to explore all aspects of the pedagogies and these observations provide a realistic indication of what is possible. Peter observed the lessons, made video and audio recordings of key moments, gathered student work samples and interviewed Rebecca before and after the lessons. The following is a discussion of the three elements of the *tasks and activities* aspect of the interactive pedagogies: the importance of having clear goals; building on what students know; and mathematical richness.

The importance of having clear goals

The importance of teacher clarity is supported by Hattie and Timperley (2007), who reviewed a range of studies on the characteristics of effective classrooms. They found that feedback was among the main influences on student achievement, the key elements of which are 'Where am I going?', 'How am I going?', and 'Where am I going to next?' The implication is that it is best if the teacher formulates specific goals for student learning, can make decisions on expectations for performance, and has some sense of where the experiences are leading subsequently. It is therefore important that the teacher establishes clear goals, so that the many interactive classroom decisions, questions and comments are made with a clear purpose in mind.

To help make the focus of teaching plain, in each of the three sets of lessons some key ideas were extracted and elaborated at the first stage of planning. The planning was iterative and took place by email some weeks prior to the teaching. To illustrate what is meant by identifying key ideas, the following were the ideas suggested after Rebecca had proposed the topic and level (Grades 3 and 4, student ages eight or nine) that were the focus of instruction.

The first sequence of lessons was on subtraction. It was proposed that the key ideas were: stating the numbers 1 and 2 before a given number; modelling numbers in terms of their parts; mental strategies that are useful for subtraction; and connecting different representations of subtraction (see Sullivan et al. 2009a). As an indication of the success of the planning and teaching, all students were individually interviewed at the end of the lesson sequence. Nearly all Grade 4 students and most Grade 3 students were able to answer the questions: 'I have eight biscuits and I eat three. How many do I have left?' and 'What is 10 take away seven?' While these are not complex tasks, the results indicate that the lesson sequence included the weaker students effectively.

Rebecca suggested that the second sequence of lessons focus on partitioning numbers, the key stages of which were proposed to be: patterns in numbers to 10 and 100; breaking numbers into parts (eg 65 is 60 + 5 as well as 50 + 10 + 5 etc); and regrouping numbers (eg 98 + 35 = 100 + ?) (see Sullivan et al. 2009b). Students were interviewed again to obtain a sense of their learning. Nearly all of the 15 students were able to count by 10s past 100; count by fives to 90; calculate 9 + 4, where the nine objects were covered, requiring counting; state the answer to 2 + 19, and most were able to answer 27 + 10. This is evidence of learning and growth.

The third sequence was about division. The key ideas suggested were: using models to represent multiplicative situations; working multiplicatively with numbers; solving problems without using models; and moving to larger numbers.

It is argued that these represent key ideas within each of these topics, and that having a clear idea of the focus of instruction is better than merely working on a collection of loosely related activities that vaguely address the topic for instruction. This clarity is helpful for choosing tasks, for explanations, for emphasising the purpose to students, for interacting with students, for interpreting their responses and for assessing their achievements. The interview assessments were not intended to measure the ceiling of learning but the extent to which students generally had learned the desired content. In this, the lesson sequences were successful.

Building on what they know

The second element also draws on Hattie and Timperley, who argue that learning is more effective when teachers identify what the students already know, so that both the activity of the task and the feedback to students can build on their prior knowledge. The confidence that students derive from working on familiar concepts can then be used as the springboard for the subsequent challenges that teachers set that lead to real learning. Perhaps paradoxically, this is an aspect that many educators find difficult.

As part of teacher learning sessions we proposed the use of contexts with which the students are familiar. These might include linking to modern ideas such as sports, or traditional ideas such as time-marking systems or the language of directions and location.

Since the development of understanding and fluency with numbers is an essential element in education for participation in modern society, a particular challenge is to identify aspects of numbers with which students are familiar. After observing students at a school fete, Rebecca commented that the students seemed to be familiar with money. The second and third sequences were developed to build on this familiarity. The following two activities show how this was enacted.

The first activity sought to build on perceptual (as distinct from conceptual) recognition of money amounts. Various combinations of $1, $2 and $5 amounts were shown for a short time and then covered. Students first whispered their answer to the person sitting next to them and then declared their answer. The observer (Peter) noted:

> The students seemed to be extraordinarily adept at doing this accurately. Given that this involves a number of key skills in combining and partitioning numbers, it created the sense of the strong foundation on which the lesson sequence could build.

This was repeated using ten 20–cent pieces first and then adding 50–cent pieces. Many of the students seemed to do this readily and it created the excitement that goes with successful completion and with challenging questions. We have video records of eight-year-old students accurately identifying money amounts as quickly as adults who have been familiar with money all their lives.

Another activity, indicating the move away from using the actual coins, was based on a well-known game, *Race to $10*, where students, starting at 0, in turn add $1 or $2, and the one who makes the total $10 is the winner. There is a winning strategy. This was then played as *Race to $1*, adding on 10 cents or 20 cents. The observer noted:

> The students were able to play the game easily, and were energetically engaged. As a review of the activity, Rebecca played this for some

time with individuals to see whether they would see the pattern, and recognise a winning strategy. Only one student did, and he was asked to report on this, but there was an emerging awareness in the others. Again, the success at the game, presumably derived from the familiarity with the money amounts, created an opportunity for engaging with the mathematical ideas. The money provided the springboard.

Using the money tasks, with which many students were familiar, created a sense of enthusiasm and success, and seemed to allow extension to straight number tasks, which was Rebecca's intent in the first place. In individual interviews after the lessons, nearly all students could recognise the total of two $2 coins and two $1 coins, shown for two seconds, and over half of the students could recognise the total of three 20-cent coins and one 10-cent coin, shown for two seconds. This both confirms the initial observations that some students were fluent with these tasks and also indicates that the lessons allowed other students to attain this fluency.

Choosing rich tasks

The third element is the choice of tasks that are mathematically rich and challenging. The nature of the tasks and associated teachers' actions are summarised in a set of recommendations for teachers (see Jorgensen and Sullivan, Chapter 4 this volume). To illustrate the nature of these tasks, the following are three examples that were used as part of the observed teaching. The first task was posed as follows:

> I am thinking of two numbers. The difference between the numbers is 2. What might be the numbers?
>
> This can be recorded symbolically as
>
> □ − □ = 2

The point is that students can explore aspects of 2 difference and even recognise the patterns of differences that appear. We want students, for example, to be able to calculate 19 − 17 as readily as they calculate 19 − 2. This type of task gives students the opportunity to make active decisions on the numbers they use and the way they record their results. It is important to emphasise that there is more than one possible answer and that it helps if the answers are written systematically. The observer noted:

> The pupils worked productively on the task, and most groups were willing and able to produce multiple solutions, some of which were

systematically organised. Making choices seemed to be engaging. In this case there was a need for extended explanations of how this would work. Perhaps in the future it will be easier to pose such tasks. The students worked in groups with particular roles. Rebecca encouraged the reporter from each group to explain the process whereby the group found their particular set of answers. Again, this reflects the focus on students explaining their strategies, supported by the teacher.

The success of the groups is indicated in the diversity of responses given by the groups. Many groups developed a range of possible solutions, indicating that they had identified patterns in the solutions and laying the groundwork for knowing the answer readily to questions such as 19 – 17.

The pedagogies associated with this task are illustrative of the approach we are advocating. The task had a variety of entry levels, it could be answered in different ways, it involved group work with roles, and it allowed a detailed and focused class discussion of strategies and patterns. The concluding review allowed the teacher to highlight particular student insights.

Another task was posed, using $1, $2 and $5. In Rebecca's words, 'Your job is to work out as many ways as you can to make $10'. The observer noted:

> This seems to be an example of the type of task that can be successful. It is complex enough to allow for multiple answers; some reasoning and problem solving is required; and it is practising a core skill toward the goal, that of ways of building to 10.

The students wrote their answers on small whiteboards. They seemed to understand the task and worked productively, with many producing multiple correct answers.

The purpose of including discussion of the third task here is slightly different. This task was presented as: 'I have three silver coins, how much money might I have?' It allows a similar diversity of responses to those of the previous tasks, but there was an interesting twist. The observer noted:

> This again is the sort of task that should work. It has a range of answers, it prompts communication, it is challenging mathematics, and it is addressing the overall theme. It did not work as intended, with many students including $1 and $2 coins in their total, making it more complex. Yet Rebecca had explained the task well. The reason for not mixing the dollars and cents is that it makes the calculation more difficult.

Only later did it emerge that the local word for coins or change is 'silver' (in Australia, there are coins for $2 and $1 and these are gold), which highlights the need to consider alternative interpretations of events and language at all times. This illustrates the importance of the interactivity implied by the pedagogical model, as well as sensitivity by the teacher to the interpretations of the students.

These three tasks illustrate that the students are willing and able to engage with such number and money investigations. They are able to identify a range of possible responses and record them systematically, which presumably lays the groundwork for developing mathematical connections.

Reflecting on opportunities and challenges with the interactive pedagogies approach

The goal of the research is to investigate the challenges and opportunities afforded by this pedagogical approach. From the lesson observations overall, it can be concluded that being clear about the goals of teaching is helpful both to the teacher and to the students. In the lessons observed, the clarity meant that the activities could be thoughtfully sequenced, each activity could build on a previous experience, and the students were clear about the teacher's goals and her expectations for them. It also appears that 'building on what the students know' was an effective strategy. In the sequence of activities that drew on the apparent familiarity and fluency of students with money, the class was extraordinarily energised and engaged; they participated actively and the experience seemed to lead to other learning. Rebecca was able to extend some of the students toward formulating some potentially powerful generalisations.

In these observations it also appeared that the students were both willing and able to engage with rich tasks that required decision making by them and allowed the construction of mathematical ideas. It seems useful to use such rich tasks with the students and to encourage them to create mathematical ideas based on those tasks.

In these examples, and the other lessons observed, there were many instances that would be judged outstanding teaching and learning in any school, and certainly demonstrated that students in remote schools can learn as well as their metropolitan counterparts. Three challenges emerged from these observations. The first is that care needs to be taken when making inferences about the extent of student engagement. In the sequence of activities based on the money questions the class seemed highly engaged. Yet in subsequent interviews, in the class observed, while most students were highly fluent with the money and equivalent number questions, there were two students who were not able to identify the value of any coins. This emphasises that there is a diversity of achievement within each class – and a diversity of readiness – and specific actions must be taken to accommodate this diversity. While we have not researched the potential in this, it seems that the Aboriginal Education Workers who are available in some schools could be better utilised. It also seems that there would be advantages in exploring ways of grouping students for instruction that maximise students' opportunity to contribute meaningfully.

A second issue relates to the conduct of class reviews after rich explorations. Rebecca patiently probed the students' thinking and invited them to explain their reasoning. Yet this was not often successful from a whole-class perspective. One example was the student who explained his strategy for winning the *Race to $10* game. He gave an extended explanation and, if you knew what he was trying to say, his explanation was insightful and illustrated clear conditional thinking and argument. Yet his explanation would not have informed other listeners. There were a number of other instances where an individual gave an excellent explanation that elaborated on the desired type of thinking, but not in a way that would engage the other children. The other students were not interested in such explanations, which may be partly a function of a lack of clarity. Rebecca was energetic and committed to the approach and had worked with the class on her expectations for participation. It is suspected that specific actions will be necessary for this aspect of the approach to realise its potential. One strategy that seemed to work was for the teacher to restate the explanations given by students and to provide additional diagrammatic support for their explanations.

A further issue is the intensity of the interactivity. In many of the observations the students became tired. Noting that these classes are quite small, students are constantly under scrutiny. Clearly, in the above, there were mathematically rich and challenging experiences in which the students participated well, even beyond expectations. But it is perhaps unreasonable to expect the students to do this for the full 90 minutes of each mathematics class. It is suggested that teachers could plan some experiences that are less intensive and less interactive and these could be used to buffer shorter and more intensive parts of the lessons. These less intensive experiences could include competitive games such as card games, some aspect of physical activity combined with a mathematical experience, drawing or storytelling.

The interactive pedagogies model clearly has potential to engage students in doing significant mathematics. Our project is now seeking to elaborate on the aspects that worked well and to revise those that did not.

References

Baturo, A; Cooper, T; Dietzmann, C; Heirdsfield, A; Kidman, G; Shield, P; Warren, E; Nisbet, S; Klein, M; Putt, I. 2004. *Teachers Enhancing Numeracy*. Canberra: Commonwealth of Australia.

Boaler, J. 2008. 'Promoting "relational equity" and high mathematics achievement through an innovative mixed ability approach'. *British Educational Research Journal* 34 (2): 167–194.

Burton, L. 2004. *Mathematicians as Enquirers*. Dordrecht, The Netherlands: Springer.

Frigo, T; Corrigan, M; Adams, I; Hughes, C; Stephens, M; Woods, D. 2003. 'Supporting English literacy and numeracy learning for indigenous students in the early years'. ACER Monograph 57. Camberwell, Victoria: Australian Council for Educational Research.

Gore, J; Griffiths, T; Ladwig, J G. 2004. 'Towards better teaching: Productive pedagogy as a framework for teacher education'. *Teaching and Teacher Education* 20: 375–387.

Grootenboer, P. 2009. 'Rich mathematical tasks in the Maths in the Kimberley Project'. In *Crossing Divides*, edited by Hunter, R; Bicknell, B; Burgess, T. Proceedings of the 32nd Conference of the Mathematics Education Research Group of Australasia. Vol. 1. Sydney: MERGA: 696–699.

Hattie, J; Timperley, H. 2007. 'The power of feedback'. *Review of Educational Research* 77 (1): 81–112.

Howard, P. 1997. 'Aboriginal voices in our schools'. Paper presented at the Annual Conference of the Australian Association for Research in Education (AARE), 30 November – 4 December 1997, Brisbane.

Jorgensen, R. 2009. 'Cooperative learning environments'. In *Crossing Divides*, edited by Hunter, R; Bicknell, B;& Burgess, T. Proceedings of the 32nd Conference of the Mathematics Education Research Group of Australasia. Vol. 1. Sydney: MERGA: 700–703.

Lokan, J; Greenwood, L; Cresswell, J. 2001. '15-up and counting, reading, writing, reasoning'. Camberwell, Victoria: Australian Council for Educational Research.

Pegg, J; Graham, L; Bellert, A. 2005. 'The effect of improved automaticity on basic number skills on persistently low-achieving pupils'. In *Proceedings of the 29th Conference of the International Group for the Psychology of Mathematics Education*, edited by Chick, H; Vincent, J. Vol. 4. Melbourne: IGPME: 49–56.

Perso, T. 2006. 'Issues concerning the teaching and learning of mathematics and numeracy in Australian schools'. *Australian Mathematics Teacher* 62 (1): 20–27.

Sarra, C. 2008. 'New narrative tells of brighter future together'. *Australian* 8 August. Accessed 20 October 2009. Available from: http://www.theaustralian.com.au/news/features/new-narrative-tells-of-brighter-future-together/story-e6frg6z6-1225759141388.

Sullivan, P. 2009. 'Describing teacher actions after student learning from rich experiences'. In *Crossing Divides*, edited by Hunter, R; Bicknell, B; Burgess, T. Proceedings of the 32nd Conference of the Mathematics Education Research Group of Australasia. Vol. 1. Sydney: MERGA: 726–732.

Sullivan, P; Youdale, R; Jorgensen, R. 2009a. 'The link between planning and teaching mathematics: An exploration in an Indigenous community school'. In *Proceedings of the Biennial Conference of the Australian Association of Mathematics Teachers*, edited by Kissane, B. Fremantle, Western Australia: MERGA: 247–256.

Sullivan, P; Youdale, R; Jorgensen, R. 2009b. 'Knowing where you are going helps you know how to get there'. *Australian Primary Mathematics Classroom* 14 (4): 4–19.

Marginalisation of Education Through Performativity in South Africa
Towards a Radicalisation of Education

Yusef Waghid
Stellenbosch University

The publication of Jean-Francois Lyotard's classic text, *The Postmodern Condition: A Report on Knowledge*, in 1984, spawned much debate and controversy about postmodern framings for education, the most significant of which were on the concepts of 'performativity', 'performance', 'incredulity', 'nihilism' and 'paralogy'. Unlike those who associate the use of these postmodern framings for education with a philosophical movement of deconstruction, which foregrounds the place of language and discourse and the challenges of foundational certainties (or grand narratives) in thought and action (Lemert in Edwards 2006, 273), or the promotion of individualism and lifestyle practices commensurate with neoliberalism (Featherstone in Edwards 2006, 273), or the offering of space for forms of radical and emancipatory politics, which bring to the fore issues of gender, race, ethnicity and sexuality (Ellsworth in Edwards 2006, 273), I wish to talk about a radicalisation of education through critique. I want to answer an ontological, ethical and epistemological question: Why should critique be considered as a postmodern purpose of education?

To perform means to 'show' and 'demonstrate' what one is doing (Usher 2006, 286). That is, one makes 'public' and 'transparent' what one is *enacting* in order to make oneself 'count' in the eyes of others (Ball in Usher 2006, 286). Through the performance of 'the postmodern condition', Lyotard made himself count publicly and transparently by conveying powerful performative meanings. One would not necessarily associate a politician's public mutterings as performances of this kind, as they might not be accountable. Learners in public schools can be considered as engaging in a 'show and tell' assessment regime because they quite anxiously want their work to be judged by educators – so they perform. Likewise, researchers in universities are increasingly held accountable for what they do through various forms of research performance assessment regimes (Usher 2006, 285), whether they are applying for an NRF (National Research Foundation) rating, publishing an article in an accredited journal or acquiring external funding for project work. As Usher (2006, 285) argues, 'What is happening here is that researchers are making themselves count in relation to the measures of excellence defined in these regimes and are at the same time and by the same means themselves held to account'.

But performing in this way can also be enabled by 'performativity' – that is, utilising those technologies that bring about systemic efficiency or the optimisation of efficient performance (Usher 2006, 280). If one's NRF rating, one's publication in an accredited journal and one's winning of external funding is about positioning the university in the 'league table of excellence', and hence about enhancing the prestige of the university, then the emphasis of research may switch from enquiry to application, from ideas to outcomes, and perhaps away from the academic virtues of 'truth' seeking and the 'disinterested' pursuit of knowledge (Usher 2006, 282). In this sense, the performance of academics becomes too performative. Performance in itself is not a problem, but performing solely for the sake of performativity – that is, 'a pragmatics of hard-headed calculation' (Usher 2006, 286), which is associated with 'how many one can produce and gain', would reduce the work of researchers to a much maligned, 'business dominated technological determinism' (Poster in Usher 2006, 283). Such technological determinism should not be the purpose of education, for that would reduce education (as we find in outcomes-based education – OBE – today) to a regime of 'mastery' (Edwards 2006, 277). Mastery represents a form of completion, an end to learning, and points towards a position of finality and closure. Further, attempts at mastery (such as through OBE) – increasingly inscribed in discourses of standards and targets – only point to the inability of many to master whatever has been prescribed (Edwards 2006, 277).

Nowadays at some institutions in South Africa one often witnesses an acceleration of academics' promotion because their performances are deemed excellent through the game of audit – that is, having so many articles, book chapters and an NRF rating. Yet it is nevertheless true that some of them might not even be able to articulate a coherent argument, or critically and playfully engage with the untidiness and complexity of the current education situation (say in South Africa). They fail to imaginatively destabilise (or what Lyotard refers to as paralogise) performative language games. They attempt to 'master' research, but dismally fail in their attempt to do so. How many learners have left our public schools, told that they have mastered the outcomes, yet go into the world with an inability to read and count? (For endless examples of impoverished schooling refer to *Toxic Mix* (Bloch 2009)).

If the purpose of education is not to perform mastery, how would performing critique help us to reconfigure it? In tackling this question I take my cue from Alasdair MacIntyre (1985) who, in *After Virtue*, notes that the Enlightenment project, though providing us with traditions of liberty, equality and democracy, has been excessively ambitious in the sense that 'its deontological justifications have proved to be flimsy, giving way to base emotivism that has deprived contemporary society of a normative vision of goodness, which has in turn been detrimental for education' (Gray 2006, 316). Education has abdicated its task of engaging in ethical deliberation and visioning about the good life and has increasingly become an instrument of performativity within the global economy, concerned solely with transmitting the knowledge and skills needed to prepare for economic productivity. It acts as a mere agent of epistemological and economic instrumentalism and has relinquished its primary mission of cultivating goodness in people (Alexander in Gray 2006, 316). I wish to take up the monumental task of reclaiming goodness by reconnecting education to critique, so that education can be meaningful and avoid instrumentalisation.

This brings me to the question: What should the discourse ethics to guide education comprise? In the main, education cannot just be about imposing one's views on others (as the acquisition of mastery requires most of the time), but entails actually engaging others by offering some justification for one's reasons. In turn, others should be persuaded or dissuaded by one's reasons. If others find one's reasons palatable or unpalatable, this could only be on the basis of their proffered justifications. A discourse-oriented education is one underpinned by norms of justification through making one's point clearer to others, who in turn offer an account of their reasons for agreeing or disagreeing with one's arguments. This kind of discourse ethics makes education more deliberative, as others are afforded opportunities to engage with or disengage from one's points of view. It is connected to what Seyla Benhabib (2006, 48) refers to as democratic iterations – those linguistic, legal, cultural and political repetitions-in-transformation. A democratic iteration is characterised by acts of reappropriation and reinterpretation. One simply has to engage in an unending debate with others through democratic self-reflection, self-determination and public defensiveness. It is a profound sense of democratic reflexivity that appeals to recursive questioning and reiterated justifications (Benhabib 2006, 48).

To my mind, democratic iteration is precisely what we require in South Africa to make sure that the education system we now have to implement has been subjected to democratic reflexivity and recursive justifications. This means listening to the views of those involved in the implementation of the National Curriculum Statement and to 'talk back'. Only then can outcomes-based mastery in education be avoided, because performing democratic reflexivity and recursive justifications would render the educational project as a narrative that is always in the making, to borrow a formulation from Maxine Greene (1996). Democratic iteration or talking back does not have to be non-belligerent or non-distressful just because we think we need to continue the conversation. Sometimes we can articulate our reasons with a sense of roughness and distress, even to the extent of making others feel uncomfortable; otherwise our conversations would be unduly policed (by ourselves and others) and often would be frivolous or useless mediations. Hence, the notion of mastery does not sit easily with democratic iterations because the latter always subject the self-mastery and mastery of the subject to incredulity (that is, an inability to believe) or a loss of faith in the regimes of mastery.

Rather than being a route to mastery, education might be better considered as a condition of 'constant apprenticeship' (Rikowski in Edwards 2006, 277). If education can be considered as the continuous perpetuation of apprenticeships, iterative learning communities would evolve in which teachers and learners engage in meaningful work, subjects studied would generate new understandings, and learning would be mediated through active experimentation (Alexander in Gray 2006, 320) or what Popper (1989, 33) refers to as 'learning through making mistakes'. In fact, learners would be encouraged to be reflective about why their way of thinking is desirable (or not), and these communities would be performing teaching as opposed to training, and engaging in genuine learning as opposed to mechanical learning (Alexander in Gray 2006, 321). Through such a discourse, ethics teaching would be understood as a moral activity that seeks to strengthen the moral agent within. It would empower students to make moral choices more intelligently on their own, which may involve some training but should culminate in understanding and independence that are expressed concretely (Gray 2006, 321).

I now attend to the question: How can critique help us to perform education non-instrumentally, that is, to radicalise education? In response to this question I take a closer look at the university today. From the outset, I want to acknowledge my personal paralytical complicity in the academic position the South African university has assumed since the first democratic elections in April 1994. When I joined the university sector two years after the establishment of the new government I witnessed, without the freedom to speak out, how the newly elected African National Congress (ANC) government legislated one higher education policy text after the other: from the 1996 White Paper on the Transformation of Higher Education, to the Higher Education Act of 1998, to the National Plan for Higher Education in 2001.

At the core of these education policy initiatives has been the government's most serious ambition to break (some would argue symbolically) with the apartheid past, while simultaneously advocating for a university (the now 23 universities and universities of technology are the result of mergers of the previous 15 universities and 21 technikons) that can satisfy utilitarian demands in the service of the government and the public. Thus one finds that the National Plan proposes the achievement of 16 outcomes, ranging from increasing student access – particularly of black communities – into the university sector, to enhancing their (students') cognitive abilities with respect to technical and professional competences, which would not only ensure greater competitiveness in an ever-evolving labour-market economy, but also increased participation as democratic citizens in service of the 'public good'. In a way, the university in South Africa has been coerced to produce what Derrida (2004, 95) refers to as 'businessmen or technicians of learning'.

Moreover, the performative role of the university is enhanced through the government's funding formula, which favours subsidising the university according to student enrolments, throughputs and research publications in what have become known in South Africa as accredited journals. This means that a faculty's funding is secured through its technical compliance with student input and output, and publication output. As a result, rigorous scholarship seems to be exchanged often for increased student throughput and publications, and the impending state subsidy. From my conversations with colleagues, it seems that academic rigour and belligerent supervision are waning and that research in the university has been 'pledged in advance to some utilitarian purpose' (Derrida 2004, 111). Too often I hear that the country requires many doctorates to be economically competitive. The old cliché 'publish or perish' has assumed a monetary priority because of technical and fiscal demands.

How odd that we are continually reminded that the university cannot survive if throughputs are not sustained! Such instrumental utilitarianism implies that the university in South Africa is an institution without autonomy. And a university without autonomy cannot by definition be a university, but rather a marginalised institution. For Derrida (2004, 104–105), a university that is autonomous 'must be able, according to Kant, to teach freely whatever it wishes without conferring with anyone, letting itself be guided by its sole interest in truth'. Contrary to such an idea of the university, the South African university has abandoned its internal quest for truth to become instead a technical agent of state bureaucracy. Annually, the subsidy gains of the university are determined by the quantity of research outputs, student enrolments and throughputs as part of the government's control of the imperatives of technological production. Recently, the vice-chancellor of a prominent university was reminded by the government's spokesperson that his institution should transform, considering the state subsidy the institution receives. Such a not-so-unusual demand from the government confirms its concern with guiding the universities towards serving the government's interests.

Of course I am not suggesting that the university in South Africa should not have ends (that is, aims and objectives). But if instrumental ends are the only outputs of the university system, then the university has lost its soul – it has been marginalised. This assessment implies that the university 'is there *to tell the truth*, to judge, to criticise in the most rigorous sense of the term, namely to discern and decide between the true and the false; and if it is also entitled to decide between the just and the unjust, the moral and the immoral, this is so insofar as reason and freedom of judgement are implicated in it as well' (Derrida 2004, 97, emphasis in the original). Some instances that confirm the erosion of the university's power and freedom to take a stand on issues of true and false, right and wrong, include: the South African university's reticence during the xenophobic violence that erupted in certain parts of the country last year; some academics' refusal to support their colleagues where voices in favour of the 'freedom to speak out' are silenced by a populist vice-chancellor; and the calculated reluctance of many former white Afrikaans-speaking universities (such as the one I am working in) to condemn publicly the humiliation of black workers by some white students, who insisted that the workers consume liquid contaminated with urine.

At the level of research, the university is in even deeper trouble. Increasingly the university can be seen as dancing to the tune of large business corporations that invest enormous sums of money in research to support utilitarian purposes. As Derrida (2004, 143) confirms, 'the end-orientation of research [I would add in South Africa as well] is limitless'. For instance, my institution has made the pursuit of research to achieve some of the United Nations' Millennium Development Goals (MDGs) an overarching strategic priority. This means that research should be aimed at achieving the following goals: combating pandemic poverty, promoting human security (from food security to peace initiatives), maintaining and promoting human dignity, promoting democracy, and promoting and maintaining environmental sustainability. If the university (with specific reference to my institution here) endeavours to pledge in advance the use of research for some techno-scientific purpose, then the possibility that fundamental or basic research might be neglected is a stark reality. Does agricultural research in poor farming communities contribute towards eradicating poverty when the produce is still under the control of the rich farmers who now become increasingly entrepreneurial? Does research in violent communities secure peace if some people are challenged to deal with the choice of engaging in drug trafficking in the face of unemployment? Does research about democracy necessarily ensure that societies behave according to the ideals of democratic action? What I am wondering is whether this kind of envisaged 'end-oriented' instrumentalist research actually achieves its desired or intended consequences. The fact of the matter is that the university in my country has been pursuing this kind of instrumentalist research for some while and very little, if any, substantive societal changes have ensued. By far the majority of people remain poor and joblessness escalates. But perhaps this is not what the university is supposed to be doing? It is for this reason that I now focus my attention on what the university ought to be doing.

In the wake of the university's technocratic commitment to produce students who can serve their communities, as indicated in the university's vision and mission statements: to produce students who can professionally, vocationally and technically be attentive to the demands of the public good (of course, as determined by the government), I now wish to elucidate what seems to distinguish 'technicians of learning' from scholars of knowledge (the latter constituting the university ideally), before moving on to a discussion of how to reconstitute the place of critique.

Following Derrida's neo-Kantian analysis, 'technicians of learning' are in fact former students of the university who have been educated to perform functions to meet the ends determined by the state and not the ends of science – the latter being the work of scholars at the university. Technicians of learning wield enormous power, not only as a result of displaying technical mastery within their professions – whether as doctors, journalists, lawyers, magistrates, accountants, geneticists, biochemists, engineers, teachers or theologians – but also as a result of their influence on and shaping of the public sphere. For Derrida (2004, 96), 'they are all representatives of the public or private administration of the university, all decision makers in matters of budgets and the allocation and distribution of resources... all administrators of publications and archivisations, publishers, journalists, and so forth'. In a way, they are technical consumers of knowledge(s), who professionally serve their own interests and those of the public. University prospectuses clearly confirm the interest of all current South African institutions in producing 'technicians of learning' who can vocationally practise their careers of benefit to the public. But, of course, herein also lies a potential danger to the university.

Technicians of learning, like most state bureaucrats involved in the technical administration of knowledge(s), often present themselves as judges and decision makers in the public practice of their careers. Mostly they usurp the right to judge and decide on the performance of their professions without being subjected to the authority and censorship of the university and its faculties (Derrida 2004, 97). How common is it today for some doctors to prescribe inappropriate medication, or for some teachers to use archaic learning strategies without conferring with the university, or for some judges to wrongly convict an innocent person? The point is that technicians of learning often use their university-acquired qualifications to parade as quintessential paragons of knowledge(s), who at any time may usurp the power of scholars of knowledge to decide and judge. Yet this is not what they have been educated to do. But perhaps the university has stripped itself of its responsibility to judge and decide on the true and the false, with the result that technicians of learning now masquerade as producers of knowledge(s).

Reconstituting the place of critique in the university is first of all an attempt at recognising and invoking critique. The value of critique finds itself rightfully associated with 'thinking' that no longer lets itself be determined by an obsession with techno-economic performativity. As for Derrida, so for me, critique is a form of dissonance and questioning that is not dominated and intimidated by the power of performativity. 'This thinking must also unmask – an infinite task – all the ruses of end-orienting reason, the paths by which apparently disinterested research can find itself indirectly reappropriated, reinvested by programs of all sorts' (Derrida 2004, 148). This thinking is always asking: 'What is at stake (in technology, the sciences, production and productivity)?' It is a kind of critique that allows us to take more risks, to deal openly with the radical incommensurability of the language games that constitute our society, and invites new possibilities to emerge. Critique is a matter of enhancing the possibility of dissent and diversity of interpretations (Burik 2009, 301); of complicating what is taken for granted, pointing to what has been overlooked in establishing identities (Burik 2009, 302); an active opening up of one's own thought structures that is necessary for other ways to find an entrance (Burik 2009, 304). In a different way, it is performing a radicalisation of education away from marginalisation because radicalising education is innately concerned with creating possibilities for dissent, diversity of interpretations, complicating the taken-for-granted and opening up to the other. Perhaps only then as educationists can we ensure that education does not remain marginalised in South Africa.

This brings me to a discussion of how a critique-based education system can actually work with reference to my own teaching. At the beginning of each academic year, I teach a module to postgraduate students in their final year of a professional teaching qualification. The title of the module is 'Theoretical Perspectives on Diversity and Inclusivity'. The module aims to teach students – about to become high-school teachers – to use aspects of democratic citizenship education in their classroom practices. The demographic composition of the class is overwhelmingly white (90 per cent). One of the reasons for this anomaly in a country where the majority of the population is black is the fact that many black people do not speak Afrikaans – considered to be the dominant *lingua franca* at the institution where I work.

For the past three years, I have employed a critique-based strategy within the module, aimed at educating the students to become deliberative inquirers. I have been teaching deliberation in relation to three issues that have gained prominence in South Africa: racism, blind patriotism and xenophobia. I introduced students to three video clips of incidents related to these phenomena. They were then asked to give an account of why racism, blind patriotism and xenophobia are societal ills that should be eradicated. Working in groups, students had to justify to one another why these societal ills are detrimental in the process of cultivating responsible citizens after decades of apartheid rule. What ensued was that some students gave explanations of why these ills surfaced and other students critically evaluated the explanations. The groups then offered their arguments against racism, blind patriotism and xenophobia to the entire class. Randomly, I asked students to respond to other students' reasons, thus taking one another's reasons into a zone of systematic controversy. Critically evaluating one another's reasons has always been done through listening to what the other had to say before agreeing or disagreeing, and this was then followed by giving an account of their own reasons. As the university teacher, I eventually considered the reasons offered by the students before giving my own reasons, after which students could evaluate those reasons. Sometimes students became annoyed with other students for what they perceived to have been an articulation of ill-conceived reasons. It was my task to emphasise that respect demands that we can disagree (even belligerently) with one another's reasons and that we have to tell one another when we think the other is wrong. Thus, through listening, evaluating and re-evaluating one another's reasons, deliberation was fostered in the university classroom.

However, what sparked much heated controversy in the class was the remark by a white student that the racial prejudice and racist actions perpetrated by five white students against elderly, black workers at a university residence in 2009 could be seen as a response to the killing of some white farmers in the country. One of these five white students urinated into a prepared meal for black workers to show how gullible and ignorant blacks are in the country. Of course, the humiliation of people should not be tolerated. Similarly, the brutal murder of some white farmers is an abhorrent and barbaric act. However, to argue that racially degrading behaviour can be justified as a response to the farm killings is not only an ill-conceived argument, but also the expression of an irresponsible view. It was at this point that even white students belligerently disagreed with the views of a fellow student. The most defensible argument raised against this ill-conceived view, promulgated by Amy Gutmann (2003), recognises that freedom of expression should not be left unconstrained when an injustice to others is perpetrated. The white student who attempted to rationalise the racist incident suffered some kind of distress, which is not unusual for the kinds of deliberations I encourage in the class. The debate became very heated and one might have expected students to leave the classroom. Yet conditions of deliberation had already been engendered in the class for some time, which meant that such an act was not necessary.

The point here is that even when deliberations are belligerent and distressful, students should continue to participate in them. Eamon Callan (1997) explains that the idea of deliberation does not entail an attempt 'to achieve dialogical victory over our adversaries but rather the attempt to find and enact terms of political coexistence that we and they can reasonably endorse as morally acceptable' (Callan 1997, 215). Through deliberation, university teachers and students disturb complacency or provoke doubts about the correctness of their moral beliefs or about the importance of the differences between what they and others believe (a matter of arousing distress), accompanied by a rough process of struggle and ethical confrontation – that is, belligerence (Callan 1997, 211). If this happens, belligerence and distress give way eventually to moments of ethical conciliation, when the truth and error in rival positions have been made clear and a fitting synthesis of factional viewpoints – such as happened in this class – is achieved (Callan 1997, 212). This is an idea of deliberation with which I agree – where no one has the right to silence dissent and where participants can speak their minds. And when university teachers and students can speak their minds, they are also prepared to take risks that will prepare them well to enhance justice in their society. University teachers and students who are prepared to challenge forms of injustice in their society, such as racism and barbaric murders, do so for the sake of achieving democratic justice – they act as responsible citizens willing to take the risk of speaking their minds.

In essence, deliberative argumentation prompts students and teachers to question meanings, imagine alternative possibilities, modify practical judgments, foster respect and develop critical engagement. Teaching students through and about deliberation would go some way in cultivating a critique-based educational discourse in South African universities.

References

Benhabib, S. 2006. *Another Cosmopolitanism*. Oxford: Oxford University Press.
Bloch, G. 2009. *The Toxic Mix: What's Wrong with South Africa's Schools and How To Fix It*. Cape Town: Tafelberg.
Burik, S. 2009. 'Opening philosophy to the world: Derrida and education in philosophy'. *Educational Theory* 59 (3): 297–312.
Callan, E. 1997. *Creating Citizens: Political Education and Liberal Democracy*. Oxford: Oxford University Press.
Derrida, J. 2004. *Eyes of the University: Right to Philosophy 2*. Trans. Plug, J. et al. Palo Alto: Stanford University Press.
Edwards, R. 2006. 'All quiet on the postmodern front?'. *Studies in Philosophy and Education* 24 (5): 273–278.
Gray, K. 2006. 'Spirituality, critical thinking, and the desire for what is infinite'. *Studies in Philosophy and Education* 24 (5): 315–326.
Greene, M. 1996. *Releasing the Imagination: Articles on Education, the Arts and Social Change*. New York: Jossey-Bass.
Gutmann, A. 2003. *Identity in Democracy*. Princeton and Oxford: Princeton University Press.
Lyotard, J F. 1984. *The Postmodern Condition: A Report on Knowledge*. Trans. Bennington, G; Massumi, B. Manchester: Manchester University Press.
MacIntyre, A. 1985. *After Virtue: A Study in Moral Theory*. 2nd edn. London: Duckworth.
Popper, K. 1989. *Conjectures and Refutations: The Growth of Scientific Knowledge*. London and New York: Routledge.
Usher, R. 2006. 'Lyotard's performance'. *Studies in Philosophy and Education* 24 (5): 279–288.

Index

$100 laptop program, the 160–2
Aboriginal art 117, 151
Aboriginal Education Workers 215
Aboriginalism 166–7, 168
Aboriginal people *see* Indigenous Australians
academics, shortage of 64
Accelerated Literacy program 205
access to knowledge 185
access to technologies 160, 163–5
accountability 91, 97, 111, 131, 139–40, 179, 180, 186
achievement, diversity of 214–15
achievement-focused teaching 135
activities 9, 33, 160, 205, 206, 208, 209, 210, 211–13, 214
African languages 57, 60, 65–6
Afrikaans 57–58, 60, 66, 182, 225
alternative education provision 45–6
alumni 15, 21, 97
Anangu students 24, 25, 31
anti-violence education 77–82
apartheid
    anti-apartheid struggle 176, 58, 182, 188–9
    end of apartheid 58–9, 88, 94
    and institutionalised racism xviii, 98–9
    as the origin of South African inequalities 56–8, 63, 100
    transition to democracy 94–102, 178, 221
apology to Indigenous Australians 17, 109, 110–11
apprenticeships 220
Arnhem Land 118–20
assessment 7, 29, 31–32, 135, 137, 140, 142–3, 206, 218
assimilation 113, 200
AtoL program 135–6
Australian writing 149–56
automaticity 207

autonomy 65, 179, 185, 222
background, of students
    connecting mathematics to 31–5
    engagement of education with 3, 27, 132–3, 206, 210–12, 214
    see also social heritage
back to basics approach 183–4
Bantu Affairs 56
Bawinanga Aboriginal Corporation 120
benchmarking 121
bias 29, 31–2, 121
    see also institutional biases
biased information search 200
bicultural education 167
bilingual education
    in Australia 7–8, 24, 122, 167
    in New Zealand 40
    in South Africa 60
Bilingual Language Program 7
Bill of Rights 10
black South Africans
    literacy 18
    matriculation rates 18, 20–1, 57–8, 59, 184
    middle class 176
    number of postgraduates 63–4
    prohibition of teaching mathematics to 19
    socioeconomic disadvantage of 17–21, 56–67, 178–9
    university attendance of 58–67, 221–2
    see also apartheid; South Africa
Blainey, Geoffrey 165
blaming the victim 200–1
blind patriotism 225–6
Bloch, Graeme 17–21, 63, 176, 181, 183, 189
Bloemfontein Conference 100
boarding schools 30
Bourdieu, Pierre 24–5, 123–4
budgets 137–9

bullying 18, 20, 76
    see also violence
bureaucracy 115
    see also education policy; managerial approach
Canberra 2
capabilities 169–70, 185–6
capacity building 139–40
careers
    career choices 6, 16, 18, 58, 151
    in research 64
    in teaching 19, 181
Caring for Country projects 117–18
Central Desert region 23, 24, 27
Centre for Aboriginal Economic Policy Research 123
Cherbourg State School 88, 195
Chisholm Report, the 184
citizenship, skills for 104, 225
Clark, Helen 39
class reviews 215
classroom interactions 136–7
classrooms
    effective classrooms 209
    as sites for education reform 131
closing the gap
    in Australia 1–11
    critiques of 112–13
    and employment 124
    information and communication technology policies 163
    as a metaphor 39–40, 170–1
    in South Africa 17–21
    see also gap, the; socioeconomic disadvantage
Closing the Gap on Indigenous Disadvantage 4–5, 109, 110–13
collaboration 8, 130, 141, 205
colonisation
    of Australia 87, 114, 115–16
    and education debt 132–3
    of New Zealand 40–1, 42–3
    teaching of 2–3
    and victim culture 199–201
communities
    involvement in education 15, 96, 207
    modernisation of 204, 205
    working productively with 198–9
communities of practice 141
community-based organisations 188
community capacity building 91–2
community leadership 203
competition 179, 180, 181
computers 158–71
Constitution of the Republic of South Africa 10, 59, 88, 94–5
content, and technology 165–6

continuity of customs 114
control 143
corporal punishment 182, 183
corporate partnerships 21
corruption 182
Council of Australian Governments (COAG) 4, 109, 111, 163
country 30, 118–19
Craven, Peter 152, 153
crime 20, 132, 138
    see also sexual violence; violence
critical thinking 65, 185
critique 217–27
critique-based education systems 225
Cuban, Larry 161
cultural context 8, 28
cultural identity 196, 199, 202–3
    see also background, of students; social context
culturalism 167–8
cultural norms 28
cultural values 3, 117
culture, internalisation of 26
Curriculum 2005 59
curriculum development
    imposition of western curricula 206
    investing in 2
    plurality in curriculum design 122
    public debate about 183–4, 188
    and troubled knowledge 102
    'two-way strong' curricula 30–2
customary knowledge 40, 114, 116, 123, 124, 132–3, 211
customary norms 112
deficit approach 33–4, 39–40, 133–4, 168, 206
definitional ceremonies 80
degree qualifications 48–50, 52–3
deliberation 225–6
democratic culture 94–5, 182, 186, 188
democratic iterations 219–20
Dessaix, Robert 152–3
Development Bank of Southern Africa (DBSA) 17, 18, 175–6
    see also Bloch, Graeme
digital divide, the 158–71
digital education resources 162
digital education revolution, the 162–5
dignity, from education 2–3
discourse ethics 219
discourse-oriented education 219
discrimination 5, 44, 60, 65, 94, 133, 183
disempowerment 3, 76
displacement of Indigenous Australians 13
Djelk Rangers 120
dysfunctional schools 189
early childhood education 46, 78

economic agenda 90, 103
  see also neoliberalism
economic growth 177–8, 180
economic reforms 90, 91
  see also globalising economy
education
  community involvement in 15, 96, 207
  contribution to economic growth 177–8
  definition of 8
  in Indigenous Australian cultures 13–14
  institutionalisation of 25, 86, 89–90, 92–4
  as an instrument of government 86, 92–4
  opportunities through 21
  public debate about 186
  radicalisation of 225
  relevance of 186, 187–8
  as a right 10, 182–5, 196
  as a social priority 19–20, 21
  and technology 165–6
educational achievement, affect of gender on 52–3
educational effort 6–7
educational work 86, 89–90, 103, 104
education debt 129–45
education departments 20–1, 59, 66
education policy
  to address education debt 144–5
  Closing the Gap on Indigenous Disadvantage 4–5, 109, 110–13
  conflicting aspirations of 143
  for education reform 137–8
  the education revolution 1–2, 162–5
  grassroots approach to 175
  human capital theory in 178
  and Indigenous education 88–94
  language of 4–5
  localised policy making 91
  for mathematics achievement 206
  No Child Left Behind 140
  priorities of 90
  and professional development 135–7
  in South Africa 19
education quality 63, 174–89
education reform at the system level 129–45
education revolution, the 1–2, 162–5
Education Roadmap, the 18–21, 174–89
efficiency 181–2
effort 6–7
eGranary 162
emotional literacy 185
employment
  prospects of 6–7
  in remote areas 121
  students' experiences of 14
  targets to improve 110–11
employment rates 3, 61
empowerment of students 40, 54

engagement of students 11, 205, 214–15
English
  in Australia 7–8, 25–7, 150, 151, 167, 208
  in New Zealand 135
  in South Africa 58, 60, 66
  see also bilingual education
ethical responsibilities 98
evidence, and education reform 131
evidence-based teaching 135
expectations
  high expectations of students 12–13, 28, 31, 33–4, 195, 196, 202–3
  and standardised testing 142
  students' expectations of school 7
experience, of students
  disjunction with institutionalised practice 25
  engagement of education with 3, 33–4, 132–3, 142
  of school 7
experiential learning 2–3
extended families 15
externalisation 79, 80
failure, as a social category 143
familiar concepts 210–12
feedback 209
fees 180
feminism 74
formative assessment 143
Foundations for Learning Campaign 183–4
Fraser, Nancy 185
Freud, Sigmund 70, 73, 77
funding
  for education reform 137–9, 144
  targeting of 187
  of universities 180, 221–2
game 26–7, 211–12, 215
gangs 20
gap, the
  in Australia 3–4, 14–16, 85–6, 93
  in New Zealand 39–40
  between rural and urban areas 59–60
  see also closing the gap; socioeconomic disadvantage
Garma Living Maths program 206–7
Garvey, Marcus 202
gender and educational achievement 52–3, 187
Gillard, Julia 155–6
girls, experiences of violence 69–77
global financial crisis, the 180
globalising economy 90, 92
goals 130, 209–10, 214
goodness 219
GPILSEO model 130–1
Group Areas Act 56
group work 207

habitus 25, 26, 27–8, 31–2, 35
helplessness 9–10, 78
Higher Education Act 59, 221
high expectations of students 12–13, 28, 33–4, 195, 196, 202–3
history
   recognition of 66
   teaching of 2–3
   see also colonisation
Hole-in-the-Wall Education Ltd 158–60
homelands (Australia) 114, 122
homelands (South Africa) 57
home language 7–8, 10, 33, 34, 183, 208
hope, and transformative education 77
human capital 1–2, 63, 91, 100, 103, 170, 174, 187
human capital theory 109, 123, 175, 176, 177–82
human rights and education 10, 182–5, 196
hybrid economy model 116, 122, 124
imprisonment rates 3
improvement infrastructure 139
incentives 139–40
inclusiveness 153–4, 186
income management 5
Indigenous art 8, 117, 151
Indigenous Australians
   and the digital divide 166–71
   experiences of education 12–16
   government apology to 17, 109, 110–11
   history of invisibility of 87–8, 103
   importance of land to 13, 30, 116, 118–19
   middle class 197
   perceptions of 196–8
   socioeconomic disadvantage of 3–4, 14–16, 85–6, 93, 102, 110–11
   see also traditional owners
Indigenous communities xv, 7, 9, 115, 119, 122, 124, 125, 163, 169, 196, 198, 199–203
   constraints faced by 201
   distribution of 114, 115
   role of schools in 7, 9
   teaching mathematics to students in 23–35, 204–15
   victim culture in 199–201
Indigenous culture
   education in 13–14
   local knowledge 123, 124
   mathematical ideas in 33
   teaching of 2–3, 8–9
Indigenous education
   challenges and opportunities in 1–11
   and remaking the social 88–94
Indigenous Education Leadership Institute 195
Indigenous history, teaching of 2–3, 8–9
Indigenous identity 197–8, 202–3
Indigenous incapacity 168

Indigenous-owned land 114, 115
Indigenous Protected Areas 118, 119
Indigenous schools, technology use in 161–2, 163
Indigenous theatre 154
Indigenous writing 149–56
individual responsibility 113
inequality, patterns of 85, 133
infant mortality 3
information and communication technology (ICT) 158–72, 186
infrastructure 114, 144
innate ability 25, 142–3
in-school facilitators 138–9
institutional biases 88–90, 92, 93, 104
institutional complicity 98, 101
institutional culture 99
institutionalisation 25, 86, 89–90, 92–4, 137–9
institutionalised racism 97–9
institutions, and education reform 130
interactive pedagogy 207–15
interculturality 116
interdependent learning opportunities 207
intergenerational legacy 131–2
internalisation 26, 30, 79
Internet, the 158–71
intervention in the Northern Territory, the 5
interventions, to improve completion rates 61–2
Irigaray, Luce 71, 72–3, 74
James, Clive 151
Jansen, Jonathan 96–102
Jose, Nicholas 149, 153–4
Ka Hikitia 144
Kimberley region 23, 24, 27
Kriol 24, 208
land 13, 30, 116, 118–19
land rights 87, 114
language
   and access to learning 24–8
   and apartheid 57
   learning in home languages 7–8, 10, 33, 34, 183, 208
   managerial language 4–5
   in South African education 59, 60, 187
   in standardised tests 29, 121
   and technology 165–6
   translation issues 25–6, 28, 213–14
Language in Education Policy 59
Language Laws 57–8
Language Policy in Higher Education 59
languages
   African languages 65–6
   Afrikaans 58, 60, 225
   Kriol 24
   official languages 66
   Pitjantjatjara 24, 25–6

te reo 40, 45–6
see also English
laptops 160–2
large-scale reform projects 141
leadership 100, 130, 139–40, 195–203, 205
learning difficulties 134
learning styles 206
Le@rning Federation, the 164
lesson sequences 209–10
libraries 19, 162, 176, 186–7
life expectancy 3, 14, 15, 110–111
lifelong learning
   for parents 9
   and participation 91
   priorities of 90
   and remaking the social 92
   as work focused 100
literacy
   autonomous model of 168
   and bilingual education 167
   of black South Africans 18
   curriculum focus on 145, 188
   in early childhood 184
   of Indigenous Australians 3–4, 8, 121
   literacy programs 15, 205
   and performance measurement 122
   targets to improve 110–11
   and technology 164, 165–6
local accountability 180
local decision making 188
loss 72, 73, 75
Lyotard, Jean-Francois 217–19
Macquarie PEN Anthology of Australian Literature 149–56
Majura Primary School 2–3, 8–9
malnutrition 186
management skills of principals 19
managerial approach 109, 112
managerial language 4–5
Manworrk Rangers 118–19
Maori
   educational attainment of 41–3, 46–7, 48–52
   educational reform for 129–45
   gender disparity in educational achievement 52–3
   measuring performance of Maori students 143
   participation in education 45
   population distributions of 42–3
   role in New Zealand identity 43
   socioeconomic status of 39–41, 43–5, 129
   te reo 40, 45–6
   tertiary participation levels 47
   tikanga Maori 40
   see also Treaty of Waitangi
marginalised universities 222

market economy 115
market-led solutions 179, 180, 181
mastery 218–19, 220
materials 186–7
mathematics
   mathematical ideas in Indigenous culture 33
   prohibition of teaching to black South Africans 19
   role of language in teaching 25–7
   structuring practices in 29–30
   teaching in remote communities 23–35, 204–15
Maths in the Kimberleys research project 204
matriculation 18, 20–1, 57–8, 59, 184
melancholia 70–1, 73, 74–5, 76–7
mentors 15, 21
Michael Rua School 18
Millennium Development Goals 223
Miller, Alice 77–8
Ministerial Taskforce on Aboriginal Affairs in Victoria 15
Ministry of Education 144
Ministry of Maori Development 40
Ministry of Social Development 46
Mitra, Sugata 158–9
Mkhize, Zweli 175
modernisation of communities 204, 205
modes of assessment 137
molestation 69
money and numeracy 31–2, 211
money economy 115
mortality 3–4, 111
multi-representational learning 208
Naidoo, Jay 175, 176
narrative pedagogy 81–2
narrative therapy 79–82
National Accelerated Literacy program 35
National Assessment in Literacy and Numeracy (NAPLAN) testing 29, 31–2, 121, 164
National Certificate for Educational Achievement 46–7, 48
National Consultative Forum 184
National Curriculum Statement 59, 220
National Education Monitoring Project 135
national education systems 85–104
National Indigenous Reform Agreement 111, 123, 125
National Partnership Agreements 111
National Plan for Higher Education 221
national testing
   bias in 29
   National Assessment in Literacy and Numeracy (NAPLAN) testing 29, 31–2, 121, 164
   No Child Left Behind 140
   see also standardised testing

native title 114, 117
negative stereotypes 6, 7, 77, 197
Negroponte, Nicholas 160–1
neoliberalism
    conflicts within the neoliberal state 123–4
    in education reform 122, 176, 178
    and the hybrid economy model 116
    and investment in remote communities 113, 125
New Zealand General Social Survey 43–4
New Zealand Living Standards Survey 44–5
NGOs 18, 21, 188
No Child Left Behind 140
normalisation 109
normative coherence 141
normative social indicators 112–13, 114
normative tests 142
Northern Territory, the
    bilingual education in 7, 24, 122, 167
    Caring for Country projects 117–18
    Central Desert region 23, 24, 27
    federal government intervention in 5
    rangers 117, 118–21, 123
numeracy
    cultural bias in testing 31–2
    curriculum focus on 145, 188
    in early childhood 184
    of Indigenous Australians 3–4, 8
    and money 31–2, 211
    numeracy programs 15
    and performance measurement 122
    in remote areas 121
    targets to improve 110–11
    see also mathematics
Nyangatjatjara College 31
Nyathi, Ronald 19
objective targets 10
occupational agency 86, 89–90, 103
official languages 59, 66
One Laptop per Child 160–2
Ontario Literacy and Numeracy Strategy 137–8
opportunities through education 21
oral storytelling 155
other, the 197–8
outcomes-based education 19, 21, 183, 188, 218–19, 220
outstations 114, 122
Overcoming Indigenous Disadvantage Key Indicators 2009 111
Own Affairs 56
ownership 131, 144–5
Pacific Islanders 45, 52
Palm Island riots 198
Pandor, Naledi 175
parents 9, 15, 180–1
participation
    improvement of 64–5, 113, 145
    and lifelong learning 91
    parity of 185
    rates of in New Zealand 41–2
    social participation 168–70
partnerships between community and government 91–2
    see also public–private partnerships
pedagogical pitfalls 34
pedagogy
    debates around 183–4
    and education reform 130
    interactive pedagogies 207–15
    narrative pedagogy 81–2
    poisonous pedagogy 78–9
    rich tasks 213
    for teaching mathematics 204–14
perceptions of Indigenous Australians 196–8
performance measurement 10, 41–2, 143, 184
performance-related pay 181
performance targets 184
performativity 217–27
personal responsibility 113
Pitjantjatjara 24, 25–6
planning of lesson sequences 209–10
poisonous pedagogy 78–9
policy *see* education policy
political appointments 66
political culture 86
political will 103
Population Registration Act 56
positive Indigenous identity 202–3
positive learning identities 142
post-school qualifications 50, 63
    see also tertiary study; universities
potential 8, 40, 54, 133, 143
power relations 81, 86, 89–90, 98, 99
preservice teacher education 130, 136–7
principals 19, 182
prior knowledge 210–12
    see also background, of students
problem solving 185
problem students 142
process models 179–80
Productivity Commission, the 111
professional development
    to address violence 82
    dynamic model of 134–6
    and education quality 181
    and education reform 130, 133–9
    funding of 144
    information and communication technology training 163
    in-school facilitators for 138–9
    and interactive pedagogies 209
    investing in 2
    Te Kotahitanga 40, 46

professional development coordinators 138–9
professional learning communities 137
professions, careers in 16, 18, 151
Programme for International Student Assessment 206
provinces, inequality between 59–60
psychometric approaches 142–3
public debate 94, 96–7, 186, 188
public policy *see* education policy
public–private partnerships 21, 182
pursuit of excellence, the 196
quality of education 63, 174–89
questions 26–7, 208
QuickSmart 207
Racial Discrimination Act 5
racial inequalities 18
racism 60, 97–9, 225–6
    see also Reitz incident, the
radicalisation of education 225
rangers 118–21, 123
rape 69
rates of return analysis 177–8
readiness, diversity of 214–15
reconciliation 87
Redfern Riots 198
Reitz incident, the 17, 97–102, 222, 226
relevance of education 186, 187–8
remaking the social 85–104
remote communities
    bias against in standardised testing 29, 31–2
    education and development in 9, 109–25
    relevant curricula for students in 33–5
    teaching mathematics in 23–35, 204–15
removal of Indigenous Australians 13
reporting back 208
representation
    modes of 34–5, 208
    of the unspeakable 73–4
research, instrumentalist approach to 222–3
research culture 60
researchers, shortage of 63–5
rich tasks 212–14
rights-based approach 182–5
    see also human rights and education
role models 15, 61
Rudd government 110–11, 162
Sarra, Chris 88, 195–203
scaling up reforms 141
scholarships 15, 25
scholastic mortality 28–9, 32, 35
school attendance rates 5–6, 14, 121, 205
school completion rates
    of black South Africans 18, 20–1, 57–8, 59, 184
    impact of outcomes-based education on 184
    of Indigenous Australians 3–4, 13, 16

school cultures 195
school effectiveness frameworks 179
school feeding 186
school reports 2
schools
    choice of 181
    classification by language 57
    fees 180
    role in Indigenous communities 7, 9
    role in South Africa's education crisis 184
    students' attitudes towards 76
science-related curricula 123
self-determination 202–3
self-esteem 7, 101, 203
self-harm 72, 73
self-loathing 72
separate development ideology 57–8
sexual abuse 69
sexual harassment 81, 183
sexual violence 69–77, 187
Silverman, Kaja 71
skills development 104, 121, 207
skills shortages 63–5, 175
Slumdog Millionaire 159
smart tools 135–6
social, remaking the 85–104
social barriers to Internet use 166
social compact for quality education 184–5
social context 3, 8, 32
social heritage 24–8, 35
social inclusion 91, 203
social indicators 39–40
socialisation 89, 90
social justice 90, 185–9, 202, 203
social leadership 100–2
social norms 112, 113
social participation 168–70
social systems and technology 165, 169–70
socioeconomic disadvantage
    and the Education Roadmap 187
    of Indigenous Australians 3–4, 14–16, 85–6, 93, 102, 110–11
    and institutional biases 92, 93
    of Maori and Pacific Islanders 39–41, 43–5, 129
    and technology use 160, 169–70
    see also closing the gap; gap, the
South Africa
    Constitution of the Republic of South Africa 10, 59, 88, 94–5
    disadvantage in 56–67, 178–9
    education as a government priority in 20, 21
    quality of education in 174–89
    remaking the social in 94–102
    university sector of 58–67, 221–2
    see also black South Africans

South African Democratic Teachers' Union 19, 175
South African National Skills Development Strategy 64–5
South African Schools Act 59
special education provision 142
spectrum of access 166
spread, and education reform 130
stakeholders 175, 188
standardised testing
    cultural biases in 29, 31–2, 121, 170
    and economic growth 178
    and expectations of students 142
    and information and communication technology 164
    and information for parents 180–1
    No Child Left Behind 140
stereotypes 6, 7, 77, 80, 197
Stolen Generations 109, 110
storytelling 81
streaming 30
strengths-based approach 8, 40, 133–4
stronger smarter philosophy 40, 195, 202–3
structuring practices 32
student achievement 135, 142–3
students
    aspirations of 14
    attitudes to mathematics 31
    capacity for learning 20
    empowerment of 40, 54
    engagement of 11, 205, 214–15
    expectations of school 7
    explanations given by 215
    goals for learning 209–10
    personal disadvantage of 19
    see also background, of students; expectations
subordination 143
success as a social category 143
suicide attempts 72
Swarup, Vikas 159
symbolic violence 28
systemic leadership 139–40
system level of education reform 129–45
system-wide communities of practice 141
tasks 208, 209, 212–14
teacher clarity 209–10
teachers
    African language teachers 66
    aspirations of 136
    attrition rate of 9
    institutional biases of 88–90
    occupational expertise of 92
    perceptions of Indigenous children 195
    role in education reform 131
    role in South Africa's education crisis 181, 184
    salaries of 181
    see also professional development
teacher shortage 181
teacher support 63
teacher training 57, 130, 136–7, 181
teacher unions 19, 59
teaching
    achievement focus 135
    as a career option 19, 181
    evidence-based teaching 135
    learner-centred approach to 182
    quality of 63, 174–89
    use of questions in 26–7
    see also outcomes-based education
technicians of learning 222–4
technology *see* information and communication technology (ICT)
Te Kauhua 138
Te Kotahitanga 40, 46, 51, 136, 138
Te Puni Kokiri 40
te reo 40, 45–6
tertiary study 47
    see also post-school qualifications; universities
theatre 154
tikanga Maori 40
Torres Strait Islanders 168
    see also Indigenous Australians
tough love 199, 200–1
toxic mix, the 19–20
Toxic Mix, The 181, 183
traditional owners 114, 120, 123
transformation 77, 99–102, 104
Treaty of Waitangi 40–1, 43, 88, 144
troubled knowledge 102
two-way learning 7, 30–2, 122, 206–7
    see also bilingual education
unions 19, 59, 175, 184
unique outcomes 80, 82
universities
    culture of 97–102
    funding of 180, 221–2
    as marginalised institutions 222
    participation of marginalised groups 14, 18
    role in education reform 137
    and social leadership 100–2
    in South Africa 58–67, 221–2
university completion rates 60, 61–3
University of the Free State 17, 96–9
    see also Reitz incident, the
utilitarianism 221–2
victimhood, culture of 19, 199–201
Victoria
    Indigenous Australians in 13
    Ministerial Taskforce on Aboriginal Affairs 15
Victorian Indigenous Affairs Framework 15

violence 18, 20, 69–77, 81, 187
    see also anti-violence education; sexual violence; symbolic violence
Vocational Education and Training 90
Warddeken Land Management Ltd 118–19
Warschauer, Mark 159–60, 165
welfare dependence 113
wellbeing 9, 185
western norms 112
Whorfian theory 26
wicked problems 91, 95, 97, 100
Wik judgment, the 87
women, experiences of violence 69–77
Working on Country program 118, 124
Wotton, Lex 198
W.W. Norton 150
xenophobia 225–6
Yunupingu, Gulumbu 7–8